# THE OFFICIAL PRICE GUIDE TO

# VINTAGE FASHION AND FABRICS

THE OFFICIAL PRICE GUIDE TO

# Vintage Fashion and Fabrics

PAMELA SMITH

HOUSE OF COLLECTIBLES
THE CROWN PUBLISHING GROUP
NEW YORK

House of Collectibles and the HC colophon are trademarks of Random House, Inc.

Published by:   House of Collectibles
                The Crown Publishing Group
                New York, New York

Distributed by the Crown Publishing Group, a division of Random House, Inc., New York, and simultaneously in Canada by Random House of Canada Limited, Toronto.

www.randomhouse.com

Printed in the United States of America

*Cover photos: 1960s André Courrèges Jacket,* green vinyl, made in France, $950. *Courtesy of Resurrection, New York, NY. Photograph by Tom Amico. 1980s Angelo Tarlazzi Dress,* hot pink strapless, matching stole, $675. *Courtesy of Enokiworld. Photograph by Madeline Meyerowitz. 1920s Pumps,* gilt leather, painted flowers, "Made by Andrew Geller, New York," $125. *Courtesy of Mary Troncale, Branford, CT. Photograph by Tom Amico. 1950s Handbag,* emerald green suede, pleated front with cinch accent, interior fully fashioned with change purse, comb, mirror, pockets, "Manon," $245. *Courtesy of Patina, New York, NY. Photograph by Tom Amico. 1990s Gene Meyer Tie,* silk, screened star in stripes design, multicolored, $75. *Courtesy of Craig Smith. Photograph by Tom Amico.*

ISSN: 1535-9603

ISBN 0-609-80813-3

10 9 8 7 6 5 4 3 2 1

First Edition: October 2001

*For My Children*

# Acknowledgments

Thank you to my editor, Dottie Harris, for her enthusiasm and support for this project. Thanks also to her assistant, Kathryn Henderson for her patience and assistance, and to senior production editor, Cindy Berman.

Sincere thanks to the many dealers, website dealers, and store owners whose cooperation and contributions made this book possible: Madeline Meyerowitz (Enokiworld), Wendy Radick (Kitty Girl Vintage), Laura Dalesandro (Isadora's), Karen Augusta (Antique Lace & Fashion), Linda Ames (Vintage Textile), Mary Troncale, Deborah Burke (Antique & Vintage Dress Gallery), Linda Kohn and Joseph Sherwood (High Noon), Art and Jenene Fawcett (Vintage Silhouettes), Tom and Margarita (The Fainting Couch), Janet Pytowski (fashiondig.com), Laura Wills (Screaming Mimi's), Patina, Pepper, Resurrection, From Around the World Vintage, Justin Vogel (Atomic Passion), Vintage by Stacy Lee, Miss Kitty & Calico Jack (Cat's Pajamas), Lynn Pastore (5 and Dime Vintage), Darlene Dull and Jennifer Parker-Stanton (Cookie's Closet), Steve Murray (Zap & Co.), and Gailen Moore and Amadeus Guy (Vintage Textiles).

Thank you to the reference librarians of the Ridgewood Public Library for their assistance in locating books, articles, and other information that was essential to the writing of this book.

Thank you to Marianna Garthwaite Klaiman, Director of the Fashion Department at Sotheby's, for sharing her knowledge of costume and her fashion insights, and to A. Newbold Richardson, costume conservator, for her conservation advice.

A special thank you to Gisele Ferrari. Her expertise in mounting costumes was important to the completion of this project. Thanks also to her husband, Lorrin and daughters, Chiara and Alessandra.

Tom Amico has again provided us with beautiful photography, thank you. Thanks also to his assistant, Mary Fredricks.

I am also very grateful to the website dealers for all the beautiful photography they provided, thank you.

Thank you Ruth Torielli for smoothing out the wrinkles and helping with the assembling and completion of this book. Thanks also to Comptime, Ramsey, New Jersey, for their technical support.

Thank you to my children, Amy and Craig, for their love, support, for helping keep me computer literate, and for their love of vintage fashion. Thanks to my parents for their encouraging words.

I am also especially grateful to friends: Sue Sargen who was always there for me and who believed in this book from the beginning, Dr. Arvin Murch for his suggestions to this manuscript, and Deborah Larkin from Kramer & Larkin, Philadelphia, for her technical assistance and availability at all hours. Thank you. There were also friends who helped with the photo shoots, returning clothing, hunting down garments and shops, proofing, and boosting my morale—thank you Ann, Jane, Sue, Lynn, Cecily, Kristin, Martha, Joyce, and Corinne.

# Contents

# PART III
## RESOURCES

# Introduction

My intention in this guide is to show the many varieties and possibilities of vintage fashion. Therefore, I have included the most casual clothing to the dressiest, the funkiest to the finest couture, the familiar to the unusual. This book does not tell you how to wear vintage or what to buy; that is left to your personal style as a collector. Rather, its purpose is to show the enormous diversity of fashion over an extended period of time, the availability of vintage fashions, and what you need to know to shop the market. Whether you are an avid collector or just beginning to appreciate vintage fashions, this guide will help you make intelligent decisions about what to purchase.

Looking back over the past one hundred years of fashion it is clear that two of the most significant influences on its development were advances in fabric technology and that very twentieth century medium, the movies. As a result I have included many of the signature fabrics for each decade in the century. This not only illustrates the general trend that occurred toward artificial or "man-made" fibers, but also helps in the identification of a vintage piece. As fabrics became more flexible and as the choice of available fabrics increased, designers were able to become more experimental. Fabric technology revolutionized both fashion design and the fashion industry.

Often movies were Hollywood's projection of the times, and in turn, they popularized many fashions. To illustrate this point and to help with the recognition of fashion designs I include references to many of those movies and movie stars that typify high-style fashions. Stars of the twentieth century like Greta Garbo, Grace Kelly, Audrey Hepburn, John Travolta, and Richard Gere made the fashions they wore in their movies memorable and influential.

Each decade of fashion described in this book includes a reference to designers and manufacturers of that era. Obviously it would be impossible to include every designer and manufacturer in this guide. I have tried to provide you with those whose styles best represent the period. For the serious costume student who might want to do further research into such matters, a resource guide, glossary, and bibliography are included at the end of the book.

In today's vintage market the trend is toward the 1960s, 1970s, and 1980s where the more practical pieces of clothing are found and where there are the greater number of pieces available. These periods provide a wide range of clothing, particularly as ready-to-wear was widely available and clothing was designed for the teen market as well. While clothing is still easy to find from these eras, the prices of vintage pieces will vary according to their popularity and availability. A quick look in a fashion magazine will give you an indication of the latest fashion trend. Many of today's popular fashions are retro-inspired and the original designs can be found in unique vintage fashion garments or accessories.

Couture and designer ready-to-wear garments are the first pieces that are bought in a new vintage market. Couture pieces are custom-made or made-to-order. Designer ready-to-wear are quality garments that are mass-produced as opposed to individually made. Fortunately, the increase in young designers toward the end of the twentieth century has greatly increased the availability of such pieces.

Internet dealers, store owners, and show dealers often have a preference for the period of fashion or type of fashions they sell. Keep this in mind when searching the resource guide for show dealers, stores, and websites. Read the descriptions of merchandise very carefully because this information has bearing upon the price; consider: condition, couture, designer and store labels, luxury fabrics, handwork, tailoring, and the uniqueness of the garment.

The vintage pieces and descriptions chosen for this guide are gathered from Internet dealers, vintage stores, show dealers, and private collectors from across the country. They represent a wide array of fashion choices for a wide audience of collectors. With so many ways to buy today and so many designs to choose from, it's easier than ever to find that special piece of vintage fashion.

# PART ONE

# An OVERVIEW

# What You Need to Know Before You Buy

## Pricing, Condition, and Market Trends

There are a few basic principles used in pricing a vintage piece. *First and foremost, pricing is dependent on the condition of the piece.* The better the condition a piece is in, the higher the price; however, you will be getting a piece with greater value. In this guide the condition of a piece is listed with its price. Generally speaking, dealers use the following terms as their standards of condition: Very good is used to describe pieces that show slight wear or signs of age. Excellent is used when there are no apparent signs of wear, staining, or imperfection. Mint, flawless, pristine, perfect, and impeccable are terms that should be used for pieces that were either never worn or used, or are entirely without flaws. There are vintage clothing pieces on the market, particularly in menswear and casual wear that are marked, "New Old Stock." These pieces are vintage stock, which have never been worn. Their condition is dependent upon how they were stored.

*The quality or uniqueness of a piece is often reflected in the price.* A piece with quality of design, fine workmanship, uniqueness of material and style, or with unusual detail or ornamentation can be important considerations in pricing. Labels also generally add to the value of a piece, particularly if the piece is in excellent condition. There are several different types of labels you may find on vintage fashions. One is the label from a couture house, indicating the piece was custom-made or made-to-order, rather than being mass-produced. Flawless craftsmanship distinguishes a piece as couture. A couture label has a passage or registration number. This number can be on a separate label attached to the back of the main designer label or stamped on the front. The number contains information about the collection, year, and client for whom the piece was made. On luxury ready-to-wear, known in France as prêt-à-porter, the designer label or the boutique label is still an indication of very good quality. Department stores like Henri Bendel, Saks Fifth Avenue, and Bergdorf Goodman had their own in-house designers who designed custom-made clothing. While not true couture, these clothes were made with the same attention to detail and quality of materials. Older Bergdorf Goodman labels often include the name of the client and date. Labels of all kinds help determine the provenance or origin of the piece, provided these are original to the piece.

*Pricing depends on where you buy.* Prices will differ according to where you buy. Usually, larger cities command higher prices, but they are also where there is the highest demand for vintage fashion and where the better pieces are often found. Attending shows and searching shops are good ways to acquaint yourself with pricing. For the perpetual shopper there has never been anything to compare to buying online. If you are familiar with fashion design and prices, you are better able to make intelligent decisions. Do not hesitate to e-mail a website dealer, just as you would ask any store owner or show dealer questions about condition, measurements, the return policy, or the price.

*Pricing fluctuates with time.* The prices in this book reflect current retail values, that is, the prices that items are currently selling for when this book went to press, or the prices they sold for at auction, or current estimated values that were provided by an auction house or an appraiser. Prices can change according to the desirability of a piece. The prices listed in this guide are to be used as guidelines to help familiarize you with vintage fashion.

## HOW TO BUY, BUYING FROM DEALERS, BUYING ONLINE

It is always best to be well informed before buying. Read as much as you can about the pieces that interest you. Acquaint yourself with the names of designers and their signature fashions. Remember, condition and uniqueness of a piece are important considerations in the price. Consider the location of where you are buying. Keep in mind how much you are willing to spend, then start your search.

Most dealers are happy to tell you what they know about the provenance of a piece. If you are well informed, you will be able to ask appropriate questions and make intelligent decisions on what to purchase.

Shopping online, a recent addition to vintage clothing shopping, offers an unlimited supply of merchandise. If you plan to shop online you will want to get to know the dealer you are working with. You can do this by watching their website for a while to become familiar with their inventory and terms of sale. You need to know your measurements before you shop. Read descriptions carefully and always check on the representation of the condition of the garment before purchasing. Some dealers give you more information about their pieces than others. Do not hesitate to e-mail the dealer about any questions you might have. The obvious drawback of this type of shopping is not being able to see the piece or try it on. It is, however, a pleasurable way to learn and shop the market. Provided in the resource guide are the websites for many dealers and shops.

## CONSERVATION GUIDELINES

It is important to have some guidelines to help you determine the wearability of a piece.

In an interview, costume conservator and appraiser Newbold Richardson shared general information about what she thought a collector should know before purchasing a piece of vintage fashion. Here is a summary of what she had to say.

The very first thing that should be considered is the integrity of the fabric. Is the fabric sturdy or not? Be sure to differentiate between the condition of the lining and the garment. Linings can easily be replaced, and stains or worn areas shouldn't be deterrents to buying if the rest of the fabric is sturdy! Following this, you must obviously check for loose seams or hems; many of these can be mended easily. Be wary, however, of tears that cannot be mended. Stains in twentieth century clothing, particularly from the 1960s through the 1990s, are difficult to clean because of the experimentation that was used in making artificial fabrics. Of course always look for care labels on the garments to determine how they should be cleaned. Dry cleaning should be done by a professional, preferably someone who does dry cleaning on the premises and does their own work. Often you can find a professional dry cleaning company by calling a local church or museum to find out how they clean their vestments or vintage pieces. The dry cleaner may recommend that you remove decorative buttons or trim before dry cleaning. These can easily be replaced after cleaning.

Bridal dresses can be cleaned by a reputable dry cleaning business. It is a good idea to ask when they will be using a clean tank of fluid and to take your gown to them at that time. Acid-free boxes and acid-free tissue can be bought from a conservation supplier. Home dry cleaning in your dryer should only be used to freshen-up or to take out musty odors in any clothing.

All natural fibers can be washed. These include cotton, linen, and silk. The exception is inexpensive silk, which often cannot be washed because of the sizing that is put on to the fabric. Sizing is a generic term for compounds applied to fabrics in some way, by adding sheen, weight, smoothness, stiffness, or strength. You can tell expensive silk from inexpensive silk by the feel. Good silk is heavy and has a good drape. All fabrics should be tested before washing for color-fastness. One must be very diligent in testing silks manufactured from the 1870s to the 1920s because of the experimental nature of dyeing fabrics during that period. If test results show the silk can be washed, then hydrogen peroxide is a good cleaning agent because it bleaches but does not affect the fiber. Look for any fading in older fabrics because this cannot be repaired by cleaning or washing.

For cleaning of natural fabrics and "whites" (lingerie dresses made from white cotton, linen, or lawn), Ivory Snow or liquid Cheer can be used. If using Ivory Snow, be sure to rinse thoroughly. Cheer is the only commercial cleaning product that does not have optical brighteners that boost the color by attracting UV rays. Sodium perborate or enzyme presoak (TR-ZYM) can be used to wash cellulose or plant fiber fabrics like cotton, linen, or christening clothes made from cotton or linen. Care must be taken to support the fabric during the washing, rinsing, and drying process. It is the weight of the water on the fibers that causes damage. Soak gently and if working on a large piece, place it in a "sling" made from an old color-fast sheet to lift it in and out of the tub. Drain the water in the tub you are using before lifting the piece. Some pieces will take many soakings. Drain the dirty water and add fresh until achieving the desired result. Do not wring any garment. Lay flat to dry, and blot gently with clean color-fast towels. Always remember to treat vintage fabric with "kid gloves."

Rayon from the first half of the twentieth century is a different rayon from rayon today in terms of care. There were many experiments made with rayon during this era in terms of dyes and fibers. For that reason, vintage rayon dresses from the thirties and forties cannot be washed. They must be dry-cleaned. This is also true of lingerie from this period, often made from a rayon sometimes known as artificial silk.

The size and fit of garments are important. Many women under the age of thirty-eight often have larger rib cages because of their participation in sports at an earlier age. Rib-cage measurement is crucial in determining the fit. In order to wear vintage garments today, it is acceptable to make small alterations, like letting out seams or altering hems. Suits from the 1940s usually are tight in the upper arm for today's generation. A conservator can add a gusset to the underarm to make it deeper. The bust measurement, however, is still the determining factor for fit. Keep in mind that clothing from the 1930s, 1940s, and 1950s were very fitted styles and meant to fit snugly. Keep in mind also that there is a fundamental forgiveness of small problems like letting out seams or hemming on a vintage piece.

Standardized sizing was regulated in the 1940s as a result of fabric rationing during World War II. Therefore, when buying clothing made earlier than 1940, sizes will vary greatly. In the early 1980s there was a sizing upward to accommodate the changing figure of women. In the 1970s, a size 12 was a 29″ waist, but in the 1980s, a size 12 was a 31″ waist. In contemporary sizing, bridal dress sizing is still two sizes smaller than regular clothing sizes. Therefore, taking measurements is still the best way to size a garment.

Labels are important. They should not be removed because they can add to the value of a piece. If you must remove them for alterations, sew them back onto the garment. When taking apart an older garment to do an alteration, take each stitch out by itself. Tweezers are good for this. Over the years, perspiration and repeated cleanings have bonded the stitches to the fabric. A curved seam ripper designed for surging stitches is also recommended. Frequently any holes that are left in the fabric where stitches have been removed can be steamed out.

Vintage clothing should be stored in the same climate that you live in. Avoid storing clothing where there are extreme temperature changes as in basements or attics. Beaded or sequined clothing should be stored lying flat because the heavy downward pull of the beads or sequins can tear the fabric if it is hung. If you choose to hang lighter vintage pieces, use padded hangers to protect the fabric from tearing. For long-term storage, use acid-free boxes and acid-free tissue which can be ordered from a conservation supplier.

When in doubt as to how to treat your vintage piece or whether your vintage piece should be worn, consult a conservator. *Conservators, conservation studios, and suppliers are listed in the resource guide.*

# PART TWO

# VALUE GUIDE: A CENTURY OF DESIGN AND DESIGNERS

*Detail of Aqua Silk Gown:*
Silk embroidery, beading,
and metallic lace.

Aqua Silk Gown. *Courtesy of Linda Ames, Vintage Textile, www.vintagetextile.com.*
*Photograph by Linda Ames.*

# 1900–1910
# Elegant and Extravagant

Fashion style at the turn of the century was referred to as Edwardian fashion, and also as the fashion of La Belle Époque. This new beginning to the century was a relatively peaceful period and was distinguished by the advances made in the arts, literature, and technology. Fashion was dictated by the wealthy, and it was common for the women of leisure to change outfits several times a day according to strict rules of etiquette. In the morning a woman wore a tailored suit if she went out or a morning dress or wrapper if she stayed at home. In the afternoon, a formal costume, called a reception gown, with a train or trailing hem was required. If she received guests at home, she wore an elaborate tea gown, and finally for evening, dinner clothing or even more formal clothing if dining out or going to the theater. The ritual of dressing was made possible only with a staff of servants to help with the preparation of attire, including laundering and sewing.

The Edwardian silhouette was intricate, requiring much planning and preparation. The S-shaped corset designed by Mme. Gaches-Sarraute entirely changed the silhouette of women. It was considered a "healthier" corset because it eliminated the severe pressure on the waist and diaphragm caused by the previous century's corset designs. Actually the new S-shaped corset was equally inhibiting, as it began low on the bust with a straight busk and extended deeply over the hips with a tightly laced back. This style of corset forced the torso into a pigeon shape. Women of this period were often compared to flowers from the images inspired by their silhouettes of slender waists, flat abdomens, protruding rears, and voluptuous chests. Women were depicted in the art of the times, that of Art Nouveau.

Over the corset, a woman wore an impressive array of elaborate under-

11

wear, all beautifully lace-trimmed and buttoned. Taffeta and silk petticoats were added; the gowns and dresses were the final touch. Elegant gowns and reception dresses were made of fancy fabrics: chiffon, lace, faille, silk taffeta, and silk satin in cream and pastel hues. For summer women wore beautiful lingerie dresses with decorative lace, tucks, or white on white embroidery. Lingerie dresses were often referred to as "whites," as they were made from white cotton, linen, lawn, or lace.

To balance her S-shaped silhouette, a lady would wear an immense hat, laden with plumage, faux flowers or fruits, and yards of ribbon. Out of necessity, hats were secured with ornate, often jeweled hat pins. A fashionably dressed woman wore her hair in a pompadour, which required hair to be piled on top of the head, and puffed on to "rats" or pads with combs.

As with hats, kid or silk gloves were always worn. An outfit was complete only with a dainty parasol of Chantilly lace, silk, or chiffon, with a carved ivory or mother-of-pearl handle. Moonstones and garnets in small drop earrings, as well as pins and rings, were fashionable jewelry. Often fans were made of painted silk, ostrich feather, or lace with tortoiseshell or mother-of-pearl sticks that were pierced or gilded. Gauze fans with sequins or spangles were also popular. Most fans were imported from Paris, London, or Vienna. The many buttons needed for these ensembles were made of Italian glass, silver, pewter, plique-à-jour, cloisonné, or covered with fabric or thread.

Art Nouveau floral motifs were chic for trim and fabric. Purses were small; chatelaines, reticules, hand-worked, and mesh bags were common. Gowns had lace-embroidered necks and long, full sleeves with tight wrists, trains, and skirts with ruching and pleating, decorated with flowers, ribbons, and lace. Evening gowns were influenced by theatrical costumes. They had deep décolletage and were beautifully and intriguingly embellished. Fox fur muffs and stoles were luxurious. The most elegant finery was the tea gown, which was a loose-fitting garment with lavish trim, worn to receive guests in the drawing room. Jacques Doucet was famous for his use of flowing fabrics typical in tea gowns.

The sport of motoring started the trend for automobile coats, known as dusters. These long and loose-fitting coats were made from linen or pongee for the summer and in wool, tweed, and fur for the winter. Large hats had silk veils over them with lace insets to protect the face from the dust of the roads when motoring.

In 1906 Paris introduced the Empire dress and the ensuing Princess-style dress, which ended the reign of the fashion of the monobosom or the single-bosom silhouette. The two-piece dress was replaced with the gore-fitted dress with a slightly raised waistline. By sewing tapered panels or gores into a skirt or dress, the hem increased in width and a flared skirt was achieved. This allowed for easier movement and a flowing design. Dresses were made in linen, lawn, or Irish crochet for warm weather. Suit jackets were now longer, and the dress and jacket combination appeared. In 1909 Mariano Fortuny, originally a textile designer, patented the Delphos dress, a loose silk, finely pleated garment that hung straight from the shoulders and was weighted at the hemline with glass beads.

Most women had their dresses individually made for them by dressmakers and then added finishing details themselves. Ready-mades were available but not widely used. Those not in society were hard-pressed to keep up with the fashionable and extravagant clothing of the devotees of King Edward's court. Women of modest means spent many hours making and remodeling clothing as well as using the assistance of a dressmaker.

Edwardian men were as conscious of their fashion tastes as their female counterparts. Proper formality was very important, and clothing symbolized wealth and status. As an *Esquire* fashion editor wrote in the book, *Esquire's Encyclopedia of Twentieth Century Men's Fashion* (p. 110), "One must look genteel, prosperous, and athletic in the broad-chested fashion of Theodore Roosevelt." The suit coats were oversized, padded, long, and loose. Trousers were pleated at the waistband and tapered down the legs. By mid-decade, trousers were cuffed, initially because of rain and mud. Vests were not only worn for warmth but for the pocketwatch and watch fob concealed in the pockets. This decade saw a modified version of the sack suit, called a business suit, which had a shorter jacket, very small lapels, and four buttons. Winter suits were often made of serge or worsted wool and were worn with a high derby hat. In summer, suits were flannel or linen, and hats were made of straw. A well-dressed gentleman always wore gloves and often carried a walking stick or cane of malacca or bamboo. For formal attire, a man wore tails, a double-breasted, white waistcoat, a white bow tie with a poke collar, and high-button shoes. A long overcoat and silk opera hat completed the look. Clothing designed for comfort would not become fashionable for another decade.

## Signature Fabrics of the Edwardian Era

Cotton, linen, lawn, faille for lingerie dresses and shirtwaists

Serge, wool, tweed, and velvet for tailor-mades

Serge and wool for men's winter suits

Lace, faille, silk satin, silk chiffon, mousseline, net, gilt lace for gowns and tea gowns

Taffeta for petticoats

Simulated silk warp prints for gowns

## Important Edwardian Designers and Manufacturers

**BOUÉ SOEURS:** In 1900, the Boué Soeurs were known for their lingerie dresses, which were all white and extremely popular because they could be easily cleaned and were practical for summer activity.

**JACQUES DOUCET:** Doucet was known for his opulent gowns made of lace, mousseline, satin, and for silk tea gowns, tailored suits, and fur-lined coats in the late nineteenth and early twentieth centuries. He used pastels and iridescent silks as well.

**DUVELLEROY:** Duvelleroy designed and produced fans for the Edwardian woman.

**FORTUNY:** Fortuny is best known for his unique pleating style, the product of a process that he patented in 1909. His pleated gowns and cloaks were dyed vivid colors with vegetable extracts. The overall effect was silk that looked like velvet. One of his most famous designs was the Delphos dress, which was sleeveless or had dolman sleeves. It was a tubular cut dress, tied at the waist with a cord. His free-flowing designs were favorites of Isadora Duncan. He also had a line of designs that were adaptations of ethnic garments: the kimono, the North African burnous and djellabah, and the sari.

**MADAME GEORGETTE:** One of the best Parisian milliners prior to World War I, Mme. Georgette trimmed wide-brimmed straw hats with ribbon, faux flowers, and veils.

**GILLET:** Gillet designed and manufactured shoes.

**GLUYS-BROUGHELL:** Gluys-Broughell designed and manufactured fans in the Edwardian period.

**HELLSTERN & SONS:** Known as fine designers and makers of women's shoes, Hellstern and his sons designed beaded evening slippers with heels and leather pumps with buckle decorations in the early part of the twentieth century.

**LIBERTY & CO.:** Liberty & Co. supplied and imported textiles with fanciful Art Nouveau motifs of flora and fauna.

**MADAME PAQUIN:** Since opening her own shop in 1891, Paquin was well known for her romantic clothes that came to be known as "Fairyland" dresses in the teens.

**PAUL POIRET:** Poiret began designing on his own in 1904. He extended the corset to the hips, thereby creating a more relaxed silhouette which became the dominant style into the next decade. Poiret's 1908 designs were simple, soft gowns that differed from the tight, corseted look so popular at the time.

His loose-looking designs were popular with the famous dancer Isadora Duncan, and others. In 1909, Poiret designed a collection that was heavily influenced by the Ballets Russes, with turbans, aigrettes, and harem pants in bold colors which became the fashion trend in the teens.

**REDFERN:** In 1908, he helped to popularize the Grecian style with a high waist for ladies' dresses.

**CAROLINE REBOUX:** Renowned for her fine millinery, Caroline Reboux was a French designer of finely made hats for ladies.

## 1900–1910
### Introduction Frontispiece

**C. 1904 AQUA SILK GOWN.** Bodice of silk crepe, the neck insert and sleeve ruffles of fine ecru lace, silk floss combined with corded floss and chenille in highly textured embroidery design, with added metallic beads and sequins, boned bodice lined with silk, hooks up back, skirt of several layers of silk chiffon over satin underskirt, the top skirt, rows of horizontal tucks, satin bands and bows outline central metallic lace panel, wide satin border hems bottom, label: "Thurn New York," very good condition, outside excellent. $1,675. (See photograph on page 10)
*Courtesy of Linda Ames, Vintage Textile.*

## MARKET TRENDS FOR THE 1900S

### Underpinnings and Lingerie

**C. 1905 PETTICOAT.** Fine cotton and linen cloth, Valenciennes lace, cotton twill drawstring, triple layers of cloth and flounces add fullness at bottom of petticoat, excellent condition. $250
*Courtesy of Karen Augusta, Antique Lace & Fashion, www.antique-fashion.com*

**C. 1905 NIGHTGOWN.** White cotton muslin, eyelet lace, fitted yoke and shoulders, three chin buttons, excellent condition. $145
*Courtesy of Karen Augusta, Antique Lace & Fashion, www.antique-fashion.com*

**C. 1900 PETTICOAT.** Fine cotton, embroidered eyelet, set waistband, excellent condition. $220
*Courtesy of Miss Kitty & Calico Jack, The Cat's Pajamas, PA, www.catspajamas.com*

**C. 1900 PANTALOONS.** White fine broadcloth, side ties, blue detail work, cutwork, and ruffled cuffs, initialed "M," excellent condition. $75
*Courtesy of The Fainting Couch, MA, www.faintingcouch.com*

"Silk and Linen Blouses," from *Vogue*, 1902. *Courtesy of Irene Lewisohn Costume Reference Library, The Metropolitan Museum of Art.*

## Blouses

c. 1905 BLACK BATTENBERG LACE BLOUSE. Bobbin lace, chemical lace medallion, silk neck band, metal snaps, exceptional, excellent condition. $265
*Courtesy of Karen Augusta, Antique Lace & Fashion, www.antique-fashion.com*

c. 1905 WHITE BATTENBERG LACE BLOUSE. Cotton floss, china silk, steel hooks and eyes, classic handmade Edwardian, perfect condition. $265
*Courtesy of Karen Augusta, Antique Lace & Fashion, www.antique-fashion.com*

## Dresses and Suits

**EDWARDIAN HOUSEDRESS.** Orchid cotton check, attached original Gilchrist Paper ticket, excellent condition. $225
*Courtesy of The Fainting Couch, MA, www.faintingcouch.com*

**C. 1900 IVORY NET DRESS.** Lace inserts, buttoned back with mother-of-pearl buttons, excellent condition. $345
*Courtesy of Miss Kitty & Calico Jack, The Cat's Pajamas, PA,*
*www.catspajamas.com*

**C. 1900 JAPANESE-INSPIRED DRESS.** Sheer cotton, red and white woven windowpane plaid, pigeon-breasted bodice with front hooks, puffed sleeves with lace ruffles, ecru polished cotton lining, skirt unlined for summer wear, very good condition. $785
*Courtesy of Linda Ames, Vintage Textile, www.vintagetextile.com*

**C. 1900 TWO-PIECE DAY DRESS.** Pale pink cotton, printed red and tan flowers, unboned blouse with front tying belt attached, four mother-of-pearl buttons, charming, excellent condition. $285
*Courtesy of Karen Augusta, Antique Lace & Fashion, www.antique-fashion.com*

**C. 1900 LINEN WALKING SUIT.** Jacket fits snugly at waist and flares out over hips, tiny watch pocket at waist, jacket and skirt lavishly decorated with dark brown soutache, dark brown piping outlines skirt pocket, collar, cuffs, and armhole seams, jacket and skirt edged with beige linen lace, excellent condition. $985
*Courtesy of Linda Ames, Vintage Textile, www.vintagetextile.com*

**C. 1908 WALKING SUIT (JACKET AND SKIRT).** Woven linen and cotton, velvet cuffs and collar, steel hooks and eyes, mother-of-pearl buttons, classic walking suit, mint condition. $495
*Courtesy of Karen Augusta, Antique Lace & Fashion, www.antique-fashion.com*

**C. 1908 EDWARDIAN WALKING SUIT.** Cream wool flannel, pink velvet, silk soutache braid, silk tassels, cream silk twill jacket lining, brass hooks and eyes, and steel snaps and eyes, handwork surface decorations, soutache worked as trailing tulips, lavish raised silk embroidery, oversized tasseled heart medallions, embroidered decorative buttons, three-dimensional Irish crocheted flowers meandering over mesh trellis, museum quality, excellent condition. $2,800
*Courtesy of Karen Augusta, Antique Lace & Fashion, www.antique-fashion.com*

## Evening Dresses and Gowns

**C. 1904 SILK TAFFETA GOWN.** French watered silk taffeta, ikat pattern, boned bodice lined in silk taffeta with front hooks, neckline draped with

"Early Spring Models" from *Vogue*, 1902. *Courtesy of Irene Lewisohn Costume Reference Library, The Metropolitan Museum of Art.*

ecru silk chiffon and blond lace, front panel inset of pleated silk chiffon outlined with lace, sleeves with wide draped border of silk chiffon, trained skirt, label: "Marie Crespin–52 rue Washington–Paris," very good condition. $1,475
*Courtesy of Linda Ames, Vintage Textile, www.vintagetextile.com*

C. 1908 LACE TEA GOWN. Valenciennes lace trimmed with handmade Cluny bobbin lace (linen) with insets of embroidered cotton lawn, 19 small mother-of-pearl buttons (close center back) very fine silk chiffon lining, known provenance, excellent condition. $1,850
*Courtesy of Karen Augusta, Antique Lace & Fashion, www.antique-fashion.com*

c. 1908 TEA GOWN. Bodice and skirt of ecru cotton lawn, Swiss embroidered lace, Cluny and Valenciennes bobbin laces, each of three different laces has circle pattern motif, sculptural eyelet flounces, label on petersham: "Mme. Rondelle Boston Mass.," known provenance, excellent condition. $750
*Courtesy of Karen Augusta, Antique Lace & Fashion, www.antique-fashion.com*

c. 1910 LAVENDER SATIN GOWN. Overdress of pale lavender net, richly decorated with silk ribbon embroidery, soutache, and beads, pale green sash wraps diagonally around hips and waist, bodice, neckline and sleeves fashioned from ecru lace, outer sleeve of pale pink dotted net with band of beaded ribbon embroidery, trained skirt, label: "Shepard Company, Providence, R.I.," very good condition. $1,525
*Courtesy of Linda Ames, Vintage Textile, www.vintagetextile.com*

## Outerwear

c. 1900 RECTANGULAR SILK SHAWL. High quality, heavy silk faille, each end of long rectangle finished with 21" wide border of plaited and knotted warp threads, ending with fringe, 122" l × 33" w, excellent condition. $285
*Courtesy of Linda Ames, Vintage Textile, www.vintagetextile.com*

EARLY 20TH CENTURY PRINTED SILK PAISLEY SHAWL. French black silk chiffon shawl, jacquard weave pattern of flowers and vines, large printed medallions in center ground have floral paisley motifs, multicolored printed border, 80" l × 42" w, pristine, excellent condition. $425
*Courtesy of Linda Ames, Vintage Textile, www.vintagetextile.com*

1895–1905 ECRU COAT. Wool, appliqués outlined in soutache on mesh ground creates lace effect, flared back, excellent condition. $985
*Courtesy of Linda Ames, Vintage Textile, www.vintagetextile.com*

1895–1905 RUSSIAN EVENING COAT. Cream wool flannel, silk velvet and passementerie, tape work inset into body of coat creates lacy effect, unusual for woolen coat, made to be worn unfastened, unlined, perfect condition. $950
*Courtesy of Karen Augusta, Antique Lace & Fashion, www.antique-fashion.com*

c. 1900 IRISH LACE CUT-AWAY-STYLE COAT. Cut-away front, flared back below waist, sleeves end in points, wide border of three-dimensional lace motifs, excellent condition. $875
*Courtesy of Linda Ames, Vintage Textile, www.vintagetextile.com*

c. 1900 ECRU WOOL COAT. Wide cape collar has cut-out pattern of lace appliqués, silk pile collar and sleeves, lavishly trimmed with hand-

made linen needle lace, metallic lace, decorated front with 8 hand-embroidered buttons and corded rosettes with long tassels, probably French, very good condition. $1,550
*Courtesy of Linda Ames, Vintage Textile, www.vintagetextile.com*

c. 1900 IRISH LACE COAT IN A FLORAL PATTERN. Allover hand-made floral pattern, row of crocheted buttons down full length of skirt, centered in circular motifs, excellent condition. $1,385
*Courtesy of Linda Ames, Vintage Textile, www.vintagetextile.com*

c. 1908 SUMMER COAT. Cream colored cotton duck, classic sailor collar, silk and cotton soutache and braid decorations, three mother-of-pearl buttons, excellent condition. $285
*Courtesy of Karen Augusta, Antique Lace & Fashion, www.antique-fashion.com*

c. 1908 SILK SATIN JACKET CUT-AWAY STYLE. Vented back, wide bell sleeves, jacket lavishly decorated with scrolling pattern of green soutache, pale green silk lining, generous size, excellent condition. $695
*Courtesy of Linda Ames, Vintage Textile, www.vintagetextile.com*

## Accessories

c. 1908 LACE AND STRAW HAT. Braided leghorn straw, wire frame covered in silk gauze, Valenciennes lace, silk ribbons, cotton covering decorated with soutache braid, embroidery, Irish crocheted roses and cotton net China silk lining, "McNulty & Co. Ladies Hatters Rochester," near-perfect condition. $1,150
*Courtesy of Karen Augusta, Antique Lace & Fashion, www.antique-fashion.com*

c. 1902 WOOL FELT HAT. Chenille trim, ostrich feathers, black and white velvet ribbon, silk lining, original silk-covered hat pin, excellent condition. $110
*Courtesy of Karen Augusta, Antique Lace & Fashion, www.antique-fashion.com*

EDWARDIAN BLACK STRAW HAT. Original trim of pink daisies, lined, excellent condition. $125
*Courtesy of Miss Kitty & Calico Jack, The Cat's Pajamas, PA, www.catspajamas.com*

c. 1900 VELVET HAT. Wide brim, dark green velvet, black velvet crown and edge of brim, feathers, ostrich plumes, and ecru satin bow decorations, original hat pin, excellent condition. $485
*Courtesy of Linda Ames, Vintage Textile, www.vintagetextile.com*

c. 1900 EVENING SHOES. Leather, jet beads, shoe buttons, three straps and beading hand-done, excellent condition. $295
*Courtesy of Karen Augusta, Antique Lace & Fashion, www.antique-fashion.com*

"Au Pesage" from *L'Art et la Mode: Journal de la Vie Mondaine*, 1907. *Courtesy of Irene Lewisohn Costume Reference Library, The Metropolitan Museum of Art.*

**1900–1910 WHITE LINEN PARASOL.** Oval lace inserts, ribs and tips of ribs in metal painted white, stick is bamboo bent at the handle with 1½″ bone tip, excellent condition. $325
*Courtesy of Karen Augusta, Antique Lace & Fashion, www.antique-fashion.com*

### Menswear

**1900s MEN'S BLACK WOOL VEST.** Black satin trim, size 40/41, excellent condition. $45
*Courtesy of Deborah Burke, Antique & Vintage Dress Gallery, www.antiquedress.com*

Embroidered Net Tea Dress. *Courtesy of Linda Ames, Vintage Textile,*
*www.vintagetextile.com. Photograph by Linda Ames.*

# 1910–1920
# Inspiration and Imagination

From 1910 to 1920, couture designers looked for new sources of inspiration for their fashions. The Ballet Russes of 1909 inspired couture designers to explore color and experiment with styles of dress. The foremost designer of the time, Paul Poiret, began using intense colors like red, orange, violet, blue, and emerald green. He designed dramatic evening dresses with Empire waists, kimono sleeves, and tunics over trouser skirts; his designs were often worn with turbans. Heavy capes of fur were worn over richly colored gowns. Madame Lanvin, equally influenced by the oriental costumes of the Ballet Russes, designed with rich materials: lamé and brocades of gold and silver.

Fashion also looked to painting for inspiration. The Fauve movement, which used vivid colors and free-flowing movement of shapes, introduced bright, solid blocks of color which were incorporated into fabric patterns. Poiret was the first to employ artists such as painter Raoul Dufy to design textiles. Dufy's beautifully colored palette lent itself to the designs of unusual and unique fabrics. Artists such as Paul Iribe and Georges Lepape used their art in fashion illustration; some of the most beautifully executed fashion drawings are from this period of Art Nouveau.

The dominant silhouette of the decade was a straight figure. To achieve this look, a corset was cut low in the bust and had a more natural waistline. It fit closely over the hips and had an additional brassiere. These changes in underclothes left clothing designers free to experiment with many skirt styles.

Poiret is credited with the "lampshade" style—a wired tunic top over a narrow skirt—which led to a minaret line of clothing in 1913. His most famous design was the hobble skirt of 1910, which was so narrowly tapered that the wearer had difficulty maneuvering and even walking. Small slits or pleats had to be added to make walking possible. The hobble skirt was followed by the pantaloon skirt, harem pants, and the popular walking "trotteur" skirt.

Necklines gradually changed from high necks to rounded collars to V-shapes. Tambour embroidery with beading and tambour lace was often used to decorate dresses and blouses. Jackets were long and loose, trimmed with fur in the winter. Some of the most beautiful coats were designed in the teens: full-length and full-cut wraps, cloaks, and capes, often cut from luxurious cloth and accented with beading, fur collars, and cuffs.

Evening clothes remained elaborate throughout most of the decade. In 1911, one of the more unusual fashion statements was a dress with an uneven hemline and fishtail train, which was divided in two and could be worn loose or pulled between the legs to the front and made into harem pants. In 1913, couples enjoyed the new dance rage, the tango, and the designer Lucile introduced her tango dress with a slightly flounced skirt and knee-length tunic. In 1915, sleeveless evening gowns were narrow at the hem and had décolleté necklines and trains. Trains continued as a fashion shown even through the wartime.

There were two daytime dress styles by 1915: semi-fitted or waisted with a full skirt. By 1916, skirts were very full and bodices on dresses were very small in contrast. Waist placement varied with designer and eventually was eliminated altogether with Chanel's loose, low-waisted chemise jersey dresses, a fashion which would be the dominant theme of the next decade.

Paris fashions were copied and sold in American department stores. Unfortunately for them, Parisian designers could not receive profits from these ready-to-wear copies of their designs. With this practice, fashion was reaching more people and couture designs were accessible to more women. Mail-order added another new dimension to fashion and ads continued to lure women with "designs from Paris."

Sports clothing gained in popularity as women participated in tennis, golf, and skating. Bloomers, knickers, and fur skating costumes were prevalent and gave a new freedom to women's dress that had a great impact on the fashions of the decade ahead.

During World War I, there was a scarcity of cotton and wool, so silk was used in abundance. Much of the silk was woven with metallic thread which made it heavier and more expensive; it was called weighted silk. Unfortunately, the weight of metallic thread also made the silk deteriorate more rapidly. It is hard to find pieces from this period which are still intact. Colored dyes were in short supply so fabrics were pale. During the war, women worked in military industries and needed an alternative dress that was casual and practical. While women learned labor skills during the war effort, fashions became more versatile and less decorous, although not changing fashion entirely.

Before the war, designers such as Poiret, Paquin, and Callot Soeurs reigned supreme with very fancy fashions. After the war, Chanel, Patou, and Vionnet came to the foreground as the next couture designers with simpler fashions. Chemise gowns in georgette, crepe, lamé, gold and silver cloth were worn for evening. Wearing all black or all white attire was a popular fashion trend. Chanel experimented with jersey, which became her signature fabric for later clothing designs. Chanel's ensemble, called the dressmaker suit, consisted of a slim, straight skirt, cardigan, loose jacket, and matching blouse. Soon, jackets were virtually shapeless with soft rounded shoulders and an optional loosely styled belt.

Early in the teens, hats were formal, decked with feathers and ribbons. These hats were thought to enhance the slimmed silhouette. As clothes took on a more relaxed feeling, hairstyles were less full and hats were closer to the head, usually of velvet and silk, with small, unadorned brims.

An evening hat was sometimes a simple large feather aigrette on a band or turban. Shoes often had high vamps and many buttons; later, the Louis heel, a thick covered heel that flared out from the mid-section, was the most popular shoe style. Handbags were larger because women needed to carry more belongings when they worked. Large knitted and handmade bags were especially common. Gradually, fashion trends began to reflect the emerging, independent, and more active roles of women in society. Women could now choose styles reflective of their changing lifestyle.

Men's fashions were also increasingly relaxed. Suits were trimly tailored with shorter jackets, narrow sleeves, and soft shoulders. Trousers were pleated and cuffed with a high waist. Evening clothes followed the same styling with noteworthy formal features like fur-collared overcoats, high silk hats, and well-tailored waistcoats. Bow ties were shown with resort outfits and straw Panama hats. Gloves and walking sticks still completed many an outfit as did button shoes and spats.

## Signature Fabrics of the Teens

Silk, weighted silk for gowns and capes

Silk satin and silk chiffon for gowns

Fur for collars and cuffs

Georgette, crepe, lamé for gowns

Jersey, the signature fabric for Chanel

Velvet and satins for Eastern-style eveningwear

Gauze, taffeta, poplin, and silk for tea gowns

## Important Designers and Manufacturers of the Teens

**RAOUL DUFY:** Dufy was an artist who worked for Paul Poiret developing dyeing techniques for fabrics in the early teens. He later became the artistic director of Bianchini-Ferier, a French fabric company for which he designed silks and brocades with strong designs and colors.

**HELLSTERN & SONS:** A Parisian shoe designer and maker, Hellstern & Sons was known for their leather and beaded pumps.

**JEANNE LANVIN:** In the teens, Lanvin's designs tended toward the romantic and feminine with her *robes de style* which remained popular through the early twenties. She also showed a line of picture dresses with decidedly Victorian-inspired shapes and embroidered ornamentation. Later in the teens, her designs reflected the influences of the Orient with her Eastern-style eveningwear of velvets and satins.

**LUCILE:** Lucile also favored feminine styles through the teens with her tea gowns in gauze, tafetta, poplin, and silk. Her name is also associated with colored underwear and pastel colors in her designs. Her hats during this decade favored more romantic styles with satin crowns and fur trim.

**MADAME PAQUIN:** Paquin's "Fairyland" dresses of the Edwardian era were still favorites with women in the teens. In 1913, she also showed day dresses that were designed to be worn into the evening. Aware of the increasingly active role of twentieth century women, Paquin's designs were a combination of draped and tailored lines that reflected women's need to be comfortable in their activities. Other well-known Paquin designs include her tango dresses, lingerie, and fur creations.

**JEAN PATOU:** Jean Patou first opened a house in his own name in 1919, after a break from fashion while serving in World War I. His first collection included shepherdess dresses with Russian-style embroidery.

**PAUL POIRET:** In the teens, Poiret continued to bring novel changes to the current silhouette. In 1911, he introduced the hobble skirt, a design which freed the hips but confined the ankles. It was not widely adopted in common dress, although it caused a great deal of controversy. Another novel design was the "lampshade" tunic which had internal wiring to make it stand away from the body. Poiret also tried to popularize harem pants as an alternative to long skirts under tunics.

**MADELEINE VIONNET:** In 1912, Vionnet opened her own couture house. She closed it during World War I and reopened after the war ended, continuing with her innovative designs. Early in her career, Vionnet pioneered cutting on the bias and draped designs. She did not work with the corset shape, but used her new cutting styles and diagonal seams to create her signature fluid lines that grew in popularity in the twenties and thirties.

## 1910–1920
### *Introduction Frontispiece*

c. 1915 EMBROIDERED NET TEA DRESS. White, lavish embroidery, crisp ruffles, neckline framed with band of delicate lace, dress closes in back with hooks, snaps, and tiny buttons, sash, aqua silk satin ribbon, woven in checkerboard pattern, excellent condition. $650 (See photograph on page 22)
*Courtesy of Linda Ames, Vintage Textile.*

## MARKET TRENDS FOR THE TEENS

### *Lingerie*

c. 1910 EMBROIDERED NIGHTGOWN. Fine linen with cotton hand-embroidery of bird, flowers, and bows, lavender silk twill ribbon, beautifully finished and hand-sewn, exceptional, made in Italy, excellent condition. $275
*Courtesy of Karen Augusta, Antique Lace & Fashion, www.antique-fashion.com*

c. 1910 EMBROIDERED CAMI-KNICKERS. Fine linen lawn, cotton floss, silk ribbons, hand-embroidered roses and rosebuds at front of camisole and at hem of knickers, original ribbons, entirely hand-stitched, perfect condition. $145
*Courtesy of Karen Augusta, Antique Lace & Fashion, www.antique-fashion.com*

c. 1910 LACE PETTICOAT. Cotton lawn, cotton floss, Valenciennes lace, beautifully hand-done workmanship in all seams and embroidery, tiny pin tucks, lace inserts, excellent condition. $285
*Courtesy of Karen Augusta, Antique Lace & Fashion, www.antique-fashion.com*

c. 1915 LACE NEGLIGEE. Fine handkerchief linen, handmade bobbin lace, Valenciennes lace, lavender silk ribbon, all hand-sewn, French seams, exquisite, perfect condition. $225
*Courtesy of Karen Augusta, Antique Lace & Fashion, www.antique-fashion.com*

c. 1914 SILK NEGLIGEE. Pale peach-pink China silk, ecru lingerie lace, silk satin binding, armholes, neckline, and hem bound with satin tape, scalloped bottom hem, completely hand-sewn, excellent condition. $95
*Courtesy of Karen Augusta, Antique Lace & Fashion, www.antique-fashion.com*

c. 1914 SILK NEGLIGEE. Light pink China silk, handmade Buckinghamshire bobbin lace, completely hand-sewn, excellent condition. $95
*Courtesy of Karen Augusta, Antique Lace & Fashion, www.antique-fashion.com*

## Summer Dresses

c. 1910 LINEN DRESS LAVISHLY DECORATED. Taupe, bodice decorated with numerous rows of pin tucks, lace inserts, and wide tucks, applied crocheted balls in lace, long sleeved, flared skirt, perfect condition. $635
*Courtesy of Linda Ames, Vintage Textile, www.vintagetextile.com*

c. 1915 AFTERNOON LACE TEA DRESS. White linen and lavish lace, pin tucks on shoulders and skirt sides, three-quarter-length sleeves, tiny mother-of-pearl buttons on top, hooks on skirt, excellent condition. $585
*Courtesy of Linda Ames, Vintage Textile, www.vintagetextile.com*

c. 1918 WHITE NET OVERDRESS. Satin-stitched embroidered panels in center front and back, sides and sleeves fashioned with loosely woven floral pattern lace, net panels at hipline, sleeves cut in one piece with side panel, very good condition. $685
*Courtesy of Linda Ames, Vintage Textile, www.vintagetextile.com*

## Dresses and Gowns

c. 1910 LAVENDER SATIN GOWN. Overdress of pale lavender net decorated with silk ribbon, embroidery, soutache, and beads, pale green satin sash wraps diagonally around hips, bodice, neckline, and sleeves fashioned in ecru lace, outersleeve of pale pink dotted net with band of beaded ribbon embroidery, label: "Shepard Company, Providence, R.I.," very good condition. $1,525
*Courtesy of Linda Ames, Vintage Textile, www.vintagetextile.com*

c. 1910 EMBROIDERED AND LACE TEA GOWN. One-piece gown of cotton lawn and eyelet embroidery, Valenciennes lace, Irish lace, chemical lace, tiny Dorset buttons on each cuff, gown closes at center back, wearable, excellent condition. $465
*Courtesy of Karen Augusta, Antique Lace & Fashion, www.antique-fashion.com*

c. 1912 SILK CHIFFON EVENING GOWN IN CLASSIC GRECIAN LINES. Sage green silk chiffon, silk charmeuse, cream silk lace, silk tulle, glass beads, and painted velvet trim, 7 stays in bodice and silk twill petersham, yellow silk gauze lining, wool flannel hem lining, classic Grecian lines, couture, museum quality, excellent condition. $1,275
*Courtesy of Karen Augusta, Antique Lace & Fashion, www.antique-fashion.com*

c. 1914 EVENING DRESS WITH BLACK CHANTILLY LACE. Satin and silk chiffon decorated with black Chantilly lace, beading, and floral embroidery, intricate layering and construction of bodice and skirt with

Manteaux de jour.

"Manteaux de jour" from *L'Art et la Mode: Journal de la Vie Mondaine*, Spring/Autumn, 1913. *Courtesy of Irene Lewisohn Costume Reference Library, The Metropolitan Museum of Art.*

three layers on bodice and two on skirt, lace on bodice front, back, and sleeves embroidered with lavender flowers in silk floss, a satin cummerbund and beaded rope cord define waist, label: "Carrear Easiman—Providence, R.I.," excellent condition. $685
*Courtesy of Linda Ames, Vintage Textile, www.vintagetextile.com*

c. 1915 ECRU NET DRESS. Bands of ecru embroidered flowers outlined with contrasting bands of black net, aqua satin cummerbund defines waist, stand-up collar, label: "Chandler & Co, Tremont St. Boston" dated 6/4/15, by hand, excellent condition. $425
*Courtesy of Linda Ames, Vintage Textile, www.vintagetextile.com*

c. 1915 BLACK NET DRESS. Allover embroidery, polka dot, layered and draped over black satin underdress, asymmetrical period style featuring panels of black jet beads from shoulder to skirt on one side, draped pan-

French Embroidered and Beaded Net Tea Dress. *Courtesy of Linda Ames, Vintage Textile, www.vintagetextile.com. Photograph by Linda Ames.*

*Detail of French Embroidered and Beaded Net Tea Dress.* Bodice of knotted net lace, with embellishments of embroidery and beads. *Photograph by Linda Ames.*

*Detail of Embroidery.* Knotted net lace combined with ribbon and cord embroidery to create floral design, with tassels and white beads. *Photograph by Linda Ames.*

**c. 1912 FRENCH EMBROIDERED AND BEADED NET TEA DRESS.** Beautiful knotted net lace combined with elaborate ribbon and cord embroidery creates design of flowers, flower baskets, and tassels, design further embellished with large white beads, underskirt front panel of very fine quality cotton batiste, delicate net forms middle tier of skirt and sleeves, top layer of skirt and neckline insert of very fine ecru lace, dress silk lined having inside boned bodice, superb quality with exquisite handwork, probably French, excellent condition. $1,265
*Courtesy of Linda Ames, Vintage Textile.*

els of netting on other side, black satin cummerbund with hanging tassels of jet beads, museum deaccession, perfect condition. $585
*Courtesy of Linda Ames, Vintage Textile, www.vintagetextile.com*

c. 1915 LACE AND SILK CHIFFON TEA DRESS. Handmade Irish lace and silk chiffon, pattern in variety of handmade floral motifs, lace forms loose overbodice ending in two long back tails, ecru net underbodice, skirt of coarse mesh with diamond grid and ecru silk lining, silk chiffon with drawn thread borders used for peplums, cummerbund, hem ruffle, label: "O'Hara, 21 West 46th St., New York," mint condition. $875
*Courtesy of Linda Ames, Vintage Textile, www.vintagetextile.com*

c. 1915 BEADED EVENING DRESS. Drop-waist bodice fashioned from combination of seed beads and bugle beads, beaded shoulder straps continue down over bodice ending in long beaded rope in front, skirt with asymmetrical design of ivory lace and net over underskirt of ecru satin, clear beads and pearls trim edge of swag, beaded appliqué of rhinestones, pearls, and gold beads decorates back, very good condition. $1,365
*Courtesy of Linda Ames, Vintage Textile, www.vintagetextile.com*

c. 1918 WINTER TEA GOWN IN PURPLE VELVET. Deep purple silk velvet, chiffon, metallic mesh, rhinestone and glass bead medallions, cream silk taffeta and purple satin lining, regal lines, rich color, perfect condition. $695
*Courtesy of Karen Augusta, Antique Lace & Fashion, www.antique-fashion.com*

## Jackets and Coats

c. 1910 LINEN COAT CUT-AWAY STYLE. Princess-line-styled front, flared back, shawl collar, lower sleeves and coat front generously decorated with scrolling pattern of soutache, Irish lace rosettes decorate bodice front and skirt back, excellent condition. $575
*Courtesy of Linda Ames, Vintage Textile, www.vintagetextile.com*

1912–1915 LACE JACKET WITH TROPICAL VINES. Off-white cotton thread, open front in Irish crochet, tropical trumpet vines and palm leaves worked into lace pattern, pristine, excellent condition. $475
*Courtesy of Karen Augusta, Antique Lace & Fashion, www.antique-fashion.com*

c. 1915 WHITE LINEN EMBROIDERED COAT. Hand-embroidered with scrolling floral pattern of satin stitch and seeding, three-quarter-length sleeves, back panel ends in fully embroidered open vents, crocheted buttons fasten front, mint condition. $865
*Courtesy of Linda Ames, Vintage Textile, www.vintagetextile.com*

## Accessories

C. 1912 BLACK STRAW HAT. Oversized with original decorations, ostrich feathers, silk roses over and under, with white ostrich feather detail, excellent condition. $545
*Courtesy of Deborah Burke, Antique & Vintage Dress Gallery, www.antiquedress.com*

C. 1915 GLASS BEADED PURSE. Glass beads in two sizes, tortoiseshell frame, brass fittings, white metal ball clasp, and navy silk faille lining, Art Nouveau flowers worked in purple, dark green, blue, orange, gold, and black beads, label: "Made in France," excellent condition. $240
*Courtesy of Karen Augusta, Antique Lace & Fashion, www.antique-fashion.com*

C. 1915 DUNHAM LEATHER SHOES. Wooden stacked heel, painted metal shoe buttons, stamped on insole, "The Dunham Shoe," excellent condition. $135
*Courtesy of Karen Augusta, Antique Lace & Fashion, www.antique-fashion.com*

C. 1910–1915 HIGH-BUTTON BOOTS. Kid leather, cotton twill lining, 1½" Cuban heel, stamped on sole, "Sherwood Good Shoes," excellent condition. $325
*Courtesy of Karen Augusta, Antique Lace & Fashion, www.antique-fashion.com*

"With the Renewal of Social Activities Dress Resumes Its Importance," from *Pictorial Review*, February 1919. *Courtesy of the author.*

Beaded Purse. *Courtesy of Isadora's, Seattle, WA, www.isadoras.com. Photograph by Jennifer A. Ledda.*

# Fringe and Frivolity

General prosperity brought social change, and with Prohibition it became fashionable to defy conventional ideas. Women won the right to vote and attitudes were changing. Fashions emphasized youth and were styled for the boyish torso. Bobbed hair, wide-open darkened eyes, lacquered nails, and made-up lips and cheeks defined the twenties woman. Clothes were simpler; heavy cotton and wool fabrics were replaced with light silks; short sleeveless dresses were fashionable. Coco Chanel challenged men's dressing and women began wearing fabrics like jersey with tailored clothing.

Early in the decade skirts were still ankle-length. The chemise-style dress was straight and long, emphasizing a low waist accented by drapery or decorative trim of bows, pockets, or embroidery. Caroline Reboux designed wide hats to flatter the line of the long chemise, suits, and coats. The chignon, a carefully pinned loose bun worn at the back of the neck, was a favored hairstyle early in the decade that complemented these hats.

Fashions and fabric designs were influenced by current events. In 1922, the ancient tomb of the Egyptian pharaoh, Tutankhamen, was discovered. Egyptomania followed; designers began employing Egyptian motifs into their collections.

The Exposition International des Arts Décoratifs et Industriels Modernes in 1925 in Paris spawned Art Deco designs in fabrics. Fabrics were defined by angled lines and motifs with cut edges. Compacts, cigarette cases, and a variety of mesh and envelope purses had Art Deco designing as well. The art movement in painting, Cubism, influenced fabric designs in the Art Deco movement and was often seen in the work of painter and fabric designer, Sonia Delaunay-Terk.

The *"robe de style"* was a full-skirted, feminine, nostalgic dress of silk or taffeta with a bertha collar and lace. Dresses designed in this style offered an alternative to the casual silhouette of the twenties and were introduced by couture designers such as Lanvin and Boué Soeurs.

The flapper of the 1920s did not want to show a full bosom. She wore a garment called a bandeau, which was designed to flatten the breasts. Coordinated with this were the cami-knickers, silk camisoles, and silk teddies. Kimonos and colorful pajama costumes were designed for comfort. There was great demand for black-seamed silk, beige silk, and clocked stockings with garters and garter buttons.

Shorter dresses made shoes more noticeable. Heels were curved and "Louis-heeled" pumps were sometimes decorated with rhinestones, enamel work, or cloisonné. Pumps with marcasite buckles, T-straps, and single-button straps were all popular for dancing.

Hats in the early twenties were turbans or brimmed hats with egret and ostrich feathers, appliqué, embroidery, beading, smocking, and often faux flowers, leaves, or fruit as trim. Picture hats made of straw or horsehair decked with silk flowers were still popular in the early twenties. However, the most renowned hat of this decade was the cloche, a cap-hat worn low over the brow often accessorized with dangle earrings. Hat pins matched brooches with rhinestones, bits of coral, or tortoise bars. By 1929, the tricorn was another popular style.

Other accessories included embroidered shawls worn as evening wraps and buttons made from René Lalique's molded glass. Clothing was accessorized with long strands of beads or pearls, glitter bracelets, and Bakelite. Irene Castle, a dancer and trendsetter, established a style in the teens by wearing a band across her forehead to hold her short haircut in place. This style was adopted by the young flappers of the twenties. As always, anything Parisian was popular: ribbons, laces, trims, beads, feathers, silk fabrics, and silk flowers.

The emphasis on sports throughout this decade inspired a variety of clothing, from tennis to bathing suits. Suntans and dieting were fashionable as more women took to the beaches. Designers used the colors tan, black, yellow, and tangerine to complement suntans. Women could now easily and affordably buy ready-made clothing in department stores. Fashion was more accessible to everyone.

In the last years of the twenties, Elsa Schiapparelli introduced hand-knitted sweaters to fashion. The coat and dress ensemble was popular daywear. Dresses were colorfully printed chiffon for summer and long-sleeved satin or silk jersey with tiny prints for fall. Uneven hemlines were chic. Coats had surplice fronts and often were trimmed with fur collars. Evening dresses were fancy, made of taffeta, mousseline, Chantilly lace, or velvet, and had details like pouf skirts, décolleté backs, asymmetrical hems, and even trains. The silhouette remained long and slender throughout the twenties with an emphasis on a low waist.

Men wore suit jackets with broader shoulders and fuller sleeves, high-rise trousers and matching waistcoats. The waistcoat of the twenties was high-cut, single- or double-breasted with six buttons, with or without lapels. The cutaway and waistcoat were formal attire. On campus, the regimental striped tie was popular and the bow tie was another option. The Oxford bags were a British fad of the mid-twenties with oversized trouser legs. Edward VIII, the Prince of Wales, made the Fair Isle sweater popular. Knickers were part of a sporting man's wardrobe in various lengths and bagginess, known as plus fours, plus sixes, and even plus eights. Pajamas replaced the nightshirt. Probably the most well-known men's garment of the decade was the raccoon fur coat. Walking sticks, canes of malacca with crooked handles, and mechanical canes were chic. Brown derby hats, the Homburg, and straw boaters were all worn. Shoes were worn with spats and oxfords were common.

## Signature Fabrics of the 1920s

Light silks, gabardine, and crêpe de chine for dresses

Silk, taffeta, or silk organdy for very feminine dresses

Silk or rayon for women's underwear

Printed chiffon for summer dresses

Satin or silk jersey for fall dresses

Jersey for Chanel suits

Taffeta, mousseline, Chantilly lace, or velvet for evening dresses

Handknit sweaters for women, Fair Isle for men

## Important Designers and Manufacturers of the 1920s

**ALEXANDRINE:** A French manufacturer of fine gloves, most popular between 1925 and 1930.

**ARGENCE:** In the twenties, Argence was most famous for their rhinestone-covered heels on pumps and boots.

**BOUÉ SOEURS:** Boué Soeurs favored the feminine look, which was also popular in the late teens, with the *robe de style* of taffeta and silk organdy with ribbon and lace trim.

**CALLOT SOEURS:** In the twenties, the Callot Soeurs added designs for day dresses to their lines of lingerie and ribbons. Their fancier dress designs were of velvet and laces with elaborate beadwork.

**"COCO" CHANEL:** In the twenties, Chanel continued to set trends with her designs and personal wardrobe. In 1920 she introduced wide-legged pants for women, known as "yachting pants." In 1922, she showed more pants for women with her wide-cut beach pajamas. These styles of pants were examples of Chanel's tendency to adapt menswear styles for women's fashions. Other examples included her belted raincoats, open-neck shirts, and blazers in beige, gray, and navy. In the twenties Chanel also first showed her signature design that remains today; jersey suits and the tweed skirt with sweater, faux pearl necklace and purse with gilt chain strap. Chanel also introduced the idea of the versatile "little black dress" in the 1920s.

**LILLY DACHÉ:** A milliner, Lilly Daché promoted the ubiquitous twenties cloche in several of her New York shops. Later in the twenties, she branched out and designed turbans with several different colors of velvet twisted together. This turban design increased in popularity in future decades.

**ROSE DESCAT:** Rose Descat, a French milliner, designed beautiful hats that were often copied in the United States.

**ECHO:** Founded during this decade, Echo made a name for themselves with their unique scarf designs.

**JOHN V. FARWELL CO.:** This Chicago-based company imported glass beaded bags from Paris. A common, inexpensive design was a reticule with a wide-striped pattern and beaded header. More expensive elements were jet or silver beads, tortoiseshell frames or silk linings. Other colors and more intricate patterns also added to the value of the bags. This particular company did not carry metal frame beaded bags in the twenties.

**FERRAGAMO:** An Italian shoe designer who moved to California in the twenties, Ferragamo was renowned for his handmade shoes. Concerned with comfort as well as design, Ferragamo took up to thirteen measurements of toes alone. His many unique twenties designs included some shoes inspired by Cubist and Futurists geometric designs, and Roman sandals with ankle straps. Ferragamo designed for Hollywood from 1923 to 1927, when he returned to Italy.

**HELLSTERN & SONS:** In the twenties, Hellstern & Sons showed three types of designs for shoes which they created in a variety of materials: bar shoes, chic boots, and pumps with 2"–3" high Louis heels. Their most frequently used materials included suede, kidskin, and dyed reptile skins. Often, they trimmed their designs with rhinestone buttons and fancy metal buckles.

Boots for day and evening were a company specialty, including fetish boots with heels up to 11″ high.

**PEGGY HOYT:** Hoyt was a milliner whose designs were fashionable with actresses of the twenties.

**CHARLES JAMES:** In 1927, James opened his millinery shop in New York City, designing hats as he had in Europe under the name Charles Boucheron. His first collection of women's fashions arrived in 1928. He showed wide-brimmed straw hats with tulle cockades in 1929.

**JANTZEN:** An Oregon-based company, Jantzen developed the elastic or "rib" stitch in the early twenties which they used to manufacture their innovative bathing suit designs. In 1921, the company introduced the "suit that changed bathing to swimming," an elastic one-piece bathing suit which allowed for more body movement as opposed to the bulky suits of other manufacturers. Jantzen showed sleeveless tunic styles with scooped necks attached at the waist to trunks for both men and women. These bathing suits were decorated with three wide horizontal stripes. This new design caused much controversy at public beaches in the early twenties. Despite the controversy, Jantzen sold these suits widely and their signature patch of a red-suited girl in mid-dive could be seen affixed to cars and other personal belongings as well as to the bathing suits.

**JEANNE LANVIN:** Lanvin was known for her romantic-style dress in the twenties, the *robe de style*. In 1921, she showed a collection with Aztec-inspired patterns and designs. Another of her famous designs was the Lanvin Breton suit of 1922, which had a short jacket, decorated with a large white collar and small buttons. The suit was usually shown and worn with a sailor style hat. Lanvin also designed the ubiquitous beaded dance dress, as well as a popular wool jersey casual dress in a gold and silver checkered pattern, and dinner pajamas.

**SALLY MILGRAM:** Milgram designed for her own house in the twenties and her lines also sold in major American department stores. Her popular advertisements featured famous actresses appearing in outfits named after them.

**JEAN PATOU:** A French designer, Patou was known in the early twenties in the United States for his sportswear. He designed golf ensembles and bathing suits as well as tennis outfits, including those worn by tennis star Suzanne Lenglen, who wore calf-length pleated skirts and long cardigans. Patou's other twenties designs included Cubism-inspired sweaters, and the 1929 Princess-line dresses which gave the illusion of high hips by raising the waistline. After 1924, Patou used his monogram on his designs.

**CAROLINE REBOUX:** A French milliner, Reboux helped to continue the popularity of the twenties cloche. In 1925, Reboux started a helmet-like version of the cloche, which was very popular. It was close-fitting but ended in a square crown, often with a fedora-like dent in the middle. These new cloches were often trimmed with oversized bows and had very small, irregular brims.

**ELSA SCHIAPARELLI:** Schiaparelli's first designs were black hand-knitted sweaters which had a white bow knit into the design, giving a *trompe l'oeil* effect. With these popular sweaters, Schiaparelli started her business and in 1928 she opened her New York City store.

**VALENTINA:** In the early twenties, Valentina showed designs with natural waistlines and covered bodices for order from her New York City shop. In 1926, she began designing costumes for stage productions. Valentina's clothing designs were known for their architectural lines and dramatic flair.

**MADELEINE VIONNET:** Vionnet's innovative cuts, which she had developed in the teens, became increasingly popular throughout the twenties. She used crêpe de chine, gabardine, and satin for afternoon and evening dresses. Her suits had bias-cut skirts and wraparound coats with side fasteners. Getting a smooth fit and shape were Vionnet's design goals.

**WHITING & DAVIS:** Whiting & Davis was the company that designed and manufactured the immensely popular mesh handbags of this decade. Their bags are almost always marked with the company trademark, either in miniature on the frame or on a tag attached to the handle or frame. Some of their most popular and widely copied designs include the 1922 "Princess Mary" purse, a silver-plated, baby-fine soldered mesh bag with pastel colored designs in patterns like the paintings of the Impressionists. Whiting & Davis purses varied in price, with sterling silver and soldered bags being more expensive because more workmanship was required.

## 1920s
### Introduction Frontispiece

**1920S BEADED PURSE.** Steel cut beads sewn onto gray knit purse, beads dangle to almost 4″ long, loops of dramatic steel cut beadwork, unknown metal frame with some floral detailing, chain link handle, pristine condition. $475 (See photograph on page 34)
*Courtesy of Isadora's, Seattle, WA.*

# Vintage Fashions of the Twenties

*Detail of Party Dress:* Black and
silver beads, petal-shaped hem.
*Photograph by Linda Ames.*

Party Dress. *Courtesy of Linda Ames,
Vintage Textile, www.vintagetextile.com.
Photograph by Linda Ames.*

**1920s Party Dress.** Black and silver beads on black net, petal-shaped
hem, black satin slip at the hipline, excellent condition. $585
*Courtesy of Linda Ames, Vintage Textile.*

French Evening
Coat. *Courtesy of
Linda Ames, Vintage
Textile, www.vintage-
textile.com. Photograph
by Linda Ames.*

*Detail of Evening Coat:* Gold and
silver metallic thread roses.
*Photograph by Linda Ames.*

**1920s FRENCH EVENING COAT.** Peach-pink silk chiffon with metallic
thread floral pattern, bands of lamé at sleeve borders and hem, white
ostrich feather collar, label: "Cadolle, no. 14 rue Cambon, Paris," very
good condition. $695
*Courtesy of Linda Ames, Vintage Textile.*

Georges Barbier. "Rosalinde Robe du Soir, de Worth" from *Gazette du Bon Ton*, 1922.
*Courtesy of Irene Lewisohn Costume Reference Library, The Metropolitan Museum of Art.*

Lace Dress. *Courtesy of Isadora's, Seattle, WA, www.isadoras.com. Photograph by Jennifer A. Ledda.*

**1920s LACE DRESS.** Classic 1920s, front of dress is slightly higher than back, back hem has slits of different lace panels which give effect of movement, pink beadwork accents around neckline with edging of rhinestones, pristine condition. $2,200

*Courtesy of Isadora's, Seattle, WA.*

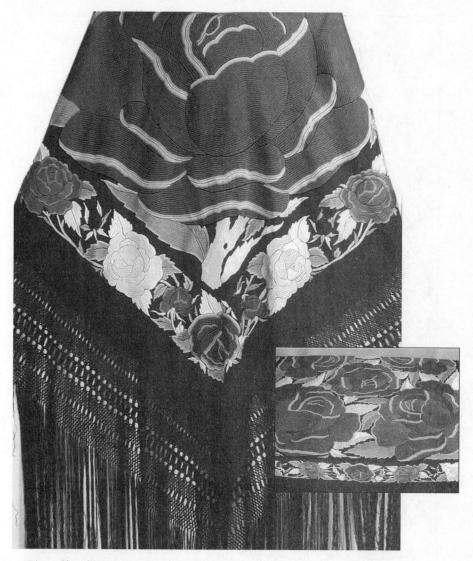

Piano Shawl. *Courtesy of Isadora's, Seattle, WA, www.isadoras.com. Photograph by Jennifer A. Ledda.*
*Detail of Piano Shawl: Roses. Photograph by Jennifer A. Ledda.*

**C. 1925 PIANO SHAWL.** Rare, fully embroidered with prominent flowers of reds, greens, peach, chartreuse, blue, magenta, and lavender, large rose measures 17½″ × 24″, silk square measures 62″ with a macramé trim of 7½″, fringe work ranges from 15–18″. A stunning contribution to any collection, pristine condition. $3,000
*Courtesy of Isadora's, Seattle, WA.*

Georges Lepape. "L'Eventail D'or," from *Gazette du Bon Ton*, March 1920. *Courtesy of Irene Lewisohn Costume Reference Library, The Metropolitan Museum of Art.*

Party Dress. *Courtesy of Linda Ames, Vintage Textile, www.vintagetextile.com. Photograph by Linda Ames.*

c. 1925 PARTY DRESS. "Henri Bendel" dramatically cut black silk velvet, bold rhinestone decoration, timeless, excellent condition. $585
*Courtesy of Linda Ames, Vintage Textile.*

*Detail of Black and Silver Dress:*
Silver sequins and black bugle
beads in Art Deco pattern.
*Photograph by Linda Ames.*

Black and Silver Dress. *Courtesy of Linda Ames,*
*Vintage Textile, www.vintagetextile.com. Photograph by*
*Linda Ames.*

1920S BLACK AND SILVER DRESS. Black net covered with silver
sequins and black bugle beads in Art Deco pattern, long fringe of marcasite beads hangs from shoulder straps, black silk crepe and black net
lining, excellent condition. $885
*Courtesy of Linda Ames, Vintage Textile.*

*Detail of Beaded Dress:* Beaded design. *Photograph by Linda Ames.*

Beaded Dress. *Courtesy of Linda Ames, Vintage Textile, www.vintagetextile.com. Photograph by Linda Ames.*

C. 1923 BEADED DRESS. Silk chiffon with a graphic design formed by small cobalt blue cut glass beads and bronze seed beads, blouson top and bateau neckline, wide sleeves bordered with gold lamé, excellent condition. $885

*Courtesy of Linda Ames, Vintage Textile.*

*Detail of Shawl:* Floral pattern.
*Photograph by Linda Ames.*

Shawl. *Courtesy of Linda Ames, Vintage Textile,*
*www.vintagetextile.com.*
*Photograph by Linda Ames.*

**1920s GOLD LAMÉ SHAWL.** Full-length, floral pattern of dusty rose,
blue, and purple, two decorative hanging tassels, reversible to dusty pink
ground with gold accents, excellent condition. $585
*Courtesy of Linda Ames, Vintage Textile.*

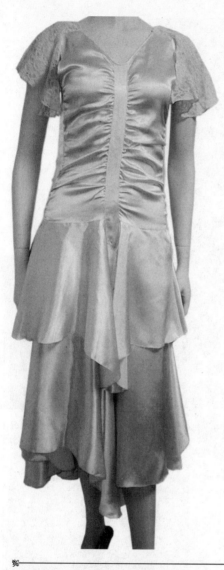

Evening Shoes. *Courtesy of Wendy
Radick, Kitty Girl Vintage,
www.kittygirlvintage.com.
Photograph by Wendy Radick.*

Champagne-Beige Tiered Gown.
*Courtesy of Wendy Radick, Kitty Girl
Vintage, www.kittygirlvintage.com.
Photograph by Wendy Radick.*

**1920s CHAMPAGNE-BEIGE TIERED GOWN.** Champagne-beige silk
satin tiered and ruched with train or tail, probably originally a wedding
dress, side hook closures, ecru lace falls gently at shoulders, excellent
condition. $265
*Courtesy of Wendy Radick, Kitty Girl Vintage.*

**1920s–1930s EVENING SHOES.** Royal blue silk, cut-out designs, gold
leather trim, fancy gold buckles decorated with little clear rhinestones;
white leather lining, well made, marked size 6½ M, 2¼″ heel, marked "HC
Capwell Oakland," very good to excellent condition. $75
*Courtesy of Wendy Radick, Kitty Girl Vintage.*

Shawl. *Courtesy of Linda Ames, Vintage Textile, www.vintagetextile.com. Photograph by Linda Ames.*

*Detail of Shawl:* Floral corner border. *Photograph by Linda Ames.*

**1920s SHAWL.** Art Deco floral print, silk crêpe de chine, mauve, hot pink, chartreuse, purple, light green, orange, beige, gray, and rusty red on a navy ground, 74″ l × 56″ w, very good condition. $300
*Courtesy of Linda Ames, Vintage Textile.*

## MARKET TRENDS FOR THE TWENTIES

### Lingerie and Robes

1920S PEIGNOIR. Pink silk crepe, lavish lace on dolman sleeves, faille ribbons, lavender and light blue rosettes, excellent condition. $125
*Courtesy of The Fainting Couch, MA, www.faintingcouch.com*

1920S PEACH CHEMISE SLIP. Fine lace bodice with tiny connecting bar, mint condition. $30
*Courtesy of The Fainting Couch, MA, www.faintingcouch.com*

1920S RAYON SLIP. Lace bodice, adjustable shoulder straps, original tags, mint condition. $30
*Courtesy of The Fainting Couch, MA, www.faintingcouch.com*

1920S CHEMISE. Short, flared, ivory, lace bodice, beautiful drape with back tie, very good condition. $30
*Courtesy of The Fainting Couch, MA, www.faintingcouch.com*

1920S NEGLIGEE. Peach silk crepe, filet lace, Irish lace, very good condition. $125
*Courtesy of Karen Augusta, Antique Lace & Fashion, www.antique-fashion.com*

### Couture

c. 1920 BOUÉ SOEURS NEGLIGEE. Pink silk, linen batiste, Mechlin lace, filet lace, embroidery, silk ribbon flowers, label: "Boué Soeurs 9 Rue de la Paix Paris 13 West 58th St. New York," very good condition. $250
*Courtesy of Karen Augusta, Antique Lace & Fashion, www.antique-fashion.com*

### Dresses

c. 1925 DOTTED SWISS SUMMER DRESS. Organdy, fabric rosettes on sleeves and at dropped waist, perfect condition. $235
*Courtesy of Karen Augusta, Antique Lace & Fashion, www.antique-fashion.com*

c. 1922 COTTON VOILE SUMMER DRESS. Silk flowers, rayon ribbon, pink voile short underbodice and deep faced hem, when worn over white slip dress has two horizontal bands of pink, muted by white dress fabric, perfect condition. $265
*Courtesy of Karen Augusta, Antique Lace & Fashion, www.antique-fashion.com*

1920S NUBBY WEAVE COTTON DAY DRESS. Bands of hand-worked cross-stitched embroidery, mother-of-pearl buttons, excellent condition. $135
*Courtesy of Karen Augusta, Antique Lace & Fashion, www.antique-fashion.com*

**1928–1930 AFTERNOON DRESS.** Attached overbodice, machine-made silk, lace, silk charmeuse lining, white metal brooch, pristine condition. $270
*Courtesy of Karen Augusta, Antique Lace & Fashion, www.antique-fashion.com*

**1920s BEADED COTTON DRESS.** Sheer pink voile ground, opaque white beads, chemise-style with added fullness in gathered skirt, hand-sewn seams, very good condition. $525
*Courtesy of Linda Ames, Vintage Textile, www.vintagetextile.com*

**1920s ROBE DE STYLE DRESS.** Silk faille, silk chiffon, silk crepe bodice lining, handsewn, rhinestones, excellent condition. $380
*Courtesy of Karen Augusta, Antique Lace & Fashion, www.antique-fashion.com*

## Eveningwear

**1920s CHEMISE DRESS.** Gold silk chiffon, black and brown velvet skirt, gold metallic thread work accenting hips and sleeves, excellent condition. $150
*Courtesy of Mary Troncale, Branford, CT.*

**1920s BLACK CHANTILLY LACE DRESS.** Black lace over pink satin, satin bows on sleeves, wide border of metallic gold lace on underskirt, high relief satin stitch embroidery defines hipline, excellent condition. $565
*Courtesy of Linda Ames, Vintage Textile, www.vintagetextile.com*

**1920s CHINOISERIE BEADED DRESS.** Colorful chinoiserie beading on light brown silk crêpe de chine, excellent condition. $675
*Courtesy of Linda Ames, Vintage Textile, www.vintagetextile.com*

**MID-1920s BLACK SILK CHIFFON DRESS.** Black silk chiffon over-dress, bold red and white roses outlined with red glass beads, green leaves outlined with metallic thread embroidery, black silk crepe slip, mint condition. $395
*Courtesy of Linda Ames, Vintage Textile, www.vintagetextile.com*

**c. 1926 BEADED PEACH CHIFFON DRESS.** Steel and silver colored beads, lined bodice, very good condition. $395
*Courtesy of Deborah Burke, Antique & Vintage Dress Gallery, www.antiquedress.com*

**c. 1927 BEADED DRESS.** Black silk chiffon, cut glass beading, graceful sleeves open at shoulder, satin rose at each hip, mint condition. $495
*Courtesy of Linda Ames, Vintage Textile, www.vintagetextile.com*

"Vous Ne Serez Jamais Prêts: Tailleur et robe de diners, de Doeuillet" from *Gazette du Bon Ton,* 1920. *Courtesy of Irene Lewisohn Costume Reference Library, The Metropolitan Museum of Art.*

**c. 1922 Beaded Dress.** Brown silk faille, glass beads, metallic thread, chiffon lining, "Adair, (Adair was a French Fashion House) the House of France, Made in France, Paris, London, Montreal, New York," mint condition. $600
*Courtesy of Karen Augusta, Antique Lace & Fashion, www.antique-fashion.com*

**c. 1922 Silk Chiffon Beaded Dress.** Carnival glass beads in burnt orange, underdress with beaded short sleeves, fabulous beading and open-work flowers, very good condition. $380
*Courtesy of Karen Augusta, Antique Lace & Fashion, www.antique-fashion.com*

**c. 1925 Ivory Beaded Dress.** Ivory silk satin, glass beading in geometric design, chiffon lining, "Made in France," excellent condition. $500
*Courtesy of Karen Augusta, Antique Lace & Fashion, www.antique-fashion.com*

**c. 1922 Black Silk Crepe Beaded Dress.** Jet beads, classic bow on hipline, hand-worked beading, excellent condition. $395
*Courtesy of Karen Augusta, Antique Lace & Fashion, www.antique-fashion.com*

**1920s BLACK SILK CHIFFON GOWN.** Asymmetrical design, gold lamé bands extend diagonally from back shoulder to front hip pointing to bias-cut draped skirt panel on other side, original black slip with bias-cut, draped skirt panel, mint condition. $495
*Courtesy of Linda Ames, Vintage Textiles, www.vintagetextiles.com*

**c. 1923 SILVER LAMÉ AND LACE EVENING GOWN.** Rhinestone design on bodice, rhinestone bow at hip, wearable size, reinforced silver lamé lining, very good condition. $845
*Courtesy of Deborah Burke, Antique & Vintage Dress Gallery, www.antiquedress.com*

## Evening Coats and Capes

**1920s METALLIC BROCADE EVENING CAPE.** Bordered with long silk fringe, fringed ties, unlined, "Julius Garfinckel, Washington-Paris," mint condition. $795
*Courtesy of Linda Ames, Vintage Textile, www.vintagetextile.com*

**1920s ROYAL BLUE OPERA COAT.** Royal blue silk velvet, metallic and silk brocade lining, gold braid, pristine condition. $495
*Courtesy of Karen Augusta, Antique Lace & Fashion, www.antique-fashion.com*

**1920s SILK VELVET EVENING CAPE.** Stand-up collar of silk roses, exquisite, excellent condition. $685
*Courtesy of Linda Ames, Vintage Textile, www.vintagetextile.com*

**1920s WRAP-STYLE EVENING COAT.** Black and gold metallic brocade in swirling pattern, velvet collar and cuffs ruched, padded, and rolled for extra fullness, bright gold silk damask lining, perfect condition. $925
*Courtesy Linda Ames, Vintage Textile, www.vintage.textile.com*

**1920s ART DECO DESIGN EVENING CAPE.** Black silk velvet combined with chenille crepe in textured design, shawl collar, black silk lining, neck closure, white plastic clasps studded with rhinestones, mint condition. $575
*Courtesy of Linda Ames, Vintage Textile, www.vintagetextile.com*

**1920s VELVET AND MINK TRIMMED COAT.** Brown corduroy type velvet cut to tan silk chiffon, mink trimmed collar and cuffs, alternating bands of velvet and bronze metallic trim form cuffs and front facing, brown silk crepe lining and interlined for added body, label inside: "St. James Shop, St. James Hotel, Philadelphia." $795
*Courtesy of Linda Ames, Vintage Textile, www.vintagetextile.com*

## Accessories

1920S ART DECO SHAWL. Lamé and satin, red on ground of black and gold, two hanging bronze tassels, 50″ square, excellent condition. $695
*Courtesy of Linda Ames, Vintage Textile, www.vintagetextile.com*

1920S PIANO SHAWL. Black silk, multicolored embroidery, wide-fringed borders, excellent condition. $900
*Courtesy of Vintage by Stacey Lee, White Plains, NY.*

c. 1925 SUMMER CLOCHE. Mesh woven raffia, red felt, celluloid flower, red lining, excellent condition. $125
*Courtesy of Karen Augusta, Antique Lace & Fashion, www.antique-fashion.com*

1920S CLOCHE. Gold lamé, lace, faux flower trim, pink silk underbrim, label: "Adelon Paris," excellent condition. $325
*Courtesy of Deborah Burke, Antique & Vintage Dress Gallery, www.antiquedress.com*

1920S SILK SHOES. Black, gold, silk damask, gold damask 3″ heel, wearable, excellent condition. $175
*Courtesy of Miss Kitty & Calico Jack, The Cat's Pajamas, PA, www.catspajamas.com*

1920S T-STRAP SHOES. White leather T-straps, perforated and cut out on top and toe, square cut-out sides, 3½″ heel, excellent condition. $75
*Courtesy of The Fainting Couch, MA, www.faintingcouch.com*

## Menswear

c. 1925 MEN'S BATHING SUIT. Wool, plastic button, all original silk woven label and two paper labels, "Jantzen Knitting Mills," men's size 38, excellent condition. $250
*Courtesy of Karen Augusta, Antique Lace & Fashion, www.antique-fashion.com*

Silk Embroidered Lounging Outfit. *Courtesy of Wendy Radick, Kitty Girl Vintage, www.kittygirlvintage.com. Photograph by Wendy Radick.*

# THE 1930s
# Glitter and Glitz

The movies, that most twentieth century medium, began to seriously influence fashion and design in the thirties. Madeleine Vionnet's signature-style bias-cut gowns were the inspiration for many Hollywood fashions. Glamorous movie stars wore lavish, backless gowns of satin or lamé. Adrian, the prominent Hollywood designer, created classic gowns that were halter-topped and backless with shimmering sequins. His shoulder-padded designs, popularized by Joan Crawford and Greta Garbo, came to signify the self-assured woman. Movies sold fashion and everyone wanted it.

Even the working girl wore a tailored, double-breasted suit with a flared or pleated skirt, and a sensational hat. Suits had slightly fitted skirts with longer hemlines below the waist-length jackets. Afternoon dresses were floral silk chiffons with long skirts that flared at the knee. Required for evening were long gowns and velvet coats trimmed with fur, wraps, or lush silver fox furs, scarves, and muffs. Silk, lace-trimmed peach-colored lingerie, negligees with beading, embroidery, or appliqué added to the glamour of the decade.

Clothing was feminine; hair was softly permed. The silhouette of clothing had a slim waist, narrow hips, and wider shoulders. Skirt lengths got longer as the day progressed: below-the-knee in the afternoon, mid-calf for tea, ankle-length for dancing and full-length for evening. The Great Depression of 1929 influenced the amount of clothing women purchased as well as what types of fabric were used. Evening gowns were made in cottons, sweaters were back for daywear, and a suit was suggested as an all-day apparel that could take on many different looks.

Sportswear was widely popular. Bare-midriff tops, lounging pajamas, playsuits, culottes, knee-length skiing and skating skirts, Lastex swimsuits and separates, the two-piece bathing suit, and molded bathing suits with bra tops were all new ideas in the thirties.

Two of the most important fashion accessories in the thirties were the belt and the hat. Mainbocher came out with the "glamour belt," a decorative accessory which enabled a woman to change the look of a dress instantly. Belt buckles were Art Deco geometric designs in paste or Bakelite with rhinestones. Rhinestone dress clips and removable collars and cuffs were also popular accessories that gave a single outfit more versatility.

Hat styles varied widely in the thirties. There were many small, knitted designs including berets of Lastex yarns, the Schiaparelli knit madcap, and tams. There were also many hat styles that were humorous, like the monster-sized cartwheel hat and Schiaparelli's shoe and lamb chop hat, the itsy-bitsy doll hat, and dunce cap style. As in other fashions, asymmetry was used for hat styles. For evening, women wore turbans and headdresses such as those designed by Chanel. The mesh chenille snood or résille caught shoulder-length hair at the nape, keeping it neat under a small hat. Veiling was often embroidered or sequined and came in four lengths: eyelash, nose, chin, and belt-buckle. Tall turbans were worn tipped forward on piles of permed curls and were held in place with a band across the back of the head. Scarves were also used to hold hats in place. Hat trims could be and were anything, including fur, ribbons, feathers, and faux flowers, fruit, and jewels. In the thirties, sandals and open-toed shoes were popular among women. Other common shoe styles were wedge-shaped heel designs and ankle strap designs. For the casual look, women wore oxfords and brogues in alligator, lizard, or suede.

There was also a large variety of purses by couture designers like Paquin, who styled a sling bag, and Schiaparelli, who designed colorful suedes, the shocking pink evening bag, and other more fanciful bags. The most common shapes for purses were back strap pouches or envelope bags, which came in cloth and skins. Straw handbags with faux fruits and vegetables were also popular, as well as top-handled purses, zippered pochettes, and crescent-shaped bags. Evening purses were smaller and decorated with a variety of materials: jewels, sequins, brocades, and needlepoint. Other fashionable accessories were celluloid and paper advertising fans which restaurants and shops manufactured to hand out to their customers. Gloves were longer and were often gauntlets; they were made in a variety of colors and textures and remained a basic part of a woman's wardrobe.

Buttons tended to be somewhat whimsical, such as Bakelite novelty buttons, catlin plastic "Style-fruit," Walt Disney characters, painted buttons with island scenes, and plastic realistics. Buttons also came in wood and glass and were sold on cards. Schiaparelli used whimsical figurine and fantasy buttons on her jackets.

Men's clothing was equally refined in the thirties. The influence on women's clothing had always been Parisian but men's styles reflected English taste. Double-breasted dinner jackets and the Windsor necktie knot were copied from the popular Duke of Windsor. The bow tie also reached its height of popularity in this decade. The narrow-shaped Indian madras bow was featured in magazines with casual wear. Hollywood-inspired neckwear, such as Humphrey Bogart's narrow, black tie was another choice. Late in the decade, polka-dotted ties were trendy. Wide knickers or plus fours and the popular Fair Isle sweater were worn for golfing. The collarless cardigan sweater, colorful handkerchiefs, argyle socks, and the camel hair coat were typical of the time. Men wore tank-top bathing suits and no-top bathing suits. Trousers featured waist pleats. Half-boots replaced high boots and the black patent dress shoe took hold. Lightweight felts and straws were popular hat styles from designers such as the American companies, Dobbs and Stetson, and the Italian firm, Borsolina.

## Signature Fabrics of the 1930s

Silk for dinner dresses

Silk chiffons for afternoon dresses

Velvet for evening coats

Cottons, crêpe de chine, gabardine, satin, and lamé for gowns

Wool and tweeds for suits

Synthetics:

    Rayon, Celanese for lingerie, hosiery

    Rayon for daydresses

    Lastex for swimwear

## Important Designers and Manufacturers of the 1930s

**ADRIAN:** Adrian's designs commonly have bold silhouettes with dolman or kimono sleeves, long, tapered waistlines, and often diagonal fastenings. Designing for actresses such as Greta Garbo and Joan Crawford gave Adrian's hats and fashions a wide audience. Some of his most well-known designs from the thirties include the "Eugénie" hat of 1930 which was designed for Garbo and had an ostrich feather that extended over one eye; and the "Letty Lynton" dress of 1939 with wide shoulders, a narrow waist, and ruffled sleeves, designed for Crawford to wear in the movie of the same name.

**AGNÈS:** A French milliner, Agnès's hat designs were very popular with women in the thirties.

**BALENCIAGA:** Balenciaga's designs used somber colors and restrained lines. In 1939, he showed suits with a dropped shoulder, narrow waist, and rounded hips.

**BELLER:** A manufacturer and designer of coats and suits, A. Beller used tweeds and fur in his designs. He showed tweed suits that had heavy tweed coats over lighter tweed dresses. For evening, he showed black velvet coats and jackets that had fur or metallic brocade trims. In 1931, A. Beller designed a culotte suit with front and back panels that hid the pants as a skirt; this design was called a "pantie suit."

**BORSOLINA:** Italian hat company renowned for their fine men's hats.

**TOM BRIGANCE:** In the thirties, Tom Brigance showed extensive sportswear collections featuring brightly colored linen separates: shorts, pants, skirts, and bare-abdomen tops.

**HOUSE OF CALLOT SOEURS:** In the thirties, the House of Callot Soeurs showed evening dresses of heavy satin and lamé.

**HATTIE CARNEGIE:** Carnegie's thirties designs were tailored suits and dresses with straight skirts. She also became known as a designer of versatile black dresses that were very popular with American women.

**CATALINA:** In the thirties, Catalina designed bathing suits for movie stars and promoted fan photos of the stars clad in their body-conscious designs. They also profited immensely by affiliating themselves with the Miss America Pageant. These publicity ideas led to increased popularity of their mass-produced bathing suits.

**"COCO" CHANEL:** In the thirties, Chanel began to commission costume jewelry whose settings imitated those of real jewels. In the early thirties, she moved to Hollywood and designed for United Artists' films. In 1939, Chanel closed her couture house because of World War II and did not reopen it until 1954.

**JO COPELAND:** Designing for Patullo Modes through the thirties, Copeland's designs were fancier than her earlier sportswear designs of the twenties. She chose elegant fabrics, such as a thin wool woven with gold sequins, and was known for her use of dynamic drapery in her dress designs.

**LILLY DACHÉ:** This milliner opened her seventh-floor shop in New York City in the late thirties. She featured profile hats, berets, turbans, and snoods as well as veiled evening hats. Daché often used intricate trimmings, with faux flowers and the occasional faux bug. In the thirties, she also had a line of hats inspired by a show of African headgear she saw in France.

**DAVIDOW:** A manufacturer of ready-to-wear clothing, Davidow specialized in coats and suits.

**DELMAN:** In the thirties, Delman was known as one of the premier shoe shops in New York. They had a contract with the famous shoe designer Vivier and featured his designs exclusively in the late thirties.

**DOBBS:** Men's hats.

**FERRAGAMO:** In the thirties, Ferragamo continued to design and produced hand-crafted shoes, such as his new wedge-shaped heels.

**GOODALL CO. PALM BEACH:** Fashionable men's suits and sportswear.

**ELIZABETH HAWES:** Hawes designed women's clothing in the thirties using natural proportions in simple designs.

**HERMÈS:** In the thirties, Hermès designed accessories often with coordinating sports clothes. He showed purses with watches set into them, and beach accessories (sunshades, hat, jacket, and handbag). In 1935, his "Kelly" bag was first introduced. Named for the actress, Grace Kelly, the saddlebag-like design became increasingly popular in the fifties when she married Prince Ranier III and became Princess Grace of Monaco.

**CHARLES JAMES:** James's 1932 culottes design was so popular that it remained in production through the 1950s. In the mid-thirties, James designed clothing and fabrics for Paul Poiret's couture house.

**JANTZEN:** More revealing and more clingy bathing suit styles led to innovative body-sculpting features such as the "Ladies Uplift," which enhances the bustline with darts and elastic while offering an adjustable skirt to hide potential figure flaws. Another daring Jantzen design of the thirties was a "Wisp-O-Weight" tunic-style bathing suit which came in flesh tones, so the wearer appeared to be naked. Many of Jantzen's thirties designs used Lastex, the exciting new rubber-based fabric.

**KORET (PURSES):** Koret manufactured purses of reptile skins and cloth in square and rectangular shapes with short straps or handles. The handbags were often shown with coordinating shoes.

**LOUISEBOULANGER:** Louiseboulanger used the famous Vionnet bias cut in her elegant thirties dress designs, which also had skirts that were shorter in the front than in the back.

**MAINBOCHER:** Perhaps Mainbocher's most renowned thirties design was Mrs. Wallis Simpson's blue wedding dress for her marriage to the Duke of

Windsor; however, his many other designs from that period include evening sweaters, dresses cut on the bias, and apron-style dresses.

**CLAIRE MCCARDELL:** McCardell's most innovative design of this decade came in 1938 with her so-called "monastic dress." She was inspired by a costume she had made for herself from an Algerian dress; the design was very full and flowed from the shoulders, with an optional belt. McCardell also had a line of sportswear in mostly solid colors.

**EDWARD MOLYNEUX:** In the thirties, Molyneux showed an oriental-inspired line of clothing designs with patterned fabrics. He also showed dirndl skirts and bias-cut dresses.

**GERMAINE MONTEIL:** Known as "American Vionnet," Monteil specialized in evening dresses.

**NETTIE ROSENSTEIN:** Nettie Rosenstein's specialty in the thirties was eveningwear of varying degrees of formality.

**ELSA SCHIAPARELLI:** In the thirties, Schiaparelli was known for her whimsical designs. She worked with fabrics designed by Surrealist artists such as Salvador Dali and Jean Cocteau. In 1933, Shiaparelli showed a pagoda sleeve on her fashions, which also became known as the Egyptian look. She showed thick evening sweaters with shoulder pads, dyed fur coats, and Tyrolean peasant–inspired fashions. Her 1935 collection included garments with plastic zippers featured prominently as decorative elements. In 1937, Schiaparelli designed especially humorous hats such as her shoe, lamb chop, and ice cream cone hats. In 1938, Schiaparelli showed a circus collection with circus theme–patterned fabrics and acrobat-shaped buttons.

**SUZANNE TALBOT:** Talbot's thirties designs were smaller hats that perched on the side or back of the head. Such designs were inspired by the French Empress Eugénie.

**VALENTINA:** Valentina worked in solid colors to make clean-lined garments of high-quality fabrics. Her thirties designs used many oriental design elements. The windy New York City streets in which she worked inspired her 1937 culotte dress.

**MADELEINE VIONNET:** In the thirties, Vionnet continued to use her signature bias cut to create glamorous dresses and gowns of gabardine and crêpe de chine that became immensely popular in Hollywood.

**B. H. WRAGGE:** A designer and manufacturer of sportswear for women, who worked with the tailored styles of menswear. Their lines of interchangeable separates in a variety of fabrics were very popular for casual dressing.

## 1930s
## Introduction Frontispiece

**1930S SILK EMBROIDERED LOUNGING OUTFIT.** Rich royal blue with colorful floral embroidery on collar and jacket front, wrap front jacket, self belt, collar cuffed sleeves trimmed in silk pleats, pants, high-waist, wide-flared leg with silk piping at hem, very good condition. $95 (See photograph on page 58)
*Courtesy of Wendy Radick, Kitty Girl Vintage.*

## VINTAGE FASHIONS OF THE THIRTIES

Art Deco Shawl.
*Courtesy of Vintage Textiles,*
*www.vintagetextiles.com.*
*Photograph by Amadeus Guy.*

**C. 1930 ART DECO SHAWL.** Gold lamé with reversible pattern. Valued at $650
*Courtesy of Vintage Textiles.*

Satin Evening Gown. *Courtesy of Wendy Radick, Kitty Girl Vintage, www.kittygirlvintage.com. Photograph by Wendy Radick.*

**1930s Satin Evening Gown.** Midnight blue silk satin, tunic-style peplum over slim-fitting skirt, puffy sleeves with a net lining at the seam, sleeves and hem of peplum are sewn with rings design, fitted bodice and waist, side snap and hook placket, belt loops, no belt, otherwise excellent. $225

*Courtesy of Wendy Radick, Kitty Girl Vintage.*

Floral Dress.
*Courtesy of Wendy Radick,*
*Kitty Girl Vintage,*
*www.kittygirlvintage.com.*
*Photograph by Wendy Radick.*

**1930s FLORAL DRESS.** Rayon seersucker, lavender embroidered neckline, embroidery below waist and above shirring, fitted waist, batwing
sleeves, semi-full skirt, side metal zipper, good wearable condition. $59
*Courtesy of Wendy Radick, Kitty Girl Vintage.*

ILLUSTRATION DEPICTS RESORT FASHIONS. For men: porkpie hat and crocodile shoes or the striped linen shirt. For women: split skirt, accentuated collar and cuffs, strappy sandals.

*Scene: The Palm Beach Casino at Cannes,* February 1936. By permission of *Esquire* magazine. © Hearst Communications, Inc. Also, Esquire is a trademark of Hearst Magazines Property, Inc. All Rights Reserved.

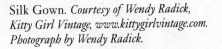

Silk Gown. *Courtesy of Wendy Radick,*
*Kitty Girl Vintage, www.kittygirlvintage.com.*
*Photograph by Wendy Radick.*

**1930s Silk Gown.** Blue and pink shell print, gathered bodice, triple
spaghetti straps, fitted waist, side metal zipper, skirt, semi-full, very good
condition. $140
*Courtesy of Wendy Radick, Kitty Girl Vintage.*

MANY HAT STYLES developed in the thirties. Here a cloche style takes on an oversized brim.

Cover illustration from the magazine, *Delineator,* August 1929. *Courtesy of Cedar Crest College Alumnae Museum, Allentown, PA. Photograph by Tom Amico.*

Gauntlet Gloves. Property of Private Collection. *Photograph by Tom Amico.*

1930s–1940s GAUNTLET GLOVES. Leather gloves with alligator gauntlets, mint condition.
*Property of Private Collection.*

Floral Print Afternoon Dress. *Courtesy of Wendy Radick, Kitty Girl Vintage, www.kittygirlvintage.com. Photograph by Wendy Radick.*

**1930s FLORAL PRINT AFTERNOON DRESS.** Sheer dogwood/floral print in coral, pink, violet, and green on sky blue ground, cap sleeves, fastens in back with hook and eye and snap closures, fitted waist, full skirt, comes with white rayon acetate slip having adjustable straps, excellent condition. $59
*Courtesy of Wendy Radick, Kitty Girl Vintage.*

*Detail of Bodice:*
Wrapped bodice and trim.
*Photograph by Deborah Burke.*

Velvet Gown. *Courtesy of Deborah
Burke, Antique & Vintage Dress Gallery,
www.antiquedress.com. Photograph by
Deborah Burke.*

**1930s VELVET GOWN.** Burgundy silk velvet bias-cut gown with
wrapped bodice, pink floral trim, tulip puff sleeves with pink flowers,
near-mint condition. $485
*Courtesy of Deborah Burke, Antique & Vintage Dress Gallery.*

Evening Dress. *Courtesy of Linda Ames, Vintage Textile, www.vintagetextile.com. Photograph by Linda Ames.*

*Detail of Evening Gown:* Shirred bodice is cut almost to waist, flared back panel. *Photograph by Linda Ames.*

**1930s HOLLYWOOD EVENING DRESS.** Bias-cut silk chiffon, two-tone design, gold fitted midriff wraps around to flared back panel, bias-cut skirt molds over hips, excellent condition. $265
*Courtesy of Linda Ames, Vintage Textile.*

ILLUSTRATION SHOWS POPULAR FASHIONS FOR MEN AND WOMEN.
For men: black Homburg and the gray flannel striped suit, both English influences. For women: mid-calf skirt, asymmetrical neckline, and smart hat.

"Something We Predicted A Year Ago," March 1935. By permission of *Esquire* magazine. © Hearst Communications, Inc. Also, Esquire is a trademark of Hearst Magazines Property, Inc. All Rights Reserved.

*Detail of Jacket:* Brown and cream diagonal pattern. *Photograph by Art Fawcett.*

Suit. *Courtesy of Art & Janene Fawcett, Vintage Silhouettes, CA, www.vintagesilhouettes.com. Photograph by Art Fawcett.*

Gentleman's Homburg. *Courtesy of Art & Janene Fawcett, Vintage Silhouettes, CA, www.vintagesilhouettes.com. Photograph by Art Fawcett.*

LATE 1930S SUIT. Brown, double-breasted with cream diagonal pattern, "New Old Stock," size 37R. $325
*Courtesy of Art & Janene Fawcett, Vintage Silhouettes, CA.*

1930S GENTLEMAN'S HOMBURG. Midnight blue "Pauson," black ribbon and brim binding, size 7⅜, excellent condition. $115
*Courtesy of Art & Janene Fawcett, Vintage Silhouettes, CA.*

Smoking Jacket.
*Courtesy of Zap & Co., PA,*
*www.zapandco.com. Photograph*
*by Steve Murray.*

Wingtips. *Courtesy of Ardis Taylor, Vintage*
*Silhouettes, CA, www.vintagesilhouettes.com.*
*Photograph by Art Fawcett.*

1930s SMOKING JACKET. Charcoal wool with brown and gray plaid lapel, cuffs, pocket trim, handsewn frog closures, excellent condition. $95
*Courtesy of Zap & Co., PA.*

1930s WINGTIPS. Two-tone, dark gray, light gray, perforated shoe body and "Spade" sole, no shoe lining, label: "Bostonians," New Old Stock, size 9C–fits 8C, mint condition. $225.
*Courtesy of Ardis Taylor, Vintage Silhouettes, CA*

## MARKET TRENDS FOR THE THIRTIES

### *Lingerie and Robes*

1930s BIAS-CUT NIGHTGOWN. Vanilla silk satin, embroidered bodice, bias cut, perfect condition. $55
*Courtesy of The Fainting Couch, MA, www.faintingcouch.com*

1930s NIGHTGOWN. Full-length, bias cut, 100% silk, dainty tie on back of waist, perfect condition. $75
*Courtesy of The Fainting Couch, MA, www.faintingcouch.com*

1930s SILK SLIP WITH EMBROIDERED BODICE. Embroidered bodice, seamless, adjustable shoulder straps, "Miss Charming," never worn. $35
*Courtesy of The Fainting Couch, MA, www.faintingcouch.com*

1930s SLIP WITH LACE BODICE. Silk and rayon blend, lace bodice, adjustable straps, excellent condition. $30
*Courtesy of The Fainting Couch, MA, www.faintingcouch.com*

1930s SLIP "STEP-IN." Lace bodice, button crotch, perfect condition. $30
*Courtesy of The Fainting Couch, MA, www.faintingcouch.com*

1930s BLACK RAYON SLIP. Adjustable straps, original store tag, perfect condition. $35
*Courtesy of The Fainting Couch, MA, www.faintingcouch.com*

1930s DRESSING GOWN. Lamé and silk chiffon, black silk chiffon top, wide kimono sleeves, base has a jacquard pattern of metallic gold thread, fully lined with gold satin, excellent condition. $685
*Courtesy of Linda Ames, Vintage Textile, www.vintagetextile.com*

1930s FLORAL WRAPPER. Delicate silk chiffon with a trained back and kimono-style sleeves, label: "Bonwit Teller, Inc.–Fifth Avenue–New York," excellent condition. $385
*Courtesy of Linda Ames, Vintage Textile, www.vintagetextile.com*

### *Separates*

1930s SUMMER ART DECO SKIRT. Cotton, green, black, and gold cotton embroidery, Art Deco motif, steel hooks and eyes, perfect condition. $55
*Courtesy of Karen Augusta, Antique Lace & Fashion, www.antique-fashion.com*

## Dresses and Eveningwear

**1930s DINNER DRESS.** Full-length, black nylon, embroidered machine lace collar and cuffs, black slip, covered buttons, very good condition. $175
*Courtesy of Mary Troncale, Branford, CT.*

**1930s DRESS AND JACKET.** Golden yellow silk, full-length jacket, short sleeves, covered buttons, nice detailing, pristine condition. $175
*Courtesy of Mary Troncale, Branford, CT.*

**1930s BIAS-CUT SATIN GOWN.** Taupe textured satin, back-draped bodice panel, trained and draped skirt, detail of rope braided trim, excellent condition. $375
*Courtesy of Linda Ames, Vintage Textile, www.vintagetextile.com*

**1930s BIAS-CUT SILK CHIFFON DRESS.** Brown silk chiffon with matching slip, draped sleeves with open shoulders, very good condition. $465
*Courtesy of Linda Ames, Vintage Textile, www.vintagetextile.com*

**1930s BLACK SILK AND NET DRESS.** Black flowered silk chiffon torso, black net skirt and cape decorated with appliquéd cutouts from floral silk, excellent condition. $685
*Courtesy of Linda Ames, Vintage Textile, www.vintagetextile.com*

**1930s BIAS-CUT FLORAL SATIN EVENING DRESS.** Back cut low to waist, butterfly sleeves, sweeping skirt, excellent condition. $395
*Courtesy of Linda Ames, Vintage Textile, www.vintagetextile.com*

**1930s SEQUINED DRESS.** Bronze crepe, bronze sequined patterning, tiered skirt, back panel drape, pristine condition. $400
*Courtesy of Mary Troncale, Branford, CT.*

**1930s SEQUINED SASH DRESS.** Black crepe, sequined side sash, side closure, pristine condition. $200
*Courtesy of Mary Troncale, Branford, CT.*

**1930s SATIN DAMASK EVENING DRESS.** Heavy black satin damask, low-cut surplice front, open back, butterfly sleeves, allover red glass beading, wearable, perfect condition. $365
*Courtesy of Linda Ames, Vintage Textile, www.vintagetextile.com*

**1930s ORGANZA EVENING GOWN.** Dove gray organza with silk crepe, orchid sequins on bodice, V neck, organza bows accent bodice, full slip, very good condition. $375
*Courtesy of The Fainting Couch, MA, www.faintingcouch.com*

**Early 1930s Silver Lamé Evening Gown.** Low-cut back, dramatic train, sleeves and skirt front hemmed with pleated ruffles, rhinestone buckle on belt, very good condition. $695
*Courtesy of Linda Ames, Vintage Textile, www.vintagetextile.com*

**1930s Black Silk Velvet Evening Gown.** Bias-cut gown with gathered bodice, keyhole back closure with marcasite arrow, puffed ribbed sleeves with bands of moss green, red, and navy matching hem, velvet belt, excellent condition. $225
*Courtesy of The Fainting Couch, MA, www.faintingcouch.com*

**Late 1930s Satin Evening Tunic over a Pleated Skirt with Train.** Mink tails decorate bodice, label: "Bergdorf Goodman," excellent condition. $835
*Courtesy of Linda Ames, Vintage Textile, www.vintagetextile.com*

**1930s Evening Dress.** Light black chiffon with gold lamé pattern, excellent condition. $575
*Courtesy of Linda Ames, Vintage Textile, www.vintagetextile.com*

**Early 1930s Bias-Cut Evening Dress.** Silk velvet, rhinestone trim at neckline and cuffs, deep V neckline, fabulous large sleeves, back slit, excellent condition. $450
*Courtesy of Linda Ames, Vintage Textile, www.vintagetextile.com*

## Evening Coats, Capes, and Jackets

**1930s Silk Evening Cape.** Aqua silk damask with chinoiserie motifs, cream silk satin lining, self fabric frog closures, excellent condition. $125
*Courtesy of Karen Augusta, Antique Lace & Fashion, www.antique-fashion.com*

**c. 1930 Black Silk Velvet Evening Cape.** Graceful peplum and double collar, top one fastening as bow at back of neck, second falls over shoulders with capelet effect, fastens at the hipline and center front, cream silk crepe lining, excellent condition. $85
*Courtesy of Karen Augusta, Antique Lace & Fashion, www.antique-fashion.com*

**1930s Evening Coat.** Black silk velvet top, teal blue windowpane taffeta skirt, sweeping hem, velvet-covered buttons, good condition. $225
*Courtesy of The Fainting Couch, MA, www.faintingcouch.com*

**1930s–1940s Black Velvet Evening Coat.** Full-length, ivory satin lining, excellent condition. $65
*Courtesy of Karen Augusta, Antique Lace & Fashion, www.antique-fashion.com*

**1930s EVENING JACKET.** Gold sequins, yellow chiffon lining, excellent condition. $285
*Courtesy of Karen Augusta, Antique Lace & Fashion, www.antique-fashion.com*

## Accessories

**c. 1939 STRAW HAT WITH FLOWERS.** Tiny chartreuse velvet flowers with speckles of lavender stamens, deep brown velvet ribbon and veiling, two matching original straw hat pins, known provenance: owned by the daughter of the Ambassador to Luxembourg, Miss H. Westlake of #1 Fifth Avenue, NYC, excellent condition. $485
*Courtesy of Deborah Burke, Antique & Vintage Dress Gallery, www.antiquedress.com*

**1930s STRAW HAT.** Wide-brimmed, light mulberry, closed band, open weave with peach ribbon band and point pleated open bow on crown, chignon back with elastic, label: "Jay's Boston, Temple Place Eleven," mint condition. $145
*Courtesy of The Fainting Couch, MA, www.faintingcouch.com*

**1930s "HOLLYWOOD PIN-UP" BEACH HAT WITH MATCHING POUCH.** Turquoise and white striped lightweight canvas, soft crown, hat brim varies from 6" to 8", width 24", original chin ties, pliable plastic strip in brim allows for folding into pouch, excellent condition. $150
*Courtesy of The Fainting Couch, MA, www.faintingcouch.com*

**1930s FELT HAT.** Gray felt with net, braided detailed brim, black bow, "NY Creations," excellent condition. $65
*Courtesy of The Fainting Couch, MA, www.faintingcouch.com*

**1930s FUCHSIA FELT HAT.** Navy net veiling, black felt self-hat pin, excellent condition. $65
*Courtesy of The Fainting Couch, MA, www.faintingcouch.com*

**1930s RED STRAW HAT.** Fine weave straw, velvet ribbon, cloth flower spray, silk gauze and grosgrain lining, 14" brim, "The French Shop Stamford, Conn and Paris," perfect condition. $145
*Courtesy of Karen Augusta, Antique Lace & Fashion, www.antique-fashion.com*

**1930s BEACH HAT.** Unsplit straw bands, woven in two-strand-braid pattern, cream silk lining, elastic hairband, whimsical, perfect condition. $125
*Courtesy of Karen Augusta, Antique Lace & Fashion, www.antique-fashion.com*

## Shoes

**1930s GILT LEATHER EVENING SANDALS.** With rhinestones, 2″ heel, "Saks Fifth Avenue Fenton Footwear," very good condition. $200.
*Courtesy of Karen Augusta, Antique Lace & Fashion, www.antique-fashion.com*

## Menswear

**LATE 1930s–EARLY 1940s, MEN'S DOUBLE-BREASTED SUIT.** Mocha and burnt orange, 1½″ windowpane pattern, never worn, never cuffed, New Old Stock, size 36R, 30″ waist. $300
*Courtesy of Art & Janene Fawcett, Vintage Silhouettes, CA, www.vintagesilhouettes.com*

**1930s ART DECO SMOKING JACKET.** Dark blue rayon, Art Deco pattern, satin blue lapels, two side pockets and left breast pocket, long fringed sash, "Roytex," very good condition. $100
*Courtesy of The Fainting Couch, MA, www.faintingcouch.com*

**1930s TUXEDO.** Three-piece, wool tux: jacket, pants, and silk faille vest, single-button jacket with satin lapels, pants with satin stripe, three-button vest, fitted, perfect condition. $145
*Courtesy of Karen Augusta, Antique Lace & Fashion, www.antique-fashion.com*

## Men's Accessories

**1930s MEN'S HAT, "PENNYS MARATHON."** Pearl gray, pearl-colored ribbon, bound edge, aluminum-colored ribbon, 2⅜″ brim, size 7¼, excellent condition. $90
*Courtesy of Art & Janene Fawcett, Vintage Silhouettes, CA, www.vintagesilhouettes.com*

**1930s MEN'S TWO-TONE SPECTATORS.** Perforated bow design, medium mahogany color with beige, white stitching, "Florsheim," size 10½ D or C, excellent condition. $195
*Courtesy of Ardis Taylor, Vintage Silhouettes, CA, www.vintagesilhouettes.com*

*Detail of "Victory Dress"*
Snappy bow, stars,
and sailor collar.

"Victory Dress" *Courtesy of Deborah Burke, Antique & Vintage Dress Gallery, www.antiquedress.com. Photographs by Deborah Burke.*

# *A*ltruism and Abundance

Wartime restrictions and limitations had an enormous impact on fashion. In the United States, regulations stipulated the amount and types of fabric that could be used in clothing designs. Such restrictions were also in effect in European nations. Nylon, wool, and silk were in short supply, so women wore rayon crepe and black faille, and for evening clothes, velvet chiffon. Rayon gabardine was used as a replacement for wool. There were also button and pocket limitations on clothing. Standardized sizing was another result of wartime fabric rationing.

In the forties, women's clothing took on its most masculine image yet: boxy suit jackets with large shoulder pads, fitted waists, sometimes with a peplum, and narrow skirts with one or two pleats. Later an A-line skirt was shown with suits.

Hollywood remained a serious source for fashion dictates and forties films were filled with the fashions that reflected the time: suits, sweaters, skirts, pants, and bathing suits. The shoulder pad image was fashioned after Adrian's design for Joan Crawford in the thirties and made popular by Elsa Schiaparelli. Sweater sets were made famous by Hollywood's Rita Hayworth and Lana Turner.

For evening, women wore beaded sweaters and jackets. Sequins were not rationed and so were widely used on evening suits. Rhinestone buttons were a trademark of forties dresses by Eisenberg & Sons. Costume jewelry was large, mostly pins and brooches. Since there was a shortage of basic metals, sterling silver was used by many costume jewelry manufacturers.

For other accessories, there were also changes made during wartime. Expensive gloves were replaced with knitted and crocheted ones. Stockings were thick rayon instead of nylon. Pocketbooks were tremendous in size and elongated. Because of the metal shortage, most handbags were made with wooden or plastic closures. Designer bags by Balenciaga and Molyneux were costly but reproductions of them could easily be found in department stores. Broadcloth or calfskin was frequently used for purses and many women crocheted their own bags with gimp or cord. Crocheted bags were also manufactured in great numbers. Envelope bags, pannier handlebags, bags made from pearlized plastic, and hatbox bags were all designs of the forties.

In dress designs, side closures with zippers were commonly used and often there was a swag or side drapery to the designs as well. The sweetheart neckline on dresses was very fashionable. For casual days, women wore pleated pants and print cotton dresses with patriotic motifs; polka dots and checks were also popular. Other fabric patterns were abstract designs in bold colors.

When many Parisian couture houses closed in 1940, United States manufacturers and designers had to act independently. American designers came to the forefront and were well known in the fashion world. American designers such as Clare Potter, Claire McCardell, and Carolyn Schnurer designed predominantly sportswear. Lilli Ann suits were made in San Francisco and Hattie Carnegie designed fine dresses for women in New York City.

California became known for its designer sportswear. Bathing suit manufacturers such as Cole, Catalina, and Mabs of Hollywood were making names for themselves. Bathing suits had foundation styling and were made from Lastex or Celanese rayon. The two-piece bathing suit had five inches of bare midriff, measured with exactitude.

Suits and dresses were accessorized with platform-soled shoes. Salvatore Ferragamo designed the popular cork wedge for use in place of leather and steel during the war. Suede and fabric platform sandals and mules were also fashionable. In Italy, Bakelite was used for soles and heels. Ballet-style capezios were worn with casual clothes.

Hats of the forties were turbans, crowned hats, calottes worn at the back of the head, snoods, and hand-knitted caps. The outrageous designer hats of the previous decade were gone in wartime. Kerchiefs tied under the chin became a chic trend and popular hairstyles were rolled or pageboys. Veils were chin length. Hats, gloves, veils, and shoes were often ornamented with the unrestricted sequins. Homemade hats were fashioned out of whatever was available, which led to very unusual combinations. Straw was unattainable during the war so a flat, pressed felt was made from fur and skim milk. French milliner Agnès even designed a hat from wood shavings. Toward the end of the war, hats became frivolous again and such styles as veiled turbans with faux fruits and flowers for decoration were designed.

Christian Dior's "New Look," shown in 1947, was a complete departure from wartime clothing. Unpadded soft rounded shoulders, wasp waists, padded hips, and full skirts were suddenly all the rage. With pleating at the waist, the calf-length skirt could be even fuller, especially when lined with crinolines. Hats were minimal, but were designed to coordinate with a specific dress. Sandals remained popular but became slimmer in the heel and toe as the Dior look became established later in the fifties. Out of the rationing and parity of wartime came affluent times and, as a result, designers showed clothing rich in fabrics and femininity.

During wartime, men's clothing also had restrictions on fabric and design. No cuffs, pleats, or overlapping waistbands were made. Vests were limited and the two-piece suit became more popular than the three-piece. The backless vest was made for eveningwear. Trousers were narrower and jackets shorter. Rayon, rayon blends, cheviot, and flannel were used. Battle jackets were popular casual wear. The zoot suit made a brief appearance, but was a waste of too much precious fabric. During its brief popularity, it was characterized by oversized coats, big shoulders, slash pockets, full knees and cuffs, trousers hiked up with suspenders, and oversized bow ties. The Hawaiian shirt, picked up by servicemen as souvenirs, became popular casual wear in the late forties.

After the war, the "Bold Look" was how men's fashion was best described. It contrasted with the frugality and somberness of wartime clothing. Postwar fashions boasted broad shoulders, wide lapels, Borsolina brimmed hats, wide-spread collars, walking shorts, and accessories such as large cuff links, plaid socks, and colorful ties. Indeed, colorful ties were the one mainstay of men's fashions throughout the forties. Patriotic colors had been popular early in the war and hand-painted and photo ties were popular during and after the war. These ties were vivid in color and inspired by Art Deco, Egyptian, African, Hawaiian, and the American Old West motifs and colors. Ties were tied in Windsor knots and were designed by Countess Mara, Tina Leser, and Jacques Fath. Arrow was a large tie manufacturer, as well as Van Heusen. After the war, Cheney manufactured pure silk ties, and luxurious clothing was again a possibility.

## Signature Fabrics of the 1940s

Faille, cotton, linen, jersey, wool jersey, and denim for daywear

Wool tweed and gabardine for suits

Velvet chiffon for eveningwear

Broadcloth or calfskin for purses

Synthetics:

Rayon crepe for daywear

Rayon gabardine in place of wool during wartime

Lastex or Celanese rayon for bathing suits

Rayon for stockings and dresses during wartime

Rayon, rayon blends, cheviot, and flannel for men's trousers.

*Outstanding examples of 1940s Hollywood designers' suits.*

*Left:* c. 1947 Irene suit made of wool twill. *Courtesy of Philadelphia Museum of Art. Gift of an anonymous donor.*
*Right:* c. 1947, Adrian suit made of wool twill. *Courtesy of Philadelphia Museum of Art. Gift of Adrian. Both objects are accessioned and part of the permanent collection.*

## *Important Designers and Manufacturers of the 1940s*

**Adrian:** After 1942, Adrian retired from Hollywood designing and sold his designs through a Beverly Hills, California, shop. His forties fashions included broad-shouldered suits with long jackets and a narrow waist, opulent ball gowns, and draped dresses for evening. He often used Pola Stout's geometric designs for fabrics as well as patterns of his own design that had animal *trompe l'oeil*, or Greek themes.

**Arrow:** In the 1880s, the Arrow Company was born of a merger between two firms which manufactured the widely popular, new detachable, starched collars for men's shirts. These collars continued to be the mainstay of Arrow's production through World War I, by which time over 400 kinds of collars were marketed. Arrow switched to the production of shirts with attached collars as the demands and styles changed. After World War II, Arrow became known for popularizing the colored shirt for men. They also manufactured ties with zany patterns of the forties.

**Balenciaga:** In the forties, Balenciaga was known for his pillbox hats, and after World War II, he featured jackets with more naturally shaped waistlines and larger sleeves.

**Fira Benenson:** Known for her use of fine dressmaker details, in 1943, Fira Benenson made the most of the L-85 regulations (wartime restrictions on clothing) with her wide circle skirts on dresses with natural shoulders and fitted waists. Her collections of evening clothes featured décolleté necklines.

**Borsolina:** Although unavailable during the war, Borsolina hats continued to top heads of every well-dressed man in the late forties.

**Tom Brigance:** Although he served in the war between 1942 and 1947, Tom Brigance's sportswear designs were very popular in his absence. His designs were playful, with wrap tops that bared the abdomen as well as trousers, shorts, wrap dresses, and bathing suits. He used synthetic jersey fabrics with cotton piqué and prints. His post-war designs consisted of more sportswear and sundresses to which he added a line of clothing suitable for city wear.

**Brooke Cadwallader:** Brooke Cadwallader was a textile designer who produced a special collection of signed scarves that had historical or current events themes. His textile designs were often used by other fashion designers. In 1947, he began designing men's silk ties and silk robes for his own label, Bronzini. All of his different designs were known for their unique color combinations; he claimed to never repeat an exact combination.

HATTIE CARNEGIE: In the forties, Hattie Carnegie had two fashion lines: an exclusive custom-design business and a ready-to-wear line called Hattie Carnegie Originals. Still remembered for her fine suits and black dresses of the thirties, Carnegie also had an interest in showing different designs. During World War II, she showed a line of clothing inspired by ethnic peasant costumes. For evening, she showed dresses that resembled black sequined schoolgirl jumpers, flapper dresses with beaded fringe, and beaded and sequined suits.

CHENEY BROTHERS: Cheney Brothers were renowned for their pure silk ties. In 1947, Tina Leser designed a line of ties for this designer.

JO COPELAND: Jo Copeland designed with lines that differed from her peers' designs. She showed clothes with a narrow fit, waist-length jackets, and asymmetrically decorated skirts. She used both natural and synthetic fabrics for her fashions. Her specialty was casual and formal evening dresses and suits.

COUNTESS MARA: Countess Mara designed a limited number of expensive ties, incorporating her initials into the designs.

DAVID CRYSTAL: David Crystal showed wool or cotton shirtwaist dresses and casual suits in the thirties. He also had a sportswear line of shorts, wrap skirts, and tops in abstract prints in rayon.

LILLY DACHÉ: In the forties, Lilly Daché continued to design stylish hats. Her hat designs featured asymmetrical crowns and brims, and side veils that tucked under the chin. Daché's wartime designs featured nap yarn hats and epaulette hats to incorporate military themes and wool restrictions. For summer, she showed hats of dressy cotton fabrics with topstitching on the brims. In 1949, she showed her first line of dresses and accessories, in addition to her hats.

DAVIDOW: Davidow manufactured wool tweed and gabardine suits in the forties.

DELMAN: As in the thirties, Delman shoes were known in the forties for their high quality and design. A shoe manufacturer that featured young shoe designers, Delman expanded their business to include the East Coast.

CHRISTIAN DIOR: Dior's 1947 "New Look" collection was perhaps the most influential fashion collection of the forties. He showed a line of shirtwaist dresses with full skirts, often lined with tulle and with small waists, accessorized by a hat worn on the side of the head. His 1948 collection called "Envol" showed skirts with shorter back hemlines and loose jackets with fly-away back panels and stand-away collars. In 1949, Dior showed slim skirts with back pleats and strapless evening dresses.

**DOBBS:** Dobbs continued to design and manufacture men's hats.

**EISENBERG & SONS ORIGINALS:** In 1941, Eisenberg & Sons expanded their clothing line of evening dresses to include casual clothes. They showed linen dresses for summer and wool tweed suits, coats, and dresses for winter. In 1949, Eisenberg created the Eisenberg Suburban line that featured casual clothing with matching costume jewelry. Throughout the forties, Eisenberg & Sons were known for their fabulous costume jewelry pieces, which were set in sterling silver during World War II.

**JACQUES FATH:** In 1949, Jacques Fath's ready-to-wear collection first appeared in the United States. He was famous for using an hourglass silhouette and his ready-to-wear line in America continued with the same curving lines. Fath was also known for popularizing stockings with Chantilly lace tops.

**FERRAGAMO:** In the forties, during wartime restrictions on metals, Ferragamo designed a platform heel of cork. In 1947, he designed the invisible shoe which had a clear nylon upper and bell heel.

**ALIX (MADAME) GRÉS:** Open for the first time in her own name after World War II, Alix Grés was famous for her draped designs that were often compared to the draped garments on classical statues. She used jersey, silk, and wool fabrics, bias cuts and dolman sleeves to create her draped evening gowns.

**IRENE:** A Los Angeles–based designer, Irene was the head costume designer for Metro-Goldwyn-Mayer from 1942 to 1949. She established a ready-to-wear line of day and evening suits with broad shoulder lines and narrow skirts in 1947. She also featured dramatic and glamorous evening dresses.

**CHARLES JAMES:** In 1945, Charles James established his own made-to-order collection in New York. His collections featured sculptured dresses and ball gowns that often combined different textured fabrics and odd colors in a single garment. He also showed sculptured coats and stoles of stiff fabrics as evening wraps.

**JOHN-FREDERICS:** In the early forties, John-Frederics' hats often had attached scarves or used scarves in their designs. In the late forties, when going hatless was growing in popularity, John-Frederics featured smaller hats and campaigned heartily for the preservation of the hat.

**KALMOUR:** Kalmour showed inexpensive evening clothes and costume jewelry. Their evening dresses were full-skirted, made of tulle and net, and decorated with sequins and faux gems.

**KNOX:** Knox designed and manufactured men's hats in the forties.

**KORET:** Koret continued to manufacture their fine line of purses.

**TINA LESER:** In 1941, Tina Leser brought her resort wear collections from Honolulu to New York City and expanded her designs. She used Tahitian and Mexican fabrics, Indian sari cloth, and prints from Japanese kimonos. She favored international styles as well as the mandarin jacket and sarongs. She continued to design mostly sportswear and resort wear but also showed full skirts for evening with dolman-sleeved shrug jackets.

**LILLI ANN:** A San Francisco manufacturer of suits and coats of European fabrics, Lilli Ann's designs were formal enough for cocktail parties. In the late forties, Lilli Ann showed suits and coats that imitated Dior's "New Look" and others who used the earlier forties silhouette which was narrower throughout the garment.

**LUCIEN LELONG:** In addition to Lelong's line of clutch purses and accessories, he showed a line of clothing in 1947. His collection included slim-skirted dresses with harem hemlines and tiny-waisted suits with broad shoulders.

**MAINBOCHER:** Mainbocher's forties designs were known for their versatility. Mainbocher designed with the idea that with quick additions, his simple black dress could go from day to evening. He introduced the "glamour belt," a belt with an attached overskirt or apron that dresses up daytime outfits. He was also known for his use of everyday fabrics for evening such as dresses of eyelet and gingham. Mainbocher also designed uniforms for the WAVES (Navy), the United States Women's Marine Corps, the American Red Cross, and the Girl Scouts.

**VERA MAXWELL:** In 1940, Vera Maxwell designed reefer suits for daytime with slim coats. In 1942, she used lumberjack shirt patterns with tailored suits. She also designed ethnic-inspired sportswear in 1942, showing shorts and tops with Peruvian jackets. In the late forties, Maxwell worked with the "New Look" silhouette, showing fuller skirts and pinched waists.

**CLAIRE MCCARDELL:** In the forties, McCardell continued to show her monk silhouette dress with an optional belt. All of McCardell's designs, from sportswear to eveningwear, shared certain design elements: bathing suits and evening dresses with halter tops, and wrap tops on dressy pants, as well as on bathing suits and dresses. Other frequent design elements on McCardell's fashions were spaghetti ties, usually meant to serve as a belt on evening and casual dresses. McCardell's sportswear was known for its practicality. She worked with large patch pockets and metal rivets as decorative elements which were also useful to the wearer. In 1942, she designed the immensely popular "popover dress" which was meant to be an all-purpose housedress. The popover dress was topstitched denim with a wrap front, large patch pocket, and attached oven mitt.

**MILLER:** In the forties, I. Miller was known in New York City for high-quality shoes.

**GERMAINE MONTEIL:** Germaine Monteil designed expensive ready-to-wear clothing. Her favored silhouette featured a full, flared skirt which emphasized the waistline. She often showed these skirts with short jackets. For evening, Monteil designed dinner suits with long skirts and ballet-length dresses.

**NORMAN NORELL:** In the mid-forties, Norman Norell showed chemise dresses and tunic blouses over slim skirts with a belted waist. In 1947, he featured colored swing coats with belted waists in various lengths. In the late forties, Norell experimented with different waistlines, using Empire waists and natural waists in the same dress. He also showed trenchcoats, pavé sequined sheath dresses for evening, and wool dresses with décolleté necklines.

**GOODALL CO. PALM BEACH:** In the forties, the Goodall Co. Palm Beach continued to manufacture fashionable men's suits and sportswear.

**MOLLIE PARNIS:** Mollie Parnis designed inexpensive dresses with feminine styles. As the decade progressed, her skirts grew fuller and her waistlines drew more attention. She used small bows to decorate the backs of her dress designs.

**PHELPS:** Phelps featured handmade belts and pocketbooks with a rough-hewn look. They are commonly considered the source for the popularization of the shoulder bag.

**CLARE POTTER:** Clare Potter was famous for her sportswear designs, pajama costumes, and loose and slim-cut pants. She would combine several contrasting colors in a single outfit. Her mid-range price designs followed a narrow, yet flowing, silhouette. She designed a forties bathing suit with bra and bloomer pants, a forerunner of the bikini.

**NETTIE ROSENSTEIN:** In the forties, Nettie Rosenstein designed day-to-evening black dresses, suits with patterned blouses, and dresses with matching print gloves.

**ELSA SCHIAPARELLI:** In the forties, Schiaparelli continued to design whimsical and humorous fashion pieces. She showed hats in the style of a fez or turban.

**CAROLYN SCHNURER:** Carolyn Schnurer designed inexpensive sportswear and bathing suits in the forties. Her casual collection included sundresses with fishnet shawls and calico bathing suits. During the war, she showed a South American-inspired line with cholo jackets. In 1947, she showed a very brief polka dotted bikini.

**STETSON:** In the forties, Stetson designed and manufactured hats for men, as they had since 1860.

**PAULINE TRIGÈRE:** Pauline Trigère was known for her coats and dramatic but simple evening dresses. Her coat designs included officers' greatcoats and long redingotes in velvet for evening and waist-length jackets for daytime. Her evening designs used wool and taffeta in a range of styles from long to ballet-length dresses to satin evening pajamas. Her designs depended on cuts to give them shape rather than tucking and shirring. Trigère introduced the idea of removable scarves and collars on dresses and coats. She also showed dresses with jewelry attached.

**VALENTINA:** Valentina's daytime dress designs in the forties had a thirties look with bias cuts in silk or wool crepe. Her other designs included linen turnouts, all-season suits, evening gowns, and dresses. Her eveningwear ranged from floor-length, black dresses to ballet-length dance dresses and opulent ball gowns with décolleté necklines.

**VAN HEUSEN:** Van Heusen ties were popular in the forties. They produced three-dimensional ties in rayon and silk blend. They also manufactured men's shirts, pajamas, and sport shirts.

**B. H. WRAGGE:** In the forties, B. H. Wragge was still designing affordable separates sportswear. His styles did not vary much beyond the annual change in color scheme and coordinating prints. Wragge's line included pleated and straight skirts, pants, jackets, dresses, and blouses. In the late forties, he added turtleneck shirts, and cap-sleeved and sleeveless jackets.

## *1940s*
## *Introduction Frontispiece*

1940s "VICTORY DRESS." Navy silk with white printed stars and sailor collar, "Lord & Taylor, 5th Avenue, NY," excellent condition. $295 (See photograph on page 82)
*Courtesy of Deborah Burke, Antique & Vintage Dress Gallery.*

## VINTAGE FASHIONS OF THE FORTIES

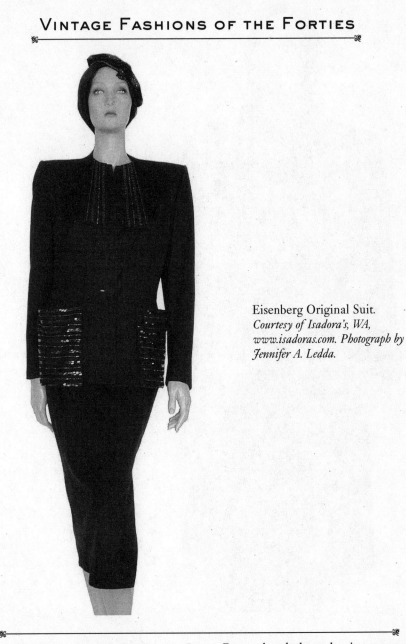

Eisenberg Original Suit.
*Courtesy of Isadora's, WA,*
*www.isadoras.com. Photograph by*
*Jennifer A. Ledda.*

**1940S EISENBERG ORIGINAL SUIT.** Brown beaded wool suit, copper-colored beadwork applied on front two pockets and lapels, skirt has fabulous side slit on left side, label inside jacket, pristine condition. $1,500
*Courtesy of Isadora's, WA.*

Persian Lamb Fur.
*Courtesy of Isadora's,*
*WA, www.isadoras.com.*
*Photograph by Jennifer*
*A. Ledda.*

**1940s PERSIAN LAMB FUR.** Three-quarter-length classic 1940s design, full cuffs, silk lined, Bakelite buttons, nicely tailored, pristine condition. $850
*Courtesy of Isadora's, WA.*

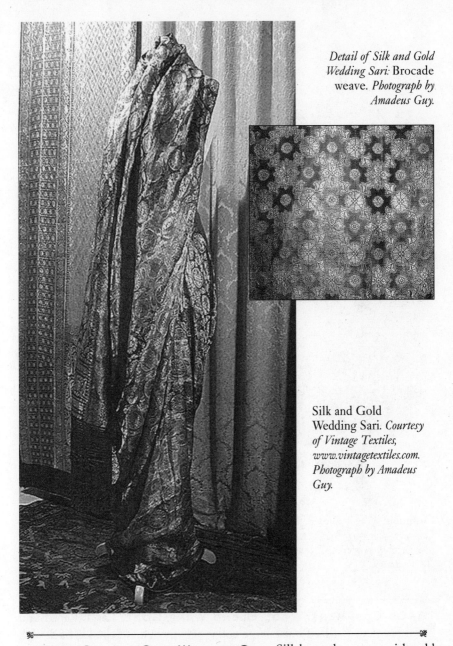

*Detail of Silk and Gold Wedding Sari:* Brocade weave. *Photograph by Amadeus Guy.*

Silk and Gold Wedding Sari. *Courtesy of Vintage Textiles, www.vintagetextiles.com. Photograph by Amadeus Guy.*

c. 1940s Silk and Gold Wedding Sari. Silk brocade, woven with gold metallic threads, design motif shows both 17th and 18th century European and Mughal influences, (a traditional hand-loomed wedding sari takes as long as one year to weave), valued at $800–$2,500 depending on age, condition, complexity, and rarity of design, as well as content of gold. *Courtesy of Vintage Textiles.*

Cashmere/Wool Blend Wrap Coat. *Courtesy of Wendy Radick, Kitty Girl Vintage, www.kittygirlvintage.com. Photograph by Wendy Radick.*

Back of Wrap Coat. *Photograph by Wendy Radick.*

1940s Cashmere/Wool Blend Wrap Coat. Large flared and cuffed sleeves, fitted waist, large collar, self-tie belt attached in back with fabric squares, lined in off-white silk satin, waist has row of vertical tucks from front to back for fitted contour, exquisite tailoring, very well made, label: "An Exclusive Fabric by Strook, 60% cashmere, 40% wool hand-tailored by Brittany," excellent condition. $375
*Courtesy of Wendy Radick, Kitty Girl Vintage.*

Floral Nightgown and Robe Set. *Courtesy of Wendy Radick, Kitty Girl Vintage,*
*www.kittygirlvintage.com. Photograph by Wendy Radick.*

**FLORAL NIGHTGOWN AND ROBE SET.** White background with multicolored floral bouquets print, lace trim, bias-cut gown with shirred
bodice and lace straps, robe, fitted at waist, puffy sleeves, three-button
closure in loops at waist, very good condition. $79
*Courtesy of Wendy Radick, Kitty Girl Vintage.*

Rose Print Sarong Dress. *Courtesy of Wendy Radick, Kitty Girl Vintage, www.kittygirlvintage.com. Photograph by Wendy Radick.*

**1940s–1950s ROSE PRINT SARONG DRESS.** Silk, beige background with large coral, red, green, and pink roses on stems with green leaves, short sleeves, fitted waist with side metal zipper, another zipper at back of neck, skirt, a true sarong, ties at the hip, below-knee length, very good condition. $72
*Courtesy of Wendy Radick, Kitty Girl Vintage.*

1940s Dinner Dress. *Courtesy of Mary Troncale, Branford, CT. Photograph by Tom Amico.*

Ceil Chapman Suit. *Courtesy of Mary Troncale, Branford, CT. Photograph by Tom Amico.*

**1940s Dinner Dress.** Black crepe, skirt with hip sash and drape, red and white sequined attached shrug, excellent condition. $175
*Courtesy of Mary Troncale, Branford, CT.*

**Late 1940s Ceil Chapman Suit.** Black crepe silk, black beads, peplum, silk-covered buttons and loop front, "Sabnias, Boston," excellent condition. $900
*Courtesy of Mary Troncale, Branford, CT.*

Cape. *Courtesy of Zap & Co., PA, www.zapandco.com. Photograph by Steve Murray.*

Fitted Jacket. *Courtesy of Zap & Co., PA, www.zapandco.com. Photograph by Steve Murray.*

Platform Shoes.
*Courtesy of Atomic Passion, New York, NY. Photograph by Tom Amico.*

**1940s Cape.** Ivory wool, stylized geometric black and ivory ornamentation, gold metallic buttons, excellent condition. $125
*Courtesy of Zap & Co., PA.*

**1940s Fitted Jacket.** Black wool, zippered front, with hand-sewn metallic ornamentation, excellent condition. $85
*Courtesy of Zap & Co., PA.*

**1940s Platform Shoes.** White, polka-dot trim, very good condition. $64
*Courtesy of Atomic Passion, NY.*

1940s Linen Dress.
*Courtesy of Mary
Troncale, Branford, CT.
Photograph by Tom Amico.*

1940s Linen Dress. Two-piece linen, geranium bow accent, covered
button back, peplum, pristine condition. $175
*Courtesy of Mary Troncale, Branford, CT.*

Suit. *Courtesy of Mary Troncale, Branford, CT. Photograph by Tom Amico.*

Herringbone Coat. *Courtesy of Wendy Radick, Kitty Girl Vintage, www.kittygirl-vintage.com. Photograph by Wendy Radick.*

**1940s SUIT.** Black wool crepe with black beaded hip swags, beaded trim on collar and cuffs, beaded covered buttons, excellent condition. $550 *Courtesy of Mary Troncale, Branford, CT.*

**1940s HERRINGBONE COAT.** Soft wool, black, gray, and white, big cuffed sleeves with matching detail to big patch pockets, black rayon satin lining, fastens with single button at neck, excellent condition. $65. *Courtesy of Wendy Radick, Kitty Girl Vintage.*

ILLUSTRATION HIGHLIGHTS EARLY 1940s FASHIONS. For men: cashmere V-neck sweater and cheviot striped suit. For women: two hat styles, the chin-length veil and the knitted beret. Square-shouldered suit jackets with slim waists.

"Tall, Dark, and Handsome," April 1943. By permission of *Esquire* magazine. © Hearst Communications, Inc. Also, Esquire is a trademark of Hearst Magazines Property, Inc. All Rights Reserved.

*Hat. Courtesy of Art & Janene Fawcett, Vintage Silhouettes, CA, www.vintagesilhouettes.com. Photograph by Art Fawcett.*

*Detail of Jacket:* Blue and cream houndstooth. *Photograph by Art Fawcett.*

Suit. *Courtesy of Art & Janene Fawcett, Vintage Silhouettes, CA, www.vintagesilhouettes.com. Photograph by Art Fawcett.*

**1940s HAT.** "Cavanaugh" classic style, gray/brown, brim 2⅓″, size 7¼, excellent condition. $85
*Courtesy of Art & Janene Fawcett, Vintage Silhouettes.*

**1940s SUIT.** Blue and cream houndstooth, single-breasted, "Anderson-Little Co.," size 38, excellent condition. $200
*Courtesy of Art & Janene Fawcett, Vintage Silhouettes.*

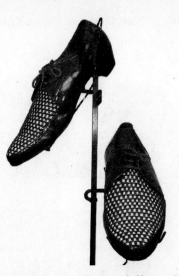

Wingtips. *Courtesy of Ardis Taylor, Vintage Silhouettes, CA, www.vintagesilhouettes.com. Photograph by Art Fawcett.*

Handmade Checkerboard Shoes. *Courtesy of Ardis Taylor, Vintage Silhouettes, CA, www.vintagesilhouettes.com. Photograph by Art Fawcett.*

Wingtip Spectators. *Courtesy of Ardis Taylor, Vintage Silhouettes, CA, www.vintagesilhouettes.com. Photograph by Art Fawcett.*

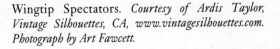

**1940S WINGTIPS.** Pointed with medallion toe, 12C/D, label: "Florsheim," excellent condition. $125
*Courtesy of Ardis Taylor, Vintage Silhouettes.*

**1940S HANDMADE CHECKERBOARD SHOES.** Mahogany and white, pointed toe and "Cuban" heel, good condition. $195
*Courtesy of Ardis Taylor, Vintage Silhouettes.*

**1940S WINGTIP SPECTATORS.** Two-tone, in leather and suede, label: "Florsheim," excellent condition. $225
*Courtesy of Ardis Taylor, Vintage Silhouettes.*

Gabardine Shirt. *Courtesy of Zap & Co., PA, www.zapandco.com. Photograph by Steve Murray.*

Photo Tie. *Courtesy of Craig Smith. Photograph by Tom Amico.*

1940s GABARDINE SHIRT. "Airman Hugster" brown with canary and cinnamon stripes, elasticized waistband, excellent condition. $150.
*Courtesy Zap & Co., PA.*

1940s PHOTO TIE. Western Glory, "Beaux Arts by Park Lane," 3¼" w, mint condition. $35
*Courtesy of Craig Smith.*

## MARKET TRENDS FOR THE FORTIES

### Lingerie and Robes

1940S BIAS-CUT NIGHTGOWN. Peach rayon and crepe, bows at neckline, "Super Fit," never worn, mint condition. $75
*Courtesy of Miss Kitty & Calico Jack, The Cat's Pajamas, PA, www.catspajamas.com*

1940S FLOWER QUILTED ROBE. Cream and peach flowered satin, shawl collar, one pocket, self-tie belt, additional inside tie, fully lined, perfect condition. $60
*Courtesy of The Fainting Couch, MA, www.faintingcouch.com*

1940S PEIGNOIR WITH MATCHING BIAS-CUT GOWN. Beige lace-trimmed peignoir, slightly padded shoulders, light pink charmeuse, matching bias-cut gown with beige lace, open back, cut low to waist, perfect condition. $365
*Courtesy of Linda Ames, Vintage Textile, www.vintagetextile.com*

1940S SHORT PINK RAYON SLIP. Pale pink, bias-cut rayon satin slip, lace bodice with appliquéd pink ribbon, spaghetti straps, excellent condition. $45
*Courtesy of Enokiworld, www.enokiworld.com*

1940S BABY BLUE RAYON BED JACKET. Pale silvery blue satin jacket, ivory lace trim, ties at neck, short wide sleeves, one triangular pocket at hip, made by Wonder Maid, excellent condition. $35
*Courtesy of Enokiworld, www.enokiworld.com*

### Separates

1940S EMBROIDERED BLOUSE. Black crepe, embroidered with silver, gold, and red cord, one-button closure at back, excellent condition. $65
*Courtesy of Art & Janene Fawcett, Vintage Silhouettes, CA, www.vintagesilhouettes.com*

### Dresses

1940S NAVY BLUE CREPE DRESS WITH STAR PATTERN. White shooting stars pattern, 6″ collar, rhinestone belt buckle, side zipper, excellent condition. $125
*Courtesy of The Fainting Couch, MA, www.faintingcouch.com*

1940S DRESS WITH MAJORETTES MOTIF. Red, white, and blue rayon, majorettes motif, mandarin collar, gathered bib front, covered buttons, excellent condition. $100
*Courtesy of Mary Troncale, Branford, CT.*

1940S FUCHSIA CREPE DRESS. Turn-out peek-a-boo sleeve accented with three covered buttons at cuff, "Stockpole, Moore, Tryon," excellent condition. $110
*Courtesy of The Fainting Couch, MA, www.faintingcouch.com*

1940S EISENBERG ORIGINAL DRESS. Taupe and white mini striped seersucker, long full skirt, self-belt in contrasting pattern, excellent condition. $175
*Courtesy of Miss Kitty & Calico Jack, The Cat's Pajamas, PA, www.catspajamas.com*

1940S FLORAL RAYON CREPE DAY DRESS. Rhinestone accents, side zipper, 6" short sleeve, mint condition. $150
*Courtesy of The Fainting Couch, MA, www.faintingcouch.com*

1940S RAYON PRINT DRESS WITH MATCHING JACKET. Blue and white PaZon rayon print, flared jacket, excellent condition. $85
*Courtesy of The Fainting Couch, MA, www.faintingcouch.com*

1950S HALTER DRESS. Polished cotton, solid blue halter with insert of blue and white stripes, full skirt gathered at waist, excellent condition. $75
*Courtesy of Art & Janene Fawcett, Vintage Silhouettes, CA, www.vintagesilhouettes.com*

## Suits

1940S WOOL GABARDINE SUIT BY JOHN PERNA. Dolman sleeves, straight skirt, camel colored, crepe lining, very good condition. $145
*Courtesy of Miss Kitty & Calico Jack, The Cat's Pajamas, PA, www.catspajamas.com*

1940S CLAIRE MCCARDELL PLAID SUMMER SUIT. Woven, wide sweeping broad bias plaid, soft textured, gilt lozenge buttons, made for Townleys, excellent condition. $375
*Courtesy of Enokiworld, www.enokiworld.com*

1940S DOVE GRAY GABARDINE CURVY SUIT. Menswear suiting wool, flecked with baby blue undertones, jacket with cornflower blue silk crepe lining, split turn-back cuffs, curved functional pockets, row of six covered buttons, straight skirt below-the-knee length, flawless condition. $210
*Courtesy of Enokiworld, www.enokiworld.com*

## Eveningwear

C. 1942 NAVY SILK EVENING SHEATH. Navy silk faille, soft front draping, navy glass beads, silk fringe, grosgrain inner waistband, metal

zipper, silk woven label: "Bergdorf Goodman on the Plaza New York," custom-fit (couture from Bergdorf Goodman), perfect condition. $395
*Courtesy of Karen Augusta, Antique Lace & Fashion, www.antique-fashion.com*

1940S BLACK CREPE DINNER DRESS WITH SWEETHEART NECKLINE. Sequined bow, tie belt, side zipper, excellent condition. $120
*Courtesy of The Fainting Couch, MA, www.faintingcouch.com*

1940S SOFT GOLD CREPE DINNER DRESS. Gold beaded front, excellent condition. $485
*Courtesy of Deborah Burke, Antique & Vintage Dress Gallery, www.antiquedress.com*

1940S BLACK CREPE EVENING GOWN. Gold sequined sleeves, low back, self-belt, label: "Bon Marche," excellent condition. $175
*Courtesy of Art & Janene Fawcett, Vintage Silhouettes, CA, www.vintagesilhouettes.com*

## Outerwear

1940S PLAID SWING COAT. Green plaid, lightweight wool, raglan sleeves, amber Lucite buttons, excellent condition. $225
*Courtesy of Miss Kitty & Calico Jack, The Cat's Pajamas, PA, www.catspajamas.com*

1940S MIDNIGHT BLUE COAT. Double-breasted lightweight wool gabardine, pleated front, silk lining, "Hochschild Kohn and Co. Baltimore," excellent condition. $145
*Courtesy of Miss Kitty & Calico Jack, The Cat's Pajamas, PA, www.catspajamas.com*

## Accessories

1940S CORAL COTTON EVENING BAG. Coral cotton, wool thread, crewel embroidered oversized tropical flowers, peach rayon faille lining, interior has change purse and three pockets, one zippered, brass and Lucite frame, "Exclusive Handbags by Ed B. Robinson," perfect condition. $125
*Courtesy of Karen Augusta, Antique Lace & Fashion, www.antique-fashion.com*

1940S GLASS BEADED PURSE. Glass beads, cotton thread, satin lining, brass frame with enameling and beading, Tambour embroidery set off by enameled frame and tiny white opalescent beads, excellent condition. $165
*Courtesy of Karen Augusta, Antique Lace & Fashion, www.antique-fashion.com*

**1940s METALLIC BROCADE EVENING BAG.** Cream satin lining, etched brass frame, excellent condition. $125
*Courtesy of Karen Augusta, Antique Lace & Fashion, www.antique-fashion.com*

**1940s VINYL SNAKESKIN PURSE.** High pouch with contrasting turned edge, snap closure accented with two round Lucite tips, brown satin lining, 6″ h × 16″ w, excellent condition. $100
*Courtesy of The Fainting Couch, MA, www.faintingcouch.com*

**1940s BLACK CORDE BARREL-SHAPED HANDBAG.** Mirror in lid, excellent condition. $125
*Courtesy of Miss Kitty & Calico Jack, The Cat's Pajamas, PA,*
*www.catspajamas.com*

**1940s PLEATED SILK CREPE CLUTCH.** Caramel colored, tiny accordion pleats, suspended from natural wooden frame, deeply carved slashes along clasp, hinged, brown rayon satin interior, with one small patch pocket, 8½″ h × 17″ w, excellent condition. $70
*Courtesy of Enokiworld, www.enokiworld.com*

**1940s COCOA PATENT POUCH WITH LUCITE CLASP.** Constructed like pouch but shaped, big chunky Lucite clasp on top, hinged sides, charcoal silk crepe lining with two patch and zippered pockets, double 6″ handles, 8″ h × 10½″ w, excellent condition. $95
*Courtesy of Enokiworld, www.enokiworld.com*

**1940s SILK FAILLE WAVY HANDBAG.** Curved and gently pleated toward center of bag, attached black coin purse "swings" out on two wide straps, black silk satin lining, double 6″ handles, 8″ h × 10″ w, flawless condition. $75
*Courtesy of Enokiworld, www.enokiworld.com*

**1940s ALLIGATOR POUCH BAG.** Supple alligator skin, gathered into a luxe pouch, chunky Bakelite clasp in deep translucent amber striped with antique brass, lined in cocoa cotton with one interior patch pocket, single 7″ handle, 6″ h × 11″ w, excellent condition. $170
*Courtesy of Enokiworld, www.enokiworld.com*

**1940s VELVET EVENING PURSE.** Black velvet with a silver rhinestone closure, excellent condition. $30
*Courtesy of Art & Janene Fawcett, Vintage Silhouettes, CA,*
*www.vintagesilhouettes.com*

**1940s "DOLL HAT."** Retro-Victorian, black silk satin ribbons, velveteen "leaves," yellow silk flowers, excellent condition. $95
*Courtesy of Deborah Burke, Antique & Vintage Dress Gallery,*
*www.antiquedress.com*

**1940S LILLY DACHÉ HAT.** Brown and olive silk satin hat with label, excellent condition. $145

*Courtesy of Miss Kitty & Calico Jack, The Cat's Pajamas, PA, www.catspajamas.com*

**1940S NAVY SILK "POUFF HAT."** Pleating and ruching all over, soft silk pouff top, "Ronnie New York," excellent condition. $115

*Courtesy of The Fainting Couch, MA, www.faintingcouch.com*

**1940S WEDGED SHOES WITH FLOWERS.** Peach, purple leather, ankle straps and leather flowers, "Fortunet Shoes with the floating step," excellent condition. $75

*Courtesy of Miss Kitty & Calico Jack, The Cat's Pajamas, PA, www.catspajamas.com*

**1940S GRAY SUEDE SHOES.** Dark gray suede "Baby Dolls," crisscross over toe, "Joseph Salon Shoes," size 6½B, ½" heel, excellent condition. $65

*Courtesy of Art & Janene Fawcett, Vintage Silhouettes, CA, www.vintagesilhouettes.com*

**1940S SLING BACKS.** White leather, "Mackey Starr," clear plastic cutouts on vamp, leather soles, Blums of Philadelphia, size 5½M, 3½" heel, excellent condition. $75

*Courtesy of Miss Kitty & Calico Jack, The Cat's Pajamas, PA, www.catspajamas.com*

**1940S POLKA-DOTTED SHOES.** Sky blue faille with raised dots, ankle straps, size 7½B, 4" heel, excellent condition. $155

*Courtesy of Miss Kitty & Calico Jack, The Cat's Pajamas, PA, www.catspajamas.com*

**1940S CHERRY RED LEATHER PUMPS.** "Fashion Craft" size 8, 3" heel, excellent condition. $145

*Courtesy of Miss Kitty & Calico Jack, The Cat's Pajamas, PA, www.catspajamas.com*

**1940S LEATHER "PARISIAN" PUMPS.** Gray with white beads, "Parisian," size 7M, 4" heel, excellent condition. $225

*Courtesy of Miss Kitty & Calico Jack, The Cat's Pajamas, PA, www.catspajamas.com*

**1940S BROWN CORDE OPEN TOE SANDALS.** Open toes, little cutouts at side of vamp, ankle straps, rayon faille heels, made by Treasure Tred, never worn, in original box, size 7AA, 3¾" heel, excellent condition. $105

*Courtesy of Enokiworld, www.enokiworld.com*

**1940S BABY DOLL TOE SUEDE PUMPS.** Brown suede, sweetheart vamp with tiny whipstitching around curvy edge, made for Lockharts in St. Louis, size 6½AA, 3″ heel, insoles and uppers flawless condition, soles show gentle wear. $60
*Courtesy of Enokiworld, www.enokiworld.com*

**1940S BUTTON AND BOW SUEDE HEELS.** Black suede peep-toe pumps, bow and button detail along top, notched throat, label: "The Foot Saver Shoe," size 8B, 2½″ heel, excellent condition. $80
*Courtesy of Enokiworld, www.enokiworld.com*

**1940S DELMANETTE BLACK SUEDE PLATFORM SANDALS.** Small platform, dressed-up black suede vamp with cutouts, size 7½ AA, 3¼″ heel, excellent condition. $90
*Courtesy of Enokiworld, www.enokiworld.com*

**1940S BROWN SUEDE AND LEATHER PLATFORMS.** Leather zigzag detail, chunky heel, made by Polly's Aristocrat, size 5½ M, 3¼″ heel, excellent condition. $75
*Courtesy of Enokiworld, www.enokiworld.com*

**1940S SUEDE PLATFORM SLINGS.** Brown suede open-toe slings, uppers with satin ribbon running diagonally, retro Art Deco design with stylized sun rays, strap crisscrosses over top of foot at ankle and slides up behind heel, made by DeLiso Debs, 9½″ inside, 3″ w, small ⅓″ platform in front, 3¼″ heel, excellent condition. $90
*Courtesy of Enokiworld, www.enokiworld.com*

**1940S BLACK SUEDE PLATFORMS WITH DOUBLE ANKLE STRAPS.** Five straps across toe, double straps at ankle, each with its own tiny buckle in jet black suede, by Carmelettes for Carmo, size 6½ M, ¾″ platform, 4¼″ heel, excellent condition. $205
*Courtesy of Enokiworld, www.enokiworld.com*

**1940S ANKLE STRAP D'ORSAY PUMPS.** Black suede, perforated and scalloped vamp, ankle straps, curved heel, scalloped detailing above heel, echoes curving edge at back, made by Rice O'Neill for Vandervoort's, size 7AAA, 3¾″ heel, excellent condition. $310
*Courtesy of Enokiworld, www.enokiworld.com*

**1940S BLACK SUEDE AND PATENT WEDGIES.** T-straps, charming triangle at open toe, made by Fortunet, size 8M, 3″-high wedge, excellent condition. $140
*Courtesy of Enokiworld, www.enokiworld.com*

**1940s BLACK SUEDE AND PLASTIC SHOES.** "Joseph Magnin" size 6½, very good condition. $55

*Courtesy of Art & Janene Fawcett, Vintage Silhouettes, CA,*
*www.vintagesilhouettes.com*

**1940s EVENING SHOES.** Open toe, cream, gold, silver, size 5M, 3½″ heel, excellent condition. $68

*Courtesy of Art & Janene Fawcett, Vintage Silhouettes, CA,*
*www.vintagesilhouettes.com*

## Menswear

**1940s MEN'S GRAY FELT HAT.** Size 7⅛, excellent condition. $75

*Courtesy of Miss Kitty & Calico Jack, The Cat's Pajamas, PA,*
*www.catspajamas.com*

**1940s MEN'S PANAMA STRAW HAT.** Size 7, 2¼″ brim, very good condition. $50

*Courtesy of Miss Kitty & Calico Jack, The Cat's Pajamas, PA,*
*www.catspajamas.com*

Ceil Chapman Dress. *Courtesy of Isadora's, WA, www.isadoras.com. Photograph by Jennifer A. Ledda.*

# Etiquette and Elvis

The fifties got into full swing after society accepted Christian Dior's "New Look." Skirts became voluminous; dress was no longer a statement on war shortage but of well-being and affluence. Ensembles featuring soft shoulders and fitted waists were complemented with small hats, white gloves, and high-heeled pumps. The fashion industry boomed as Parisian and American designers provided women with new fashions every season to make up for the uniformity of the past decade. Balmain's black taffeta strapless ball gowns, Balenciaga's wide-collared evening coats, and Givenchy's extravagant cocktail dresses were lush in colors, fabrics, and accessories. Evening gloves were elbow-length and even cocktail dresses had coordinating hats. Mink stoles were used as evening wraps. Women also wore cashmere sweaters with fur collars and jeweled embroidery for evening. The "New Look" grew even more popular and with it skirts were mid-calf and pleated at the waist to give the desired fullness.

Women left their wartime factory jobs and returned to homemaker roles. There was a desire for a contented, conservative suburban lifestyle. Families thrived in the suburbs with station wagons, picture windows, backyards, casseroles, and Emily Post. The focus was on the "ideal" American family. Happy role models were found on every television program. Donna Reed wore the standard daytime shirtwaist with full circle skirt, belted waist, and stiff upright collar. A fancy apron was added to wear at home in the kitchen. She never left the house without the regulation short white gloves, flowered hat at the back of the head, and suitable handbag. A more glamorous fashion ideal was typified by Grace Kelly in Alfred

Hitchcock's film classic, *Rear Window*. Kelly appeared in a variety of divine "New Look" dresses.

In the fifties Chanel returned to fashion designing, continuing with her signature cardigan suit and low sling-back heel. Emilio Pucci designed silk scarves, dresses, blouses, and stretch bathing suits in bold patterns of purple, blue, pink, and crimson.

For casual looks, large bows accented shirtwaist dresses, gathering in the front or back. Midriffs were lightly corseted and the uplift bra gave women a new, bustier silhouette. Poodles were top dog and appeared on skirts and jewelry. The parure and costume pearls were most popular for everyday jewelry. Rhinestone-studded sunglasses were a natural part of an outfit, and toreador or capri pants and ballet slippers were worn for casual wear. Daytime sweaters were appliquéd with different motifs.

Toward the end of the decade, two entirely different silhouettes were shown. Dior designed the "sack" dress, which later led to the chemise, a no-waisted dress that was short and narrow at the hem. Yves Saint Laurent produced the second innovation of the fifties in 1958 with the trapeze dress. It had narrow shoulders and a triangular shape, again with no waist.

As the decades progressed, shoes became higher and heels slimmer. Dior's feminine look actually accentuated the foot. In 1955, Roger Vivier working with Dior, designed the stiletto heel, a shoe with a very high, thin heel reinforced with metal, and a pointed toe. The stiletto style was used in fantastic designs for shoes and sandals with embroidery, feathers, lace, beading, rhinestones, satin, and even fur. The allure of the stiletto was perpetuated by several Hollywood stars like Marilyn Monroe and by fashion models like Suzy Parker.

Two design elements typical of the decade were the "ornamental" neckline and the dolman sleeve. Necklines could take on a variety of edgings from ruffling to halters whether on a playsuit or evening dress. The dolman sleeve required more fabric to make than other sleeve styles. It was seen on dresses as well as coats and suits.

Colored eye shadow, penciled eyebrows, and short haircuts were framed by many different hat styles, which reflected clothing designs in matching and contrasting colors and trim. Many women wore half hats with their suits and cocktail outfits. Bubble turbans, cloche styles, coolie chapeaux, wig hats, and feather helmets were all made in a variety of fabrics including satin, velvet, jersey, and fur. Short veils were shown on flowered hats and, in summer, novelty beach hats were popular.

The Wilardy Lucite box-shaped handbags were popular throughout the fifties. Clutch bags were used for evening and came in a variety of fabrics, and had jeweled clasps. Sets of purses and belts or purses and shoes were best sellers. Alligator handbags with handles, lizard and snakeskin purses were also fashionable. Caviar beaded bags and decorated wooden box bags were among the sturdier bags of the decade. Straw animal handbags were smart novelty designs of the fifties.

Bathing suits were designed to sculpt the figure with elastic fibers, boned torsos, and structured bras. Rose Marie Reid was the initiator of many of the highly structured styles. Cole of California mass-produced bathing suits, making the industry even larger. Hollywood screen stars now posed in swimsuits, as well as in gowns, for publicity photos.

Menswear in the fifties took a conservative turn after the "bold" look of the postwar forties. The "Mr. T" silhouette was the trim look of the decade, with narrow lapels and soft construction. Men chose gray or blue flannel suits worn with pinpoint collared shirts and narrow, small-knotted stripe or solid ties. The all-dacron suit appeared and rayon was now used year-round. Hats were *de rigueur* for men, usually with tapered crown and narrow brims.

To sport the casual look, men of the fifties had many choices. The Eisenhower jacket of 1950 was a waist-length, blouse-style jacket with slant pockets, a turned-down collar, and a zipper closure made in many color variations or two tones. Madras sport jackets, polo shirts, Bermuda shorts with native prints, colorful, tapered resort slacks, and Hawaiian shirts were all designed for the fifties. The Ivy League look was popular with button-down collared shirts in a variety of fabrics and colors.

The newest trend of the fifties was the change in fashions for youth. The American teenager was style-conscious and for the first time fashions were designed with teens in mind. Rock and roll star, Elvis Presley, and actor, James Dean, became fashion idols for teenagers. Rock and roll songs started fads in haircuts, suede shoes, and felt skirts. Girls wore sweaters buttoned backwards and accented them with costume jewelry scatter pins. Cinch belts, bobby socks, cuffed jeans, and hair set in rollers completed the chic teenage scene. Boys wore pink shirts and khaki pants or leather jackets and greased hair. The beaches, drive-in movies, and soda fountains were the new centers of teenage activity. The fifties led the way to the upcoming "youth explosion" of the sixties.

## Signature Fabrics of the 1950s

Silk shantung, tie silk, sheer wools, wool and silk mixtures and jersey for women's daywear

Taffetas, faille, moiré, heavy satin, velvets, ottoman, and chiffon for women's eveningwear

Brocades for cocktail suits

Synthetics:

Nylon tricot for lingerie

Nylon for men's socks, stockings, and dresses

Nylon tulle for evening gowns

Dacron for "wash and wear" men's shirts

Orlon for sweaters, coats

Orlon satin for designer gowns

Acrilan for men's raincoats

Terylene for shirts

Polyester blends for sportswear

Rayon and acetate for evening costumes

## Important Designers and Manufacturers of the 1950s

**ADOLFO:** Adolfo's fifties millinery designs for Bergdorf Goodman spanned hat styles from miniature caps to the popular cartwheel hats.

**ADRIAN:** In the fifties, Adrian had a line of suits and evening clothes as well as a line of men's shirts and ties.

**BALENCIAGA:** Balenciaga showed sack dresses and varied his hemlines so that they were longer in the back than in the front. Many of his garments worked with colored block-patterned lambswool.

**PIERRE BALMAIN:** In 1951, Pierre Balmain's fashions were brought to the United States. A French designer who had the reputation of bringing French style to American sizes, Balmain's collections included tailored suits, evening gowns, and sheath dresses with jackets. He used stole wraps as well as Cossack-styled capes in day and evening fashions.

**BILL BLASS:** In the fifties, Bill Blass was the head designer for Anna Miller, who merged with the couture house of her brother Maurice Rentner in 1959. Blass got his design inspiration from thirties movies and so favored glamorous looks in his fashions. His 1959 collection featured halter necks, sequins, and long culottes.

**TOM BRIGANCE:** As a designer for Frank Gallant, Tom Brigance created mostly sportswear and bathing suits. His bathing suits were strapless or halter-topped with bloomer bottoms in a variety of fabrics. These stylish suits often looked like cut-off evening dresses. In 1951, Brigance designed a corduroy pantsuit of loose pants, jacket, and top that consisted of a band of cotton fabric that went behind the neck, covering the breasts and attaching to the pants at the waistline. The effect was a bare look that left the abdomen partially revealed.

**Pierre Cardin:** Throughout most of the fifties, Pierre Cardin had a reputation as a designer of menswear and costumes for theater productions. His first collection of men's fashions emerged in 1954; his first for women was in 1957. This new line included coats with a loose hanging back panel and bubble skirts on chemise dresses.

**Hattie Carnegie:** In the fifties, Hattie Carnegie was known for her suits and dresses. Her bright-colored wool suits had waist-length jackets and straight skirts. These suits were not meant to be worn with blouses, but with necklaces. Her dresses were beaded or sequined on linen in summer, or crepe in winter. In 1956, Hattie Carnegie died and her couture house did not continue long after her passing.

**Bonnie Cashin:** In 1952, Bonnie Cashin showed "layered dressing" which meant a more casual sheath dress that could be dressed up with fancy aprons. She showed sleeveless and sleeved coats in layers as well. In the mid-fifties, Cashin designed a purse-pocket raincoat with an interior pocket designed to hold one's purse. In 1956, she featured canvas duck fabric with leather piping for pants, coats, and apron skirts.

**Oleg Cassini:** Cassini was known for his ultra-feminine styles in the fifties; tiny waistlines and wide skirts in taffeta and chiffon. He also showed glamorous sheath dresses, knitted suits, and cocktail dresses.

**"Coco" Chanel:** Chanel reopened her couture house in 1954, showing suit sets similar to those she showed in the thirties, coordinating tweed ensembles with pearls and gilt chain purses.

**Ceil Chapman:** Ceil Chapman was famous for her evening dresses and gowns. Most of Chapman's designs had fitted bodices that were often strapless, with small waists and full skirts. Her dresses often came with coordinated stoles to complete an outfit. Chapman's designs of 1956 and 1957 experimented with straighter skirts and looser bodices with V necks.

**Lilly Daché:** By the fifties, Lilly Daché designs could outfit a woman head-to-toe. She showed tiny hats, designed dresses and coats, and featured low-heeled fabric shoes with costume jewelry, all of her own design.

**Davidow:** Davidow was still a well-known manufacturer of suits. Their suits were respected for fine detailing such as repeating the rounded shape of a lapel on the cut-away hems on suit jackets.

**Jane Derby:** Jane Derby specialized in designs for petites. Her looks were somewhat conservative, with day and afternoon dresses in soft-colored tweeds and crepes. Derby often combined traditional day and evening fabrics in an outfit.

**JEAN DESSÈS:** Jean Dessès's fifties evening designs looked like Grecian robes with heavy drapery. He also showed sheath dresses with fitted jackets.

**CHRISTIAN DIOR:** Dior continued to be a trend-setting designer. In 1950, he shortened skirts and put horseshoe collars on his dresses. Dior also used Princess lines in his dress-jacket ensembles. In 1952, Dior designed a three-piece suit in pastel colors with three-quarter-length sleeves on a cardigan-style jacket. He also featured sheath dresses with spaghetti straps and coolie hats. In 1954, his H-line collection featured a white handkerchief, and lawn jacket with soft pleats for evening. In 1955, his A- and Y-lines showed V-shaped collars and gigantic stoles as well as long chiffon sheath dresses with spaghetti straps. Dior's 1957 collection centered around vareuse dresses. He also showed khaki bush jackets with flap pockets, and tunic dresses in black, navy blue, and white.

**ESTÉVEZ:** In 1955, Estévez started to design for Grenelle under his name and his collections were widely popular. He specialized in black and white cocktail and evening dresses. Estévez's collection was North African–inspired, showing clothing with burnous sleeves and hoods, as well as prints that featured tiger and zebra stripes.

**ANNE FOGERTY:** In the fifties, Fogerty designed dresses and coats for the junior market under the name of Margot Dresses. Fogerty later designed for Saks Fifth Avenue and then opened her own business. Her signature styles include her ballet-length cotton dresses with stiffened net petticoats, the tea-cosy dress where a full skirt fell from a dropped waist, an Empire silhouette, and many blouses with ruffles.

**GALANOS:** Galanos was famous for his fabulously detailed evening dresses and gowns. His designs repeatedly used chiffon to lavish excess with fifty yards to a skirt and layered cut-away collars. However, Galanos also designed narrow silhouettes with sheath and sack dresses, although he attached drapery that gave fluidity to the designs. In daywear, Galanos was one of the first designers to show horseshoe necklines on suits.

**RUDI GERNREICH:** In the fifties, Rudi Gernreich was known for sportswear, casual clothing, and bathing suits. He used supple fabrics such as jersey in solid and geometric patterns. In 1952, he used the twenties maillot-style bathing suit without an interior foundation which was in stark contrast to the highly constructed figures of other bathing suits of the day.

**HUBERT DE GIVENCHY:** Givenchy's fifties designs included bettina blouses, elegant evening dresses and gowns, and exaggerated sack-shaped, kite dresses.

**GOODALL CO.:** In the fifties, the Goodall Company dropped the Palm Beach company name of the thirties and forties. Regardless of the name change, Goodall continued to design fashionable suits and coats for men.

**EDITH HEAD:** Edith Head was a costume designer in Hollywood from the thirties through the fifties. One of her most widely copied designs, however, was her strapless evening dress of tulle and green satin with appliquéd white violets worn by Elizabeth Taylor in *A Place in the Sun*, in 1951; Head won an Oscar for costume design for that film. Her Hollywood designs also popularized South American–styled clothing such as shirts, scarves, and ponchos.

**CHARLES JAMES:** Charles James's fifties designs focused on fine cuts and masterful shaping for visual interest. His evening dresses rarely had or needed any ornamentation. Department stores treated James's couture designs as they did Parisian designs, buying one couture dress design and making many quality, though less expensive copies. James also designed suits, dresses, and coats for everyday wear. He used wool fabrics, dolman sleeves, and stand-away collars.

**KORET:** Koret manufactured fifties-style purses throughout the decade.

**TINA LESER:** In the fifties, Tina Leser continued to look abroad for her fashion inspiration. Her 1950 collection was Spanish-inspired, with black toreador pants that ended just below the knee, ruffled white blouses, black velvet suits with red satin-lined skirts, and black cloaks. Leser's sportswear designs in the fifties included sundresses shaped like Tahitian pareos, taffeta and Latex bathing suits, and Lurex pajamas in ethnic-patterned fabrics.

**MAINBOCHER:** In the fifties, Mainbocher designed simple yet dramatic ball gowns, versatile dresses that had optional overskirts and aprons for dressing up, and day and evening suits with boxy jackets and narrow skirts. His more casual designs for summer included coats of mattress ticking and gingham, shift dresses with appliqué and bows, and other dresses in linen and taffeta. Mainbocher also designed costumes for Broadway stage productions in the fifties.

**VERA MAXWELL:** Most of Vera Maxwell's designs in the fifties featured coats and jackets in ensembles as suits or with dresses. She used warm colors and lined coats with prints to match the coordinating dresses. She used midi jacket cuts, Princess-line coat dresses, and Chesterfield coats in her ensembles.

**CLAIRE MCCARDELL:** Claire McCardell's designs reflected her fashion interests in versatility and comfort. She continued to show her monastic dress designs as well as the popular popover dresses. Most of her dress designs were no-waist, and included a length of spaghetti piping to serve as a belt, wherever the wearer wanted it to be. She used wool jersey, corduroy, and cottons in her designs, as well as fancier fabrics in subdued colors. Many of her designs used topstitching, patch pockets, and brass fasteners as functional decorations. McCardell's bathing suits were of shape-retaining fabrics and had halter necks, hoods, and wrap waists. She also showed a line of short dresses and skirts for sportswear that presaged the much shorter miniskirts of the sixties. McCardell died in 1958.

**NORMAN NORELL:** Norman Norell's designs in the fifties varied widely. In 1950, he showed straight chemise dresses worn with flattening bras. In 1951, he designed narrow dresses with pinched waists and short spencer jackets. Norell's 1952 designs included suits with Norfolk jackets and hip belts as well as his famous sequined "mermaid" dresses. In 1955, he showed pea jacket suits and, in 1958, showed straight, high-waisted dresses called parachute chemises because of the straight front and bubbled back. Norell's later designs combined day and evening fashion elements such as full-skirted shirtwaist dresses in watered silks or lace and tweed jackets over satin evening gowns.

**CLARE POTTER:** Clare Potter designed youthful, moderately priced sportswear in the fifties. One of her most common and popular looks was a hand-knit cardigan sweater over a cotton dress or with a full, pleated skirt. She was also known for her sundresses, halter tops, and bathing suits.

**EMILIO PUCCI:** During the fifties, Pucci designed sportswear with slim pants, capri pants, shorts, and resort wear. His signature fabrics were brightly colored silks with bold patterns. His designs, especially his blouses, were popular throughout the decade and into the sixties.

**ROSE MARIE REID:** One of Rose Marie Reid's most well-known designs was her bathing suit with conical bosoms.

**NETTIE ROSENSTEIN:** In the fifties, Nettie Rosenstein used the narrow-waisted, full-skirted silhouette not only for shirtwaist dresses, but also for evening gowns and suits. She made these designs with European fabrics which had been designed specifically for her use.

**YVES SAINT LAURENT:** In 1958, Yves Saint Laurent designed his trapeze dress which had narrow shoulders and a short skirt. In 1959, he showed a shorter version of the hobble skirt.

**SCAASI:** Scaasi's specialty in the fifties was eveningwear: dramatic designs with "table-top" necklines in chiffon, slipper satin, and velvet. He often showed equally dramatic evening wraps that were lined to match the gowns. In 1958, Scaasi made a daring design of a knee-length evening dress with a bubble hem, the first instance of evening fashions being so short.

**CAROLYN SCHNURER:** Carolyn Schnurer designed mass-produced sportswear that was very affordable. She showed day dresses in French-inspired printed cottons, sleeveless sheath dresses in wool, and circle skirt ensembles with wool tube tops and matching cardigans. She quit the fashion world in the late fifties.

**ADELE SIMPSON:** In the fifties, Simpson designed a chemise dress with attached belts that could be worn tied in the front or back.

**PAULINE TRIGÈRE:** In the early fifties, Pauline Trigère was renowned for her seamless Princess-line cuts in dresses and skirts. She rarely used shirring or tucking in her designs, instead she depended on darts and carefully cut panels of fabric to give her clothes shape. In the mid-fifties, she designed short, strapless black dresses with a floor-length drape, as well as tunics in day suits, evening dresses, and wool day dresses.

**VALENTINA:** Valentina's fifties designs included suits with circle skirts and loose jackets, faille and taffeta skirts with jersey blouses, and evening gowns with optional overskirts. In the late fifties, Valentina featured her "convertible clothing" designs that allowed a travel suit to evolve into resort wear by removing a jacket and skirt to reveal shorts and a top. In 1957, Valentina closed her couture house.

**WILARDY:** This was a New York company which produced some of the most interesting and expensive Lucite purses of the fifties.

**KAY WILSON:** A Los Angeles designer, Kay Wilson made wool cardigan sweaters with felt appliquéd notions of particular themes.

**B. H. WRAGGE:** In the fifties, B. H. Wragge marketed their designs for suburban women. They showed linen sheath dresses with pongee coats and straight flannel dresses with rhinestone button fronts. Wragge's pants, shorts, and sweaters were also very popular. Their practical fashions were affordably priced.

## 1950s
### Introduction Frontispiece

1950S CEIL CHAPMAN DRESS. Designer label, silk moiré, strapless, boned, 15 covered buttons center back, high slit front, inner bustles at hips and front waistline, pristine condition. $850 (See photograph on page 114)
*Courtesy of Isadora's, WA.*

## VINTAGE FASHIONS OF THE FIFTIES

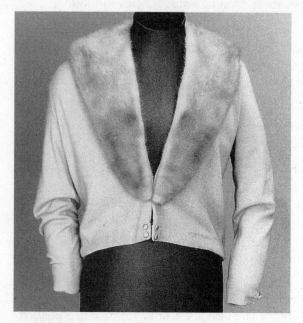

Cashmere Sweater.
*Courtesy of Patina, New York, NY. Photograph by Tom Amico.*

No-Heel Pump.
*Courtesy of Sothebys.com. Photograph by Monica Anchin.*

**1950s SWEATER.** Beige cashmere, soft mink collar, excellent condition. $175
*Courtesy of Patina, NY.*

**c. 1955 NO-HEEL PUMP.** Paramount red satin, excellent condition. $1,540
*Courtesy of Sothebys.com*

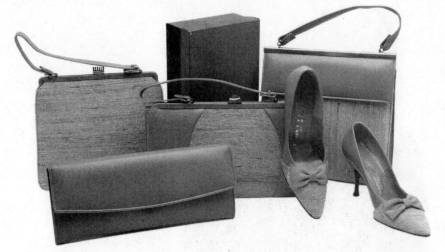

La Rose Leather Set. *Courtesy of Sothebys.com. Photograph by Monica Anchin.*

Alligator Purse.
*Courtesy of Isadora's,
WA, www.isadoras.com.
Photograph by Jennifer A. Ledda.*

**c. 1955 La Rose Leather Set.** Raw silk/green leather, one pair of shoes and four matching handbags, excellent condition. $605
*Courtesy of Sothebys.com*

**1950s Alligator Purse.** Deep red color with simple gold clasp, three pockets inside and one zippered pouch, by French manufacturer, Madelaine Bags, made in Holland, 9½″ h × 9½″ w and opens to approximately 6″ d, strap is 19″ l and 1″ w, pristine condition. $575
*Courtesy of Isadora's, WA.*

Handbag. *Courtesy of Vintage by Stacey Lee, White Plains, NY. Photograph by Tom Amico.*

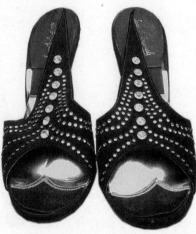

Springolators. *Courtesy of Isadora's, WA, www.isadoras.com. Photograph by Jennifer A. Ledda.*

**1950s HANDBAG.** Floral carpet, interior with zippered pocket, excellent condition. $135
*Courtesy of Vintage by Stacey Lee, NY.*

**1950s SPRINGOLATORS SORRENTO ORIGINAL.** Black suede, highly crafted with dramatic point that follows the instep, heavily encrusted with rhinestones following point and draping foot, continuing pattern on heel, excellent condition. $575
*Courtesy of Isadora's, WA.*

*The Exceptional in a 1950s Resort Ensemble and Bathing Dress.*

*Left:* 1955–56 Emilio Pucci printed cotton resort ensemble once worn by Lauren Bacall. *Courtesy of Philadelphia Museum of Art. Gift of Miss Lauren Bacall. Right:* 1953 Claire McCardell wool knit bathing dress with hook-and-eye closures. *Courtesy of Philadelphia Museum of Art. Gift of Miss Rubye Graham. Both objects are accessioned and part of the permanent collection.*

Snakeskin Box Purse.
*Courtesy of Wendy Radick,*
*Kitty Girl Vintage,*
*www.kittygirlvintage.com.*
*Photograph by Wendy Radick.*

Leopard Pumps. *Courtesy of Cecily*
*Greenaway. Photograph by Tom Amico.*

**1950s LEOPARD PUMPS.** Beige and brown velvet, "Bloomingdale's Beekman Place Shoes," excellent condition. $175
*Courtesy of Cecily Greenaway.*

**1950s SNAKESKIN BOX PURSE.** Reptile green snakeskin, gold-toned frame, clasp, and handle fixtures, black rayon faille lining, marked "DeLiso," 6″ h (without handle) × 7″ w × 4″ at base, excellent condition. $60
*Courtesy of Wendy Radick, Kitty Girl Vintage.*

Kelly Green Circle Skirt.
*Property of Private Collection.*
*Photograph by Tom Amico.*

Doll Circle Skirt. *Property of Private*
*Collection. Photograph by Tom Amico.*

**1950s Circle Skirt.** Kelly green felt with three-dimensional appliquéd lobsters, seaweed, and clams with attached faux pearls.

**1950s Circle Skirt.** Striped cotton with "dolls" wearing striped circle skirts of red, yellow, blue, orange, and green.
*Property of Private Collection.*

Beaded Cardigan. *Courtesy of Darlene Dull and Jennifer Parker-Stanton, Cookie's Closet, www.cookiescloset.com. Photograph by Sanders Stanton.*

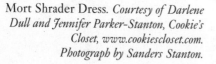

Mort Shrader Dress. *Courtesy of Darlene Dull and Jennifer Parker-Stanton, Cookie's Closet, www.cookiescloset.com. Photograph by Sanders Stanton.*

**1950S BEADED CARDIGAN.** Red wool, white beads, red pearlized buttons on front, fully lined, excellent condition. $55
*Courtesy of Darlene Dull and Jennifer Parker-Stanton, Cookie's Closet.*

**1950S MORT SHRADER DRESS.** Purple, olive green, black, gray, and red plaid wool, pleated skirt, covered buttons at neck and side closure, very good condition. $72
*Courtesy of Darlene Dull and Jennifer Parker-Stanton, Cookie's Closet.*

La Rose Set. *Courtesy of Sothebys.com. Photograph by Monica Anchin.*

Springolator Mules. *Courtesy of Wendy Radick, Kitty Girl Vintage, www.kittygirlvintage.com. Photograph by Wendy Radick.*

Box Purse. *Courtesy of Darlene Dull and Jennifer Parker-Stanton, Cookie's Closet, www.cookiescloset.com. Photograph by Sanders Stanton.*

**c. 1955 LA ROSE SET.** Yellow and black plaid, shoes and two handbags, excellent condition. $1,540
*Courtesy of Sothebys.com*

**1950s SPRINGOLATOR MULES.** Pearly pink leather, pink leather lining, open toe, "CH Baker of California," size 6½ M, 3″ heel, good condition. $46.
*Courtesy of Wendy Radick, Kitty Girl Vintage.*

**1950s BOX PURSE.** Bamboo and Lucite, 7½″ h × 8″ w × 3″ d, very good condition. $185
*Courtesy of Darlene Dull and Jennifer Parker-Stanton, Cookie's Closet.*

Polka-Dot Party Dress.
*Courtesy of Wendy Radick,*
*Kitty Girl Vintage,*
*www.kittygirlvintage.com.*
*Photograph by Wendy Radick.*

**1950s POLKA-DOT PARTY DRESS.** Sheer red with tiny polka dots, scoop neckline, peek-a-boo sleeves accented with bows, appliquéd skirt, fully lined in net crinoline, fitted waist, back metal zipper, matching belt, very good to excellent condition. $49
*Courtesy of Wendy Radick, Kitty Girl Vintage.*

Cocktail Dress. *Courtesy of Darlene Dull and Jennifer Parker-Stanton, Cookie's Closet, www.cookiescloset.com. Photograph by Sanders Stanton.*

Arnold Scaasi Evening Dress. *Courtesy of Deborah Burke, Antique & Vintage Dress Gallery, www.antiquedress.com. Photograph by Deborah Burke.*

**1950s COCKTAIL DRESS.** Red satin, bell skirt, spaghetti straps, pleated front, two roses at bustline, very good condition. $98
*Courtesy of Darlene Dull and Jennifer Parker-Stanton, Cookie's Closet.*

**1960s ARNOLD SCAASI EVENING DRESS.** Silk satin, red dahlia floral print, strapless, bouffant dress with tulle underneath, red silk satin coat, matching silk floral print lining, excellent condition. $1,195
*Courtesy of Deborah Burke, Antique & Vintage Dress Gallery.*

Knitted Shell. *Courtesy of Art & Janene Fawcett, Vintage Silhouettes, CA, www.vintagesilhouettes.com. Photograph by Art Fawcett.*

Sir Norman Hartnell Couture Dress. *Courtesy of Deborah Burke, Antique & Vintage Dress Gallery, www.antiquedress.com. Photograph by Deborah Burke.*

**1950s KNITTED SHELL.** Blue knit, allover iridescent sequins, clear beads form diamond pattern, beaded fringe with pearl ends, very good condition. $65

*Courtesy of Art & Janene Fawcett, Vintage Silhouettes, CA, www.vintagesilhouettes.com*

**1950s SIR NORMAN HARTNELL COUTURE DRESS.** Fully beaded net dress, silver bugle beads and round beads over white silk lining, near-mint condition. $5,000

*Courtesy of Deborah Burke, Antique & Vintage Dress Gallery.*

Single-breasted Suit. *Courtesy of Art &*
*Janene Fawcett, Vintage Silhouettes, CA,*
*www.vintagesilhouettes.com. Photograph by*
*Art Fawcett.*

*Detail of Fabric:* Windowpane pattern.
*Photograph by Art Fawcett.*

Gentleman's Fedora. *Courtesy of*
*Art & Janene Fawcett,*
*Vintage Silhouettes, CA,*
*www.vintagesilhouettes.com.*
*Photograph by Art Fawcett.*

**1950s Single-breasted Suit.** Chocolate with red fleck and silver 1″
windowpane pattern, New Old Stock, 40L, excellent condition. $340
*Courtesy of Art & Janene Fawcett, Vintage Silhouettes.*

**1950s Gentleman's Fedora.** Gray, dark slate blue ribbon, cavanaugh
edge, size 7⅜, 2⅝″ brim, "Dobbs" gray color has brown tint, renovated. $105
*Courtesy of Art & Janene Fawcett, Vintage Silhouettes.*

Sports Jacket. *Courtesy of Art & Janene Fawcett, Vintage Silhouettes, CA, www.vintagesilhouettes.com. Photograph by Art Fawcett.*

Detail of Jacket.
*Photograph by Art Fawcett.*

**1950s SPORTS JACKET.** Navy and purple, "Palm Beach," size 40L, excellent condition. $75
*Courtesy of Art & Janene Fawcett, Vintage Silhouettes.*

Sports Jacket. *Courtesy of Art & Janene Fawcett, Vintage Silhouettes, CA, www.vintagesilhouettes.com. Photograph by Art Fawcett.*

Detail of Jacket.
*Photograph by Art Fawcett.*

**1950s Sports Jacket.** Tweed, interwoven brown and cream with orange, "Bud Giles," size 42R, excellent condition. $75
*Courtesy of Art & Janene Fawcett, Vintage Silhouettes.*

Sports Jacket. *Courtesy of Art & Janene Fawcett, Vintage Silhouettes, CA, www.vintagesilhouettes.com. Photograph by Art Fawcett.*

Detail of Jacket.
*Photograph by Art Fawcett.*

Stetson. *Courtesy of Art & Janene Fawcett, Vintage Silhouettes, CA, www.vintagesilhouettes.com. Photograph by Art Fawcett.*

**1950s SPORTS JACKET.** Mocha with burnt orange, orange with light fleck, Western cut, "H Bar C," leather buttons, size 40R, excellent condition. $75
*Courtesy of Art & Janene Fawcett, Vintage Silhouettes.*

**1950s STETSON.** Tan, dark brown ribbon, cream brim ribbon, size 7⅜, 2⅞" brim, renovated. $85
*Courtesy of Art & Janene Fawcett, Vintage Silhouettes.*

Bill Blass Sports Jacket. *Courtesy of Vintage Apparel, New York, NY. Photograph by Tom Amico.*

Shirt, Jacket, and Tie. *Courtesy of Zap & Co., PA, www.zapandco.com. Photograph by Steve Murray.*

**1950s BILL BLASS SPORTS JACKET.** Wool, matching plaid, red designer logo lining, inside pocket, excellent condition. $100
*Courtesy of Vintage Apparel, NY.*

**1950s SHIRT, JACKET, AND TIE.** Shirt, salmon-colored gabardine, excellent condition. $65

Jacket, gray wool with black fleck, "Robert Hall," excellent condition. $45

Tie, burgundy and salmon, excellent condition. $30
*Courtesy of Zap & Co., PA.*

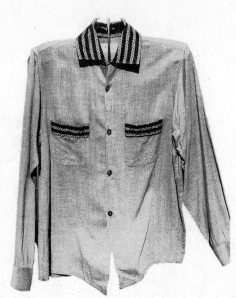

Gabardine Shirt.
*Courtesy of Zap & Co., PA,*
*www.zapandco.com. Photograph by*
*Steve Murray.*

Gabardine Shirt. *Courtesy of Zap &*
*Co., PA, www.zapandco.com. Photograph*
*by Steve Murray.*

**1950s GABARDINE SHIRT.** Chocolate with black striped and chocolate
zigzag collar and pocket trim, "Styled by Luigi for B.V.D.," excellent condition. $65
*Courtesy of Zap & Co., PA.*

**1950s GABARDINE SHIRT.** Gray, inset V-shaped wool panel with gray,
black, red, and white striped pattern trimmed with black rayon, "Essley,"
very good condition. $45
*Courtesy of Zap & Co., PA.*

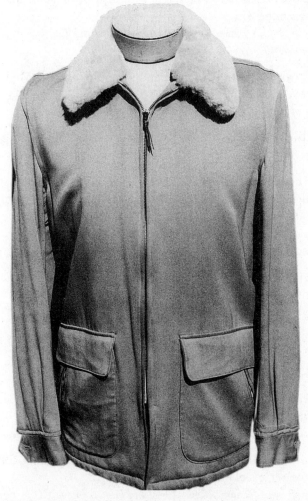

McGregor Gabardine Jacket. *Courtesy of Zap & Co., PA,*
*www.zapandco.com. Photograph by Steve Murray.*

**1950s McGregor Gabardine Jacket.** Gray, white mouton collar,
excellent condition. $125
*Courtesy of Zap & Co., PA.*

# MARKET TRENDS FOR THE FIFTIES

## *Separates*

1950s CIRCLE SKIRT. Black felt with a print of colorful leaves and pegasuses, mint. $75
*Courtesy of Art & Janene Fawcett, Vintage Silhouettes, CA.*
*www.vintagesilhouettes.com*

1950s CIRCLE SKIRT. Hand-painted, multicolored, Mediterranean design, excellent condition. $125
*Courtesy of Zap & Co., PA.*

1950s CIRCLE SKIRTS. Cotton, Paris scenes, excellent condition. $75 each
*Courtesy of Screaming Mimi's, New York, NY.*

1950s SEQUINED CIRCLE SKIRT. Black, blue, and white stripe skirt with gold and copper painted leaves accented by silver sequins, excellent condition. $75
*Courtesy of Art & Janene Fawcett, Vintage Silhouettes, CA,*
*www.vintagesilhouettes.com*

1950s SILK NAVY DOT BLOUSE. Short cap sleeves, pert ties at neck, excellent condition. $25
*Courtesy of www.fashiondig.com*

1950s COTTON FLORAL PLEATED SKIRT. With pockets, label: "Jo Collins," excellent condition. $120.
*Courtesy of www.fashiondig.com*

1950s GRAY SILK SWEATER. Knitted, crystal beads, faux pearls, label: "NINI Originals," mint condition. $90
*Courtesy of Karen Augusta, Antique Lace & Fashion, www.antique-fashion.com*

1950s CASHMERE AND MINK SWEATER. Black cashmere, full mink fur collar sweater, excellent condition. $150
*Courtesy of Lynn Pastore, Avenue 13–5 and Dime Vintage, CO,*
*www.510vintage.com*

1950s VINTAGE CAPRI PANTS. Capri pants, lavender color, never worn, New Old Stock. $40
*Courtesy of Lynn Pastore, Avenue 13–5 and Dime Vintage, CO,*
*www.510vintage.com*

1950s CASHMERE SWEATER WITH FELT APPLIQUÉ. Camel color 100% cashmere, two colorful felt appliquéd figures, one of a mother, other of a daughter with poodle, excellent condition. $145
*Courtesy of Kristin North.*

## Dresses

1950s PARTY DRESS. Black satin, off-the-shoulder sleeve, plaid lining in a peek-a-boo pointed collar, label: "Minx Modes Junior," excellent condition. $75
*Courtesy of Screaming Mimi's, New York, NY.*

1950s SWING DRESS. Gold painted pattern, bead and rhinestone detail at neckline, side zipper, excellent condition. $100
*Courtesy of Lynn Pastore, Avenue 13–5 and Dime Vintage, CO,*
*www.510vintage.com*

1950 SWING DRESS. Peach swing-style dress under shear floral patterned front, excellent condition. $50
*Courtesy of Lynn Pastore, Avenue 13–5 and Dime Vintage, CO,*
*www.510vintage.com*

1950s SUMMER WEIGHT SWING DRESS. Light blue floral pattern with button-up front and Lucy-style collar, rhinestone buttons, sleeveless, never worn, with original tags, excellent condition, "New Old Stock." $40
*Courtesy of Lynn Pastore, Avenue 13–5 and Dime Vintage, CO,*
*www.510vintage.com*

1950s LIGHT BLUE SUMMER DRESS. Polished cotton, draped neckline, Princess line, full skirt, very good condition. $75
*Courtesy of Art & Janene Fawcett, Vintage Silhouettes, CA,*
*www.vintagesilhouettes.com*

1950s RUFFLED COTTON SUNDRESS. Urn print in cocoa brown and black, ruffle at bodice, sash tie at waist, excellent condition. $87
*Courtesy of www.fashiondig.com*

1950s SUZY PERETTE SUNDRESS. Yellow and white checked, organza-like fabric with a white taffeta attached underdress, square neckline, low-pointed V waistline, full skirt, bows in back that snap across metal zipper, excellent condition. $185
*Courtesy of Deborah Burke, Antique & Vintage Dress Gallery,*
*www.antiquedress.com*

## Dresses and Party Wear

GREEN TAFFETA GOWN. Blue, pink, and yellow tiny squares of velvet, V-shaped bodice, wide ruffle on back cascades from waist down, ruffle edged in velvet, spaghetti straps, excellent condition. $210
*Courtesy of Art & Janene Fawcett, Vintage Silhouettes, CA,*
*www.vintagesilhouettes.com*

**1950s COCKTAIL DRESS.** White chiffon flocked with black velvet flowers, scalloped bodice and hem edges, tiered skirt, black velvet shoestring straps, excellent condition. $110
*Courtesy of Art & Janene Fawcett, Vintage Silhouettes, CA, www.vintagesilhouettes.com*

**1950s PINK TAFFETA COCKTAIL DRESS.** Sweetheart neckline, sleeveless, full skirt, back of dress has pouf resembling bustle, label: "Harry Keiser," excellent condition. $140
*Courtesy of Art & Janene Fawcett, Vintage Silhouettes, CA, www.vintagesilhouettes.com*

**1950s NAVY LINEN STRAPLESS COCKTAIL DRESS.** Cord leaves and white beaded design on bodice and upper portion of skirt, fitted boned bodice, full skirt, built-in slip, label: "Frank Starr Original," excellent condition. $75
*Courtesy of Art & Janene Fawcett, Vintage Silhouettes, CA, www.vintagesilhouettes.com*

**1950s BLACK AND WHITE FLOCKED COCKTAIL DRESS.** White chiffon flocked with black velvet flowers, scalloped bodice and hem edges, tiered skirt, black velvet spaghetti straps, excellent condition. $110
*Courtesy of Art & Janene Fawcett, Vintage Silhouettes, CA, www.vintagesilhouettes.com*

**1950s EVENING GOWN.** Black lace with a 19" double net ruffle at hemline, taffeta lining, very good condition. $250
*Courtesy of Art & Janene Fawcett, Vintage Silhouettes, CA, www.vintagesilhouettes.com*

**1950s ORIENTAL PRINT COTTON GOWN.** Strapless, black and white oriental print gown with circle skirt and boned bodice, bodice sprinkled with rhinestones, excellent condition. $95
*Courtesy of Miss Kitty & Calico Jack, The Cat's Pajamas, PA, www.catspajamas.com*

**1950s ORGANDY EVENING GOWN.** Fitted bodice with a pleated inset at bust, white with pink roses, excellent condition. $95
*Courtesy of Miss Kitty & Calico Jack, The Cat's Pajamas, PA, www.catspajamas.com*

**c. 1958 CEIL CHAPMAN SILK COCKTAIL DRESS.** Salmon-colored, figured silk, metal zipper, rayon faille lining, six boned stays, woven label includes "Ceil Chapman" and Sincerely Jenny (store name), perfect condition. $285
*Courtesy of Karen Augusta, Antique Lace & Fashion, www.antique-fashion.com*

**Fall 1959 Galanos Warp-Printed Silk Party Dress.** Warp-printed silk, satin, printed silk chiffon, grosgrain ribbon and gold silk organza, skirt lining has built-in petticoat in olive green net and Dupioni silk, boned bodice with built-in bra, woven silk labels, excellent condition. $825
*Courtesy of Karen Augusta, Antique Lace & Fashion, www.antique-fashion.com*

**1950s Ceil Chapman Floral Cocktail Dress.** Light gray silk floral dress, bell skirt, draped bodice and skirt, excellent condition. $685
*Courtesy of Deborah Burke, Antique & Vintage Dress Gallery,*
*www.antiquedress.com*

**1950s Anne Fogarty Black Linen Dress.** Simple T-bodice, gathered skirt welted over each hip, heavily gathered under piping, parts from dress in back forming shoestring bow, excellent condition. $180
*Courtesy of Enokiworld, www.enokiworld.com*

**1950s Traina-Norell Chiffon Cocktail Dress.** Black, bodice of gathered pleats, cut traditionally through bodice with satin-banded waist, with satin flower in small of back, black silk crepe lining, excellent condition. $695
*Courtesy of Enokiworld, www.enokiworld.com*

**1950s Maurice Rentner Wool "Apron" Dress.** Tailored gray wool, bodice backed in charcoal silk crepe, stand-up band collar, one curved pocket near collarbone, echoing one at opposing hip. Two skirts: actual skirt attached to the bodice, other lined in silk satin and lays against body like an apron, covered back buttons, thin matching belt, excellent condition. $240
*Courtesy of Enokiworld, www.enokiworld.com*

**1950s Carlye Black Cotton Eyelet Dress.** Square neckline, completely open eyelet, unlined, made by Carlye, excellent condition. $165
*Courtesy of Enokiworld, www.enokiworld.com*

**1950s Gold Dress and Jacket.** Satin, rhinestone-studded collar, label "Carlye," very good condition. $85
*Courtesy of Screaming Mimi's, New York, NY.*

## Suits

**1950s Ben Reig Velvet Collared Suit.** Simple black wool gabardine suit, maraschino cherry silk lining, velvet collar, jacket has notched sides and split cuffs lining, both in excellent condition. $160
*Courtesy of Enokiworld, www.enokiworld.com*

**1950s SCALLOPED BLACK WOOL CREPE SUIT.** Basic black suit with scalloped hem, flared bracelet-length sleeves, black silk lining, concave matching covered buttons, excellent condition. $140
*Courtesy of Enokiworld, www.enokiworld.com*

**1950s EMERALD WOOL BELTED "EDITOR'S" SUIT.** Finely woven bouclé emerald wool with abbreviated waistline, three-quarter-length sleeves, gigantic buttons, made by Herbert Sondheim in New York, excellent condition. $205
*Courtesy of Enokiworld, www.enokiworld.com*

**1950s WOOL PLAID SUIT.** Resembles Burberry's plaid, wine, camel, black, and ivory, shaped with row of matte charcoal buttons at placket and little back vent, flapped pockets at each hip, extra decorative flap above right hip, black rayon satin lining, excellent condition. $155
*Courtesy of Enokiworld, www.enokiworld.com*

**1950s FLANNEL BELTED SUIT WITH FUR COLLAR.** Combination of camel wool flannel with sheared coyote collar, jacket with peach silk crepe lining, buttons along placket with row of swirled iridescent peach buttons, belts at waist with matching sash, little pockets inseam at hips, straight skirt, zippered back, Montaldo's tag, excellent condition. $115
*Courtesy of Enokiworld, www.enokiworld.com*

**1950s LILLI ANN SUIT.** Green, black, and white heavy tweed bouclé wool, labeled Italian Fabric, very well made, excellent condition. $545
*Courtesy of Deborah Burke, Antique & Vintage Dress Gallery, www.antiquedress.com*

## Outerwear

**1950s BLACK AND WHITE PLAID WOOL COAT.** Removeable panel at neck matches narrow rib-knit undersleeves, bias-cut large bell oversleeves, low slung back belt with large square buttons matching two large buttons on front, excellent condition. $65
*Courtesy of www.fashiondig.com*

## Accessories

**1950s EMBROIDERED GLOVES.** Stretchy cotton sateen, mercerized cotton, hand-done tambour embroidery, excellent condition. $90
*Courtesy of Karen Augusta, Antique Lace & Fashion, www.antique-fashion.com*

**1950s WHITING & DAVIS GOLD MESH BAG.** Gold armor-mesh bag suspended from gilt metal openwork frame, pale peach silk satin lining, 5¼" h × 8" w, single 4½" rope chain handle, excellent condition. $125
*Courtesy of Enokiworld, www.enokiworld.com*

**1950s STRAW TOTE WITH RAFFIA FLOWERS.** Natural cotton lining, 6¾" h × 8½" w, double 5" handles, excellent condition. $65
*Courtesy of Enokiworld, www.enokiworld.com*

**1955 EVANS CARRYALL.** Swirled pattern "High Tide," opens from both sides to reveal compartments, one side has small tortoise comb in holder, powder and puff, lipstick holder, and tiny spring-loaded holder for coins, other side holds cigarettes and matching lighter, gold mesh strap, original felt bag and box 3¼" h × 3¼" w × 1¼" d, excellent condition. $135
*Courtesy of Enokiworld, www.enokiworld.com*

**1950s LEOPARD AND SATIN MUFF.** Soft fur on front, backed with burgundy ruched satin, cocoa silk satin lining with hidden zippered pocket, 10" h × 15" w, excellent condition. $170
*Courtesy of Enokiworld, www.enokiworld.com*

**1950s BLACK SATIN EVENING BAG.** Black satin, gently pleated with soft rayon satin strap, mermaid jeweled clasp set with six marquise and three round stones, peach satin lining made by Bobbie Jerome, 7" h × 9¼" w with single 6" handle, excellent condition. $35
*Courtesy of Enokiworld, www.enokiworld.com*

**1950s BLACK PATENT WEDGE PURSE.** Slight curve at bottom, gilt metal frame, single strap, black rayon satin lining, 8" h × 8" w, single 7½" handle, excellent condition. $45
*Courtesy of Enokiworld, www.enokiworld.com*

**1950s NAVY LEATHER BAG WITH TORTOISE HANDLES.** Gucci-inspired version, twin braided faux tortoise ring handles, cherry red moiré lining, two outer compartments flank main one, snaps shut with small brass clasp, 7¼" h × 10¼" w, double 3½" handles, excellent condition. $50
*Courtesy of Enokiworld, www.enokiworld.com*

**1950s MADELEINE PAGE BROWN ALLIGATOR HANDBAG.** Polished gilt hardware, brown leather lining, one zipper, two patch and one snap pocket, 9" h × 10" w with single 6" handle, very good to excellent condition. $180
*Courtesy of Enokiworld, www.enokiworld.com*

**1950s AUTO BODY FINISH PATENT PUMPS.** Made by Kalmon Paramount, size 6N with padded insole, 3¼″ stiletto heel, original box, excellent condition. $60
*Courtesy of Enokiworld, www.enokiworld.com*

**1950s DAISY RAFFIA SPIKES.** Navy burlap spike heels, squiggles of grass green across toe, white and navy 3-D daisies around outside of shoe, made by Sabrina, sold by Joseph Magnin, size 6AA, excellent condition. $45
*Courtesy of Enokiworld, www.enokiworld.com*

**1950s HERBERT LEVINE POINTY SUEDE STILETTOS.** Brown suede with small inset of thicker and more textured darker suede tucked into throat, echoing point of toe, size 5½B, heels 4″ h, excellent condition. $105
*Courtesy of Enokiworld, www.enokiworld.com*

**1950s ALLIGATOR BABY DOLL PUMPS.** Breasted alligator pumps with rounded little baby doll, slightly V-shaped vamp, made by Martinique, size 8A, 3¼″ heel, excellent condition. $115
*Courtesy of Enokiworld, www.enokiworld.com*

**1950s HERBERT LEVINE SILK "BLACK TIE" STILETTOS.** Black silk stilettos, patent leather toes, sculpted patent leather heels, one rhinestone-studded button on top of shoe, fire-engine red silk lining, size 9AA, 4″ heel, excellent condition. $265
*Courtesy of Enokiworld, www.enokiworld.com*

**1950s BLACK VELVET CHAPEAU.** Velvet with draped silk, stiff ribboned organza veil dotted with black chenille, crowned with arrangement of silver bugle beads, multicolored aurora sequins, clusters of white pearls, pristine condition. $65
*Courtesy of The Fainting Couch, MA, www.faintingcouch.com*

**1950s BLACK VELVET TOQUE.** Ornamented with oversized pink roses with "dew drops," "Toni–California," excellent condition. $165
*Courtesy of Deborah Burke, Antique & Vintage Dress Gallery, www.antiquedress.com*

**1950s BEADED HANDBAG.** Handbag is entirely covered in multicolored round beads, gilt metal coil handle and frame, burnished gilt thistle-like closure, lined in patterned beige, "Made in Italy for Rosenfeld," perfect condition. $135
*Courtesy of The Fainting Couch, MA, www.faintingcouch.com*

**1950s RED VINYL PURSE.** Round with hard sides in red quality vinyl, flip lid with snap closure, mirror in lid, matching change purse, "Gertz," 6½" d, excellent condition. $50
*Courtesy of The Fainting Couch, MA, www.faintingcouch.com*

**1950s KORET LUCITE PURSE.** White Lucite with red Lucite handles, quality vinyl interior with three compartments, center zipper, excellent condition. $75
*Courtesy of The Fainting Couch, MA, www.faintingcouch.com*

**1950s WAVE PATTERNED BATHING CAP.** Green textured rubber in excellent condition. $85
*Courtesy of www.fashiondig.com*

**1950s BROWN REPTILE PUMPS.** "Rhythm Step," size 6½, excellent condition. $89
*Courtesy of www.fashiondig.com*

## *Menswear*

**1950s VINTAGE SILK HAWAIIAN SHIRT.** Silk Hawaiian shirt, label: "Paradise," Hawaiian seal stamped on buttons, matched pocket, no plastic stays in the collar, excellent condition. $200
*Courtesy of Lynn Pastore, Avenue 13–5 and Dime Vintage, CO, www.510vintage.com*

**1950s RAYON HAWAIIAN SHIRT.** Classic Hawaiian shirt with images of pineapples and palm trees, horizontal buttonholes, top button loop, label: "Made in Japan, South Pacific," excellent condition. $100
*Courtesy of Lynn Pastore, Avenue 13–5 and Dime Vintage, CO, www.510vintage.com*

**1950s RAYON BOWLING SHIRT.** Shirt with bowling pin buttons, top button loop, strike marks around shoulders and sleeves, label: "Air Flow," excellent condition. $125
*Courtesy of Lynn Pastore, Avenue 13–5 and Dime Vintage, CO, www510vintage.com*

**1950s BOWLING SHIRT.** Bowler embroidered on the collar, bowling ball and pins on front pocket, cool yellow vents, top button loop, label: "King Louie," excellent condition. $100
*Courtesy of Lynn Pastore, Avenue 13–5 and Dime Vintage, CO, www.510vintage.com*

**1950s ELVIS-STYLE GABARDINE JACKET.** Rare reversible gabardine jacket with great detail and fleck pattern, excellent condition. $250
*Courtesy of Lynn Pastore, Avenue 13–5 and Dime Vintage, CO,*
*www.510vintage.com*

**1950s MEN'S SUMMER-WEIGHT SUIT.** Single-breasted, blue/gray with turquoise and white fleck, silver thread interweave, patch pockets, "Manchester Clothes," never worn, never cuffed, 39L, "New Old Stock," excellent condition. $300
*Courtesy of Art & Janene Fawcett, Vintage Silhouettes, CA,*
*www.vintagesilhouettes.com*

**1950s MEN'S SINGLE-BREASTED SUIT.** Light mocha brown and cream, nubby texture, "New Old Stock," waist 32, inseam 33½, drop 46″, excellent condition. $225
*Courtesy of Art & Janene Fawcett, Vintage Silhouettes, CA,*
*www.vintagesilhouettes.com*

**1950s MEN'S SPORTS JACKET.** Two-button, chocolate brown, cream check with blue/orange fleck, patch pocket, 33½″ sleeve, 40R, excellent condition. $75
*Courtesy of Art & Janene Fawcett, Vintage Silhouettes, CA,*
*www.vintagesilhouettes.com*

**1950s MEN'S SPORTS JACKET.** Three-button, brown and cream check, patch pocket, 43L, excellent condition. $85
*Courtesy of Art & Janene Fawcett, Vintage Silhouettes, CA,*
*www.vintagesilhouettes.com*

## Men's Accessories

**1950s MEN'S "DOBBS" HAT.** Tan brim binding, chocolate crown ribbon, renovated, size 7⅝, 2⅛″ brim, very good condition. $95
*Courtesy of Art & Janene Fawcett, Vintage Silhouettes, CA,*
*www.vintagesilhouettes.com*

**1950s MEN'S "BORSOLINA" HAT.** Gray, lightweight, black ribbon, unbound edge, size 7¼, 2⅛″ brim, excellent condition. $110
*Courtesy of Art & Janene Fawcett, Vintage Silhouettes, CA,*
*www.vintagesilhouettes.com*

**1950s MEN'S "ROYAL STETSON" HAT.** Leather sweatband, in original box, size 7, very good condition. $65
*Courtesy of The Fainting Couch, MA, www.faintingcouch.com*

1950s MEN's GRAY STRAW "BRYON" HAT. Blue-striped ribbon, leather sweatband, size 7, original hatbox, excellent condition. $60
*Courtesy of The Fainting Couch, MA, www.faintingcouch.com*

1950s MEN's ALLIGATOR SHOES. "Monk" straps with split "French" toe, fits 11–11½ B/C w, label: "Nettleton," excellent condition. $295
*Courtesy of Ardis Taylor, Vintage Silhouettes, CA, www.vintagesilhouettes.com*

Roberta di Camarino Coat. *Courtesy of Enokiworld,*
*www.enokiworld.com. Photograph by Madeline Meyerowitz.*

# $\mathscr{F}$lamboyant and Free

A youth-oriented and future-minded society propelled us into the sixties. Fashion designs were streamlined. The young John F. Kennedy was elected president and Jackie Kennedy's fashionable style of dress was embraced by women across the country. John Glenn orbited the planet and designers like Pierre Cardin and André Courrèges brought into the fashion sphere the space-age look, complete with helmet hats.

It was also a volatile time, and by the end of the decade we saw anti-Vietnam War demonstrations, assassinations, riots, and anti-establishment flower children on our television each day. Mini, maxi, and midi skirts all had their heyday in fashion, as women experimented with a variety of skirt lengths. Fads came and went daily. Twiggy personified the British mod look with her Sassoon haircut, hairpieces, lithe silhouette, miniskirt and long legs in white lace tights. The Beatles were the "in" group for the decade and fashion looked to London for the trends of Carnaby Street.

Oleg Cassini was Jackie Kennedy's favorite designer. He designed her high Princess-style, unbelted sleeveless dresses in solid sherbert colors, as well as suits with short jackets and large, matching fabric-covered buttons. Accessories were minimal; usually an envelope pocketbook, low-heeled shoes, a pillbox hat on a slightly teased bouffant, and simple "shortie" white gloves completed the ensemble.

Hubert de Givenchy designed sleek, carefully constructed styles for Audrey Hepburn for both on-screen and off. His understated designs were well suited for Hepburn's role as Holly Golightly in *Breakfast at Tiffany's* (1961); Holly wore a black wide-brimmed hat, simple black sheath dress, sunglasses, and carried a cigarette holder.

Mary Quant was the hottest designer in Britain and the most influential. She energized the fashion industry with her mod-style clothing for the decade's "youth." Crowds of young shoppers purchased clothing in the new London boutiques, changing shopping into a different and fun experience. Flat visor hats introduced by the Beatles, shifts with cutouts and mesh midriffs, vintage clothing, boots, Op Art minis, and tights were fashions that were found in boutiques. As skirts climbed higher, tights took the place of stockings and boots were made higher to meet the mini and the short-lived micro skirt. Late in the decade, Pierre Cardin showed body stockings and catsuits. Hot colored bikinis and black mesh suits topped with flowered swim caps dominated swimsuit fashions. Lilly Pulitzer customized polished cotton fabric and made it into shifts, slacks, and bathing suits in tropical colors. Emilio Pucci produced colorful, swirling silk prints on dresses, blouses, and scarves. Bonnie Cashin designed very functional clothing using canvas, tweed, suede, poplin, and leather.

Shoes came in bright colors with round or square toes and low heels. Beth and Herbert Levine, influenced by the art of Andy Warhol, were innovative shoe designers of the decade who used Pop Art styling. Plastics, imitation alligator, and patent leathers were new materials for shoes. The wet look was also popular for shoes and other accessories. Boots of all lengths were especially fashionable in the sixties. Shoe designer Vivier designed footwear for Yves Saint Laurent, who showed a Mondrian-inspired line of clothing, shoes, and hats. Vivier's most copied shoe was the pilgrim buckle for Laurent in 1964.

Psychedelic prints, fake fur, body painting, false eyelashes, white lipstick, hip-huggers, and bell-bottoms were all fashion trends of the time. Outrageous fashions such as the see-through blouse and Rudi Gernreich's topless bathing suit appeared. Throwaway paper fashions were sold as inexpensive chic. Accessories included wide-strap watches, Lucite jewelry, fishnet stockings, chain belts, granny glasses, and hairpieces. Imitation plastic fabric was used to make funky handbags. The handmade fashions of the hippies were displayed in crocheted vests, macramé, and tie-dye. Fashion focused on the spirited young and their new ideas.

Men's fashions always make transitions with less fervor than women's. The sixties, however, saw a marked change in men's fashions. The double-breasted suit had a new look; English styling was again very influential—wider lapels on a lightly padded jacket with side vents or a high-cut, center vent. Wide, bold ties and pointed collars accessorized the fashions. Trousers went from tapered to flared with beltless waistbands and by the end of the decade appeared in a full range of fabrics and colors. Even blue jeans were made with flared legs. Jams, a Bermuda-length swimsuit in tropical print with pajama drawstring waist, were an instant success with men. Golfing trousers were in bright plaids and colorful patchwork. For casual wear, coats varied also, as suburban men participated in many types of activities. Ski jackets, parkas, suede coats, the commuter zip-out-lining coat, and stadium coats were part of the wardrobe. Trenchcoats were shown in both midi and maxi lengths.

Men had their fashion fads as well. The leisure suit and the Nehru suit were entirely new looks in Western men's clothing. Introduced in 1966, the Nehru jacket was an exact copy of the jacket worn by Prime Minister Jawaharlal Nehru. It was copied in many fabrics for day or eveningwear, featuring velvet tuxedos with ruffled shirts and cuffs. The variety in men's clothing was never wider and men could choose their own individual style of dress.

### Signature Fabrics of the 1960s

Wool jersey for ready-to-wear

Wool, cottons, and leather for separates

Heavy silks for shifts

Taffeta and chiffon for evening dresses

Synthetics were especially apparent in knitwear

Synthetics:

> Plastic and vinyl for accessories
>
> Bonded nylon jersey for rigidity in fashions
>
> Polyvinyl chloride (PVC) for plastic coats; signature fabric for Mary Quant, (the "wet" collection)
>
> PVC and bonded jersey tunics
>
> Lurex for dressy dresses
>
> Quiana for wedding gowns
>
> Polyester for mod men's suits
>
> Crimplene for dresses
>
> Nylon for lingerie
>
> Lycra for late-sixties swimwear, ski pants

### Important Designers and Manufacturers in the 1960s

**ADOLFO:** In the sixties, Adolfo was known for the "Panama planter's hat," a mannish, brimmed straw hat, and velour, fur Cossack, and pillbox hats. For evening, he designed feathered headdresses. In 1966, Adolfo began designing clothing as well as hats. His early lines were simple, such as the suede dress with low waist, gingham dirndl skirt with cotton blouse, jersey jump-

*The Uniqueness That Comes with Experimenting with New Materials.*

1969 Paco Rabanne dress made of Rhodoid plastic and metal. *Courtesy of Philadelphia Museum of Art. Gift of Miss Rubye Graham. This object is accessioned and part of the permanent collection.*

suit, and organdy jumper. In the later sixties, Adolfo showed large fur berets, and Renaissance and peasant looks with harem pants, vests, and blouses.

**LARRY ALDRICH:** He was known for his illusionistic, Op Art fabrics, as well as his more practical wool or wool jersey dinner dresses with jackets. In 1966, he showed mini dresses covered with beads. In 1969, Aldrich designed bare-abdomen outfits with harem pants and full trouser styles in Quiana. In 1972, his company dissolved.

**BALENCIAGA:** In the sixties, Balenciaga showed looser, fuller jackets with dolman sleeves and was one of the first designers to feature body stockings. Many associate his name with large buttons on suits and stand-away collars on jackets. He retired in 1968.

**PIERRE BALMAIN:** Balmain's designs, featured Empire waistlines on dresses, simple shifts, and T-line dresses with cuffs and collars.

**BORSOLINA:** An Italian hat company renowned for their men's hats.

**GEOFFREY BEENE:** In 1963, Geoffrey Beene first began designing independently. His clothing designs were praised as youthful and spirited. Beene showed Cossack-style dresses for evening, worn with curés' hats, as well as short skirts with long jackets, high-waisted jersey dresses, and sequin-covered football sweaters for evening.

**BILL BLASS:** In 1963, Bill Blass's simple summer dress with ruffling at the hem and neckline was a bestseller, echoing the feminine simplicity of his earlier spaghetti-strapped evening dress of 1960. In the mid and late sixties, Blass's designs for women adopted menswear tailoring with double-breasted, wide-notched lapels, and blazers with suits and dresses. Despite the omnipresent mini skirt, Blass rarely showed any skirt that was above the knee. In 1967, he began to design for men, showing a brown velvet dinner jacket over black wool pants.

**DONALD BROOKS:** In 1959, Brooks designed costumes for film, theater, and television. In the early sixties, he showed plain chemise dresses, trimmed coats, and stoles. In the mid-sixties, his designs grew bolder with Op Art color block suits and coats, and designs with appliquéd pony skin. Brooks also designed generously cut pajama styles, hooded, bias-cut wool evening dresses embroidered with sequins or bugle beads, and hippie-inspired turnouts.

**PIERRE CARDIN:** Cardin's designs were bright and somewhat wild. He showed colored wigs, cutout dresses, body stockings, bias-cut spiral dresses, and flared coats with large patch pockets. In 1962, he opened a boutique in Bonwit Teller featuring his men's designs. Cardin's 1964 collection was called "Space-Age" and featured knit catsuits, tight leather pants, helmets, and jumpsuits. In the late sixties, Cardin brought necklines to new depths both in front and in back in women's fashions and then shortened his skirts another four inches.

**BONNIE CASHIN:** Cashin designed practical uncomplicated fashions. She excelled at mixing fabrics and often designed in canvas, leather, suede, poplin, and tweed. Her best-known work is from the fifties and sixties. She designed canvas and poplin raincoats, kimono coats piped with leather, ponchos, oriental-style jackets over dresses, and her signature funnel-necked pullover sweater with a neck doubling as a hood.

**OLEG CASSINI:** In 1961, Oleg Cassini became the official designer for Jacqueline Kennedy. His styles were simple and somewhat fitted. Two of his most widely copied designs were the sleeveless, high-waisted evening dress with a single fabric rose for decoration, and a boxy jacketed suit with fabric-covered buttons. He also had a ready-to-wear line which carried evening and cocktail dresses along the same line as the designs he did for the first lady. In 1963, Cassini included bathing suits, sportswear, under-clothes, and accessories in his fashion lines. He also designed for men in the sixties.

**GABRIELLE "COCO" CHANEL:** In the sixties, Chanel continued to show her signature suit ensembles.

**OSSIE CLARK:** Ossie Clark is known for his revealing designs of satin jersey and chiffon with deep necklines. In the later sixties, he also showed designs in metallic leather and snakeskin.

**COLE:** In the sixties, Cole of California's most exciting design was the "Scandal Suit" with its cutout sides and deep V-shaped neckline that extended below the waist. The theme of the collection was "New but not nude" as the cutouts on Cole's bathing suits were filled with wide-mesh netting.

**ANDRÉ COURRÈGES:** In the early sixties, Courrèges designed very short mini skirts and dresses in white and silver to be worn with high boots and goggles. His futuristic designs were referred to as "Space Age." He used contrasting colors on his trapeze dresses and trims. Courrèges's late sixties designs were markedly softer, tending toward curves, rather than the angular look of his earlier collections. He showed knit catsuits and see-through and cutout dresses.

**LILLY DACHÉ:** In the sixties, Lilly Daché designed cartwheel, lampshade, pouf hats, and feathered organdy coifs, tiny pillboxes, and space age helmets.

**OSCAR DE LA RENTA:** Oscar de la Renta is known for his theme design collections that tend toward the outrageous. In the sixties, his collections were inspired by Belle Époque, abstract art, and oriental design. He used these themes in his cocktail dresses and beautiful ball gowns. In the late sixties, de la Renta also had a line of designs that were inspired by the youthful style of the hippies, with fringed ponchos, pants, and vests. His designs for daywear included softly fitted cuts of mohair and wool with stand-away collars and attenuated seams.

**ROBERTA DI CAMARINO:** In 1965, di Camarino began designing handbags under her own name. She designed striped velvet bags, leather pieces, and later scarves and other accessories. Di Camarino also designed fabrics and clothing in the sixties under the label: "Roberta."

**GALANOS:** Galanos was known for his evening dresses and pantsuits. He favored a slim silhouette and used classical draping in chiffon, silks, cut velvet, and brocades for his designs. He made intricate beaded embroidery decorations on his fashions and often used hand-painted silk prints by Raoul Dufy. In addition, Galanos designed pantsuits and pajama costumes. His fashions are admired for their quality of workmanship, especially considering these are ready-to-wear fashions, not individually made.

**RUDI GERNREICH:** Gernreich was best known for his sportswear separates and bathing suits in the sixties. He designed shirtwaist dresses, see-through blouses, and mini dresses with vinyl insets. His many bathing suit designs included the novel topless bathing suit for women with straps that went over the shoulder, attached to the waist at the front and the back. In 1964, Gernreich worked for Warner's designing foundation styles that could adapt to the new backless, frontless, and sideless fashions.

**HUBERT DE GIVENCHY:** In 1961, Givenchy designed Audrey Hepburn's costumes for the movie, *Breakfast at Tiffany's.*

**HALSTON:** It was not until 1966 that Halston began to design ready-to-wear fashions. He gained his reputation in the late sixties and early seventies as a designer of knitwear with a line of sweaters, wide-legged pants, and turtlenecks. He designed simple clothing that clung to the body. Halston also used tie-dyed fabrics.

**BETSEY JOHNSON:** In the sixties, Betsey Johnson was a young designer who had a knack for youthful designs. Some of her most sensational designs included a clear vinyl dress that came with do-it-yourself stickers, silver motorcycle gear, noisy dresses with grommets at the hems, cowhide wrap mini skirts with thigh-high boots, and dresses such as those worn by actress Julie Christie, with long, pointed collars.

**CHARLES JOURDAN:** In the sixties, Jourdan and his three sons opened a boutique in Paris. At the end of the decade Dior granted the company a license to design shoes for the House of Dior. There are two styles Jourdan became famous for: "Maxime" a low-heeled court shoe with a satin bow, and "Madly," a platform shoe with a high vamp in red or black patent leather.

**ANNE KLEIN:** Anne Klein & Co. opened for business in 1968. A popular sportswear designer, Klein designed functional separates, blazers, blouson tops, matching dresses and jackets, and jersey dresses.

**LACOSTE:** René Lacoste, a.k.a. "Le Crocodile," was a French tennis star of the twenties and early thirties, who started a business in the thirties selling short-sleeved, white shirts with a crocodile logo of his own design. These cotton shirts were worn widely in the sixties and seventies.

**GUY LAROCHE:** Laroche worked for Jean Dessès in Paris for eight years before opening his own studio in 1957. His first designs were couture pieces which he followed with a ready-to-wear collection. Laroche is credited for his skill of cutting and fine tailoring.

**KARL LAGERFELD:** In the sixties, Lagerfeld designed mole, rabbit, and squirrel fur coats and jackets which were dyed in bright colors. Other coat designs included reversible fur coats, leather, and fabric jackets.

**MARIMEKKO:** A company known for their bright and colorful prints, Marimekko produced the Jokapoika in the late fifties, followed by shift dresses in non-figurative prints, and in the sixties, jersey dresses.

**NORMAN NORELL:** Norell's first collection of the sixties featured culotte walking skirts, harem pants, and pantsuits with tailored silhouettes. He was known for his extravagant fabric choices for décolleté evening dresses, his sequin-covered sheath dress, and his evening jumpsuit with calf-length knickers and sleeveless overcoat. In the late sixties, Norell showed several different lengths for dinner dresses: midi, floor-length and above-the-knee.

**ORIGINALA:** The Originala Company was known in the sixties for their classic coats which were expertly made from woven wools.

**EMILIO PUCCI:** In the 1960s, Pucci showed psychedelic patterns in vivid colors on silks—dresses, cruise wear, separates, scarves, and handbags. In the 1990s his prints were reintroduced by his daughter, Laudomia, into leggings, catsuits, and stretch polos.

**LILLY PULITZER:** Pulitzer is famous for the "Lilly," a shift-style dress in a polished cotton chintz of tropical colors.

**MARY QUANT:** In the sixties, Mary Quant was recognized for her youthful and affordable clothing designs. She featured miniskirts, colored, opaque tights, skinny ribs, and hip belts. In the late sixties, her designs were carried by JC Penney.

**BEN REIG:** In the sixties, Ben Reig was known for his suits and coats.

**SCAASI:** In the sixties, Scaasi designed evening gowns and clothes for custom order. He used outré materials for his designs such as aluminum-colored cellophane and sheer silk covered with huge sequins. His gowns relied on simple but well-cut shapes and helped their wearers make striking entrances.

**KEN SCOTT:** Scott opened a salon in Milan, Italy, in the late fifties. In the sixties he was known for his boldly colored fabrics which he often designed in caftan and tunic styles. Scott also designed silk jersey body stockings and printed scarves.

**ADELE SIMPSON:** In 1964, Simpson's company, Adele Simpson, Inc., made a special collection of Givenchy for Bloomingdale's. In the sixties, Simpson designed coordinating suits with coats, and dresses with jackets. She also had a collection derived from Indian sari fabrics.

**JACQUES TIFFEAU:** In the late fifties, when Tiffeau began designing independently, his specialty was sportswear. His sixties designs also tended toward more casual activity. In the mid-sixties, Tiffeau designed boxy jacket and tight pant ensembles. Other designs included heavily sculpted garments of wool and cotton, Western-style shirts with squared armholes, suits and other designs in corduroy, wide plaid wools, and silks. In the late sixties, Tiffeau designed jersey dresses with Empire waists, which were worn with thigh-high boots and long skirts.

**VALENTINO:** Valentino was an Italian designer known for elegant, tasteful designs.

**SALLY VICTOR:** Sally Victor was a premier milliner whose couture designs could cost as much as $1,000 apiece when they included fur and jewels. Some of her other sixties designs included striped berets, patent leather visors, and floppy organza hats. Her ready-to-wear designs were sold under the "Sally V" label.

**ROGER VIVIER:** Vivier designed for many major manufacturers of shoes, including Miller and Delman in America. In the sixties, he designed a shoe with mother-of-pearl, tortoiseshell, or silver buckle. Vivier is known for his construction of high-fashion heels.

JOHN WEITZ: In the sixties, Weitz designed men's fashions.

YVES SAINT LAURENT: Yves Saint Laurent's first collection of the sixties showed gold buttoned navy pea jackets, and workman's smocks in jersey, silk, and satin. Later designs included thigh-high boots, Mondrian-inspired color block dresses, tuxedo jackets for women, and velvet knickers.

## 1960s
## Introduction Frontispiece

1960s ROBERTA DI CAMARINO COAT. Printed velvet, from Giuliana; slash pockets, slit at knee, lined in printed "Roberta" silk, excellent condition. $2,100 (See photograph on page 152)
*Courtesy of Enokiworld.*

## VINTAGE FASHIONS OF THE SIXTIES

Straw Handbag and Straw Hat. *Courtesy of Patina, New York, NY. Photograph by Tom Amico.*

1960s STRAW HANDBAG ($125) AND STRAW HAT ($115), with golf motifs, excellent condition.
*Both: Courtesy of Patina, NY.*

*Detail of Hanae Mori Evening Sweater:* Glass stones and bugle beads embellishment. *Photograph by Linda Ames.*

Hanae Mori Evening Sweater. *Courtesy of Linda Ames, Vintage Textile, www.vintagetextile.com. Photograph by Linda Ames.*

**1960S HANAE MORI EVENING SWEATER.** Heavy two-ply cashmere, rib knit, plunging V neckline, embellished with rhinestones, colored glass stones, and black bugle beads, mint condition. $185
*Courtesy of Linda Ames, Vintage Textile.*

Adele Simpson Evening Dress. *Courtesy of Isadora's, WA, www.isadoras.com. Photograph by Jennifer A. Ledda.*

**1960s ADELE SIMPSON EVENING DRESS.** Deep blue silk, strapless, fitting straight across the bodice, asymmetrical hem, front slits at knee 6″ shorter, pristine condition. $750
*Courtesy of Isadora's, WA.*

Helen Rose Couture Gown. *Courtesy of Deborah Burke, Antique & Vintage Dress Gallery, www.antiquedress.com. Photograph by Deborah Burke.*

*Detail of Helen Rose Gown:* Bodice with floral beaded design. *Photograph by Deborah Burke.*

**1960s HELEN ROSE COUTURE GOWN.** Beaded allover, square neckline, floral beaded design at neckline, straps, waistband, and knee, "carwash hemline," near-mint. $1,750

*Courtesy of Deborah Burke, Antique & Vintage Dress Gallery.*

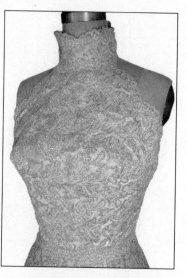

*Detail of Don Brown Halter Gown:* Iridescent floss lace. *Photograph by Deborah Burke.*

Don Brown Couturier Halter Gown. *Courtesy of Deborah Burke, Antique & Vintage Dress Gallery, www.antiquedress.com. Photograph by Deborah Burke.*

**1960s DON BROWN COUTURIER HALTER GOWN.** Gold metallic and iridescent floss lace, elliptical hemline, silk lining, excellent condition. $795

*Courtesy of Deborah Burke, Antique & Vintage Dress Gallery.*

Galanos Cocktail Dress. *Courtesy of Darlene Dull & Jennifer Parker-Stanton, Cookie's Closet, www.cookiescloset.com. Photograph by Sanders Stanton.*

**1960s GALANOS COCKTAIL DRESS.** Stellar gold, copper, and black metallic silk brocade, V neck, six-pleat skirt, excellent condition. $495
*Courtesy of Darlene Dull and Jennifer Parker-Stanton, Cookie's Closet.*

Velveteen Knit Dress. *Courtesy of Wendy Radick, Kitty Girl Vintage, www.kittygirlvintage.com. Photograph by Wendy Radick.*

Patent Leather Bow Pumps. *Courtesy of Wendy Radick, Kitty Girl Vintage, www.kittygirlvintage.com. Photograph by Wendy Radick.*

**1960s VELVETEEN KNIT DRESS.** Large floral print in fuchsia, pink, purple, and olive, keyhole-like neckline decorated with rhinestone sew-ons, short-sleeved, fitted waist, side metal zipper, tulip hem exposing knee, excellent condition. $55
*Courtesy of Wendy Radick, Kitty Girl Vintage.*

**1960s PATENT LEATHER BOW PUMPS.** Leather having iridescent quality, multicolored jewel tones; labels: "Johanson Lewis Designs" and "Lewis Salon shoes Tucson Phoenix," marked size 6½N, pristine condition. $44
*Courtesy of Wendy Radick, Kitty Girl Vintage.*

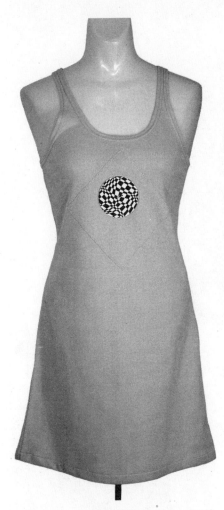

Papagallo Shoes and Handbag. *Courtesy of Sothebys.com. Photograph by Monica Anchin.*

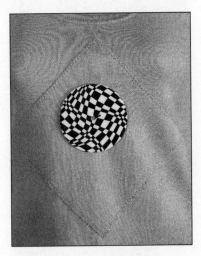

Rudi Gernreich Mini Dress. *Courtesy of Linda Ames, Vintage Textile, www.vintagetextile.com. Photograph by Linda Ames.*

Detail of Rudi Gernreich Mini Dress: Geometric prints, whimsical large black and white plastic button on bodice. *Photograph by Linda Ames.*

---

**1960s RUDI GERNREICH MINI DRESS.** Synthetic stretch knit, geometric designs, whimsical black and white large plastic button, mint condition. $485
*Courtesy of Linda Ames, Vintage Textile.*

**1960s PAPAGALLO SHOES AND HANDBAG.** Set, rose turtle skin, excellent condition. $1,200/set.
*Courtesy of Sothebys.com*

---

*Bonnie Cashin Handbag.*
*Courtesy of Sothebys.com.*
*Photograph by*
*Monica Anchin.*

Bonnie Cashin Suit. *Courtesy of Patina, New York,*
*NY. Photograph by Tom Amico*

**1960s BONNIE CASHIN SUIT.** Brown wool tweed, suede trim, brass
   toggle clasps, excellent condition. $475
   *Courtesy of Patina, NY.*

**1960s BONNIE CASHIN HANDBAG.** Bonnie Cashin for Coach bag,
   excellent condition. $605
   *Courtesy of Sothebys.com*

Mod Dress Coat. *Courtesy of Wendy Radick, Kitty Girl Vintage, www.kittygirlvintage.com. Photograph by Wendy Radick.*

1960s MOD DRESS COAT. Purple on beige abstract print, wide lapel collar, full-length sleeves, fitted Empire waist, flared A-line skirt, side inset pockets, two matching purple buttons closure, lined, mint condition. $95
*Courtesy of Wendy Radick, Kitty Girl Vintage.*

Dress. *Courtesy of From Around the World Vintage, New York, NY. Photograph by Tom Amico.*

**1960s DRESS.** Green wool, Princess style, bow with fringed panel, "Vanina, Paris–Made in France," excellent condition. $250
*Courtesy of From Around the World Vintage, NY.*

Roberta di Camarino Handbag.
*Courtesy of Enokiworld,*
*www.enokiworld.com.*
*Photograph by Madeline Meyerowitz.*

Bonnie Cashin Suede Coat. *Courtesy of*
*Enokiworld, www.enokiworld.com. Photograph by*
*Madeline Meyerowitz.*

**1960s BONNIE CASHIN SUEDE COAT.** Lime green, lined in lime
green wool jersey, made for Phillip Sills & Co, excellent condition. $510
*Courtesy of Enokiworld.*

**1960s ROBERTA DI CAMARINO HANDBAG.** Printed cotton velvet,
leather trim and handle, 9½″ h (including handle) × 9″ w, black leather
lining, inside pockets, excellent condition. $650
*Courtesy of Enokiworld.*

Trenchcoat. *Courtesy of Vintage by Stacey Lee, White Plains, NY. Photograph by Tom Amico.*

Pauline Trigère Coat. *Courtesy of Darlene Dull and Jennifer Parker-Stanton, Cookie's Closet, www.cookiescloset.com. Photograph by Sanders Stanton.*

1960s TRENCHCOAT. Red plaid cotton, double-breasted, "Fairbrook, New York," mint condition. $350
*Courtesy of Vintage by Stacey Lee, NY.*

1960s PAULINE TRIGÈRE COAT. Winter white, soft wool, tie neck, dolman sleeves, seam work detail reminiscent of Courrèges, bound button holes, bound front pockets, hand finished, crepe lining, label off-white satin with red signature, label: "Saks Fifth Avenue," excellent condition. $225
*Courtesy of Darlene Dull and Jennifer Parker-Stanton, Cookie's Closet.*

Handbags. *Courtesy of Vintage by Stacey Lee, White Plains, NY. Photograph by Tom Amico.*

Handbags. *Courtesy of Screaming Mimi's, New York, NY. Photograph by Tom Amico.*

**1960S HANDBAGS.** Bonnie Cashin, baquette-style handbag in pony, excellent condition. $500

Large pony handbag, excellent condition. $325
*Courtesy of Vintage by Stacey Lee, NY.*

**1960S HANDBAGS:** Brown snake with crown clasp, excellent condition. $125

Light brown snake with bar and curl clasp, very good condition. $75

Gray ostrich bucket bag with bar and curl clasp, suede interior, excellent condition. $110

Gray kangaroo handbag, made in Australia, excellent condition. $75
*Courtesy of Screaming Mimi's, NY.*

Sheepskin Jacket. *Courtesy of Darlene Dull and Jennifer Parker-Stanton, Cookie's Closet, www.cookiescloset.com. Photograph by Sanders Stanton.*

Western Shirt. *Courtesy of Vintage Apparel, New York, NY. Photograph by Tom Amico.*

**1960s SHEEPSKIN JACKET.** Suede outside, sheepskin lining, waist-length, snap front, "The Sheepshack of Boise, Idaho," excellent condition. $168
*Courtesy of Darlene Dull and Jennifer Parker-Stanton, Cookie's Closet.*

**1960s WESTERN SHIRT.** Women's, blue cotton scattered with flowers, fitted, "H Bar C," excellent condition. $100
*Courtesy of Vintage Apparel, New York, NY.*

Lilly Beach Jacket. *Courtesy of Darlene Dull and Jennifer Parker-Stanton, Cookie's Closet, www.cookiescloset.com. Photograph by Sanders Stanton.*

Sports Jacket. *Courtesy of Darlene Dull and Jennifer Parker-Stanton, Cookie's Closet, www.cookiescloset.com. Photograph by Sanders Stanton.*

**1960s LILLY BEACH JACKET.** Women's, orange and yellow, 100% cotton, self-tie, good condition. $78
*Courtesy of Darlene Dull and Jennifer Parker-Stanton, Cookie's Closet.*

**1960s LILLY PULITZER SPORTS JACKET.** Men's, preppy rose pattern, Lilly lions-head gold buttons; half-lining in Lilly lion print fabric, 42R, good condition. $98
*Courtesy of Darlene Dull & Jennifer Parker-Stanton, Cookie's Closet.*

*Detail of Fabric:*
Houndstooth
pattern. *Photograph by*
*Art Fawcett.*

Sports Jacket. *Courtesy of Art & Janene Fawcett,*
*Vintage Silhouettes, CA, www.vintagesilhouettes.com.*
*Photograph by Art Fawcett.*

Gentlemen's Fedora. *Courtesy of Art*
*& Janene Fawcett, Vintage Silhouettes,*
*CA, www.vintagesilhouettes.com.*
*Photograph by Art Fawcett.*

**1960s SPORTS JACKET.** Black and white houndstooth, mother-of-pearl
buttons, size 40R, excellent condition. $55
*Courtesy of Art & Janene Fawcett, Vintage Silhouettes, CA.*

**1960s GENTLEMEN'S FEDORA.** Blue/gray with black ribbon, "Stetson
Sovereign"—stetson 20 (meaning sold for $20 in the 1960s), size 7⅛,
excellent finish and condition. $85
*Courtesy of Art & Janene Fawcett, Vintage Silhouettes, CA.*

Gentlemen's Homburg. *Courtesy of Art & Janene Fawcett, Vintage Silhouettes, CA, www.vintagesilhouettes.com. Photograph by Art Fawcett.*

Shoes. *Courtesy of Ardis Taylor, Vintage Silhouettes, CA, www.vintagesilhouettes.com. Photograph by Art Fawcett.*

Gentlemen's Fedora. *Courtesy of Art & Janene Fawcett, Vintage Silhouettes, CA, www.vintagesilhouettes.com. Photograph by Art Fawcett.*

**1960s Shoes.** Cap toe (French) with simulated alligator, "New Old Stock." $165.
*Courtesy of Ardis Taylor, Vintage Silhouettes.*

**1960s Gentlemen's Homburg.** Gray, mauve crown and brim ribbon, "Stetson," some tracking on the underbrim, excellent condition, size 7⅝. $120
*Courtesy of Art & Janene Fawcett, Vintage Silhouettes, CA.*

**1960s Gentlemen's Fedora.** Medium brown, "Stetson," porkpie block, green/brown ribbon with red/black orange feather, size 7¼, 2½" brim, renovated. $85
*Courtesy of Art & Janene Fawcett, Vintage Silhouettes, CA.*

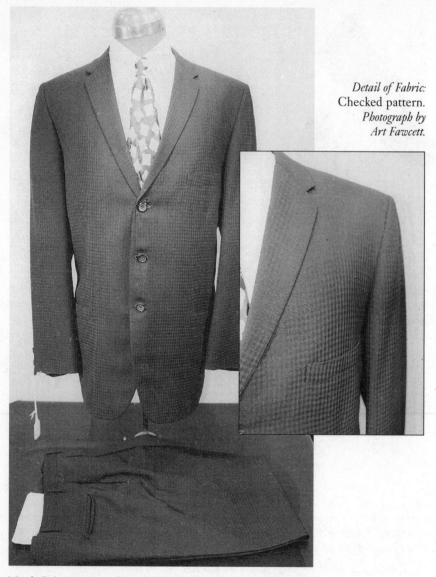

*Detail of Fabric:*
Checked pattern.
*Photograph by*
*Art Fawcett.*

Men's Suit. *Courtesy of Art & Janene Fawcett, Vintage Silhouettes,*
*CA, www.vintagesilhouettes.com. Photograph by Art Fawcett.*

1960s MEN'S SUIT. Sharkskin, three-button, checked pattern,
Hollywood high-rise, cuffed, size 42, excellent condition. $175
*Courtesy of Art & Janene Fawcett, Vintage Silhouettes.*

## MARKET TRENDS FOR THE SIXTIES

### *Lingerie*

**1960S PSYCHEDELIC PRINT SLIP.** Nylon, mint green, and chocolate psychedelic print, mint condition. $75
*Courtesy of From Around the World Vintage, New York, NY.*

### *Separates*

**1960S MINI SKIRT.** Mustard leather, excellent condition. $150
*Courtesy of From Around the World Vintage, New York, NY.*

**1960S ANNE KLEIN HIP-HUGGER PANTS.** Wool tweed, contoured below waistband, mint condition. $150
*Courtesy of Linda Ames, Vintage Textile, www.vintagetextile.com*

**1960S VERA "DAISY AND TULIP" COTTON BLOUSE.** Lemon, mustard, and green with basic black and white, hidden zipper and wide-pointed collar, excellent condition. $90
*Courtesy of Enokiworld, www.enokiworld.com*

**1950S PINK WOOL BEADED TOP.** Pink top with beads, excellent condition. $45
*Courtesy of Lynn Pastore, Avenue 13–5 and Dime Vintage, CO, www.510vintage.com*

**1960S–1970S LEVI'S STRIPED HIP-HUGGERS.** Rare vintage Levi's (Big E), striped pattern, flared leg, excellent condition. $75
*Courtesy of Lynn Pastore, Avenue 13–5 and Dime Vintage, CO, www.510vintage.com*

**1960S MIDI SKIRT.** Cotton, flower power pattern in hot pink, orange, and yellow on black ground, "Alex Coleman, California," excellent condition. $100
*Courtesy of From Around the World Vintage, New York, NY.*

**1960S CHINESE JACKET.** Blue silk, pink, and red embroidery, "Made in China," excellent condition. $185
*Courtesy of Vintage by Stacey Lee, White Plains, NY.*

**1960S RUFFLED WOOL WRAP SKIRT.** Fine wool crepe, placket and hem pleated and ruffled, wraps and fastens at the left hip, inseam pocket over each hip, black silk crepe lining, made by Divisions, excellent condition. $165
*Courtesy of Enokiworld, www.enokiworld*

**1960s EMILIO PUCCI SILK BOLERO JACKET AND SKIRT.** Abbreviated top and longer-length skirt, stylized grapes and foliage in silver, coral, brown, and pale peach on black, excellent condition. $615
*Courtesy of Enokiworld, www.enokiworld*

**1960s BANFF FLORAL BEADED WOOL SHELL.** Ribbed like corduroy, black wool shell decorated with diamond-shaped floral design, black bugle and seed beads, zippered back, black silk crepe lining, excellent condition. $80
*Courtesy of Enokiworld, www.enokiworld.com*

**1960s LAURA ASHLEY STRIPED COTTON PULLOVER.** Striped poplin mod pullover alternating popsicle orange and tangerine wide stripes, patch pocket, big stand-up zippered collar, made in Wales, excellent condition. $140
*Courtesy of Enokiworld, www.enokiworld.com*

**1960s ANNE KLEIN IKAT MOTIF WOVEN JACKET.** Japanese-inspired, one-tie closure in front, abbreviated sleeves, all cotton and richly woven, not printed, Elizabeth Arden tag, excellent condition. $115
*Courtesy of Enokiworld, www.enokiworld.com*

**1960s BONNIE CASHIN FELT AND LEATHER BUCKLE SKIRT.** Double-faced heavyweight felt trimmed in dark chocolate leather, dog leash clasp on side, hidden magnetic snaps behind the placket, deep inseam pockets at each side, wool jersey lining, "Sills and Co.," excellent condition. $280
*Courtesy of Enokiworld, www.enokiworld.com*

**1960s BONNIE CASHIN CASHMERE SKIRT, SHELL, AND CARDIGAN.** Classic twinset and sweater skirt in heather blue, shell with cap sleeves, skirt has wide waistband, slate blue silk crêpe de chine lining, three-quarter-length sleeve cardigan with buttons of matte gilt metal flowers with clusters in center, mint condition. $495
*Courtesy of Enokiworld, www.enokiworld.com*

**1960s MARIMEKKO GRAPHIC COTTON TUNIC.** Magenta and green with shots of lemon yellow on front side only, elbow-length sleeves, cut simply, slight flare at hem, zips at placket, excellent condition. $175
*Courtesy of Enokiworld, www.enokiworld.com*

**1960s ANNE KLEIN TANGERINE JERSEY TWINSET.** Leotard jersey twinset with cap-sleeved scoop-neck bodysuit and matching slinky cardigan, triple snap crotch and ribbed banding around neckline and wrists, excellent condition. $80
*Courtesy of Enokiworld, www.enokiworld.com*

**1960s MR. DINO PALAZZO PANTS AND BLOUSE.** Bright clear pink and red poppies palazzo pants and matching slim blouse, excellent condition. $105
*Courtesy of Enokiworld, www.enokiworld.com*

**1960s LOLLIPOP FLOWER SNAP FRONT SKIRT.** Navy poly gabardine skirt with lollipop-faced "flowers" in shades of lime, lemon, tangerine, and white, contrast stitched edging, matte silver snaps, made by Sir James, excellent condition. $65
*Courtesy of Enokiworld, www.enokiworld.com*

**1960s PUCKERED METALLIC SHELL.** Puckered black metallic Lurex shell, zips from waist to nape in back, black rayon crepe lining, excellent condition. $70
*Courtesy of Enokiworld, www.enokiworld.com*

**1960s ANNE KLEIN FLORAL "JEAN" JACKET.** Cropped floral jacket in natural cotton twill, printed with peonies and fuchsia, with curling tendrils and ivy, in shades of peach, baby blue, celery, and pink, styled like abbreviated jean jacket, buttoned breast pockets, opaque white buttons along placket, excellent condition. $95
*Courtesy of Enokiworld, www.enokiworld.com*

**1960s EMILIO PUCCI SILK SKIRT.** Pink silk lower calf-length skirt, double waistband, buttons down front under hidden placket, yellow based pink with swirling flowers and foliage in shades of lilac and indigo with touches of pastel aqua and chartreuse, made in Italy for Stix, Baer and Fuller, excellent condition. $225
*Courtesy of Enokiworld, www.enokiworld.com*

**1960s MOD STRIPED HIP-HUGGERS.** Low-waisted, slightly flared, goldenrod yellow, royal, navy blue, and cocoa stripes on white cotton, zippered front, 3″ belt loops, excellent condition. $40
*Courtesy of Enokiworld, www.enokiworld.com*

**1960s METALLIC GOLD WOOL FLOOR-LENGTH SKIRT AND SHIRT.** Three quarters wool and the rest metallic thread, skirt slim through waist and hips, widening out toward hem with slit in back extending above knee, blouse skinny fitting with button cuffs and pointed collar, both pieces with original hangtags, unworn condition. $165
*Courtesy of Enokiworld, www.enokiworld.com*

**1960s LANVIN PALAZZO ONE-PIECE PANTSUIT.** Vivid clown print, à la Peter Max, in nylon crepe, one-piece palazzo pajamas, wide legs, high natural waist, matching sash belt, zippered back, excellent condition. $315
*Courtesy of Enokiworld, www.enokiworld.*

**1960s EMBELLISHED PINK CARDIGAN.** Baby pink acrylic, white lace appliqué sweeping down from right shoulder, polished glass dome mirror-like buttons, made by Betty Higgins, flawless condition. $65
*Courtesy of Enokiworld, www.enokiworld.com*

**1960s PARAPHERNALIA SUEDE WRAP MINISKIRT.** Fawn suede mini skirt wraps and ties at the side with a trio of slits through which to slide the skinny sash, superwide belt loops at hip level, excellent condition. $205
*Courtesy of Enokiworld, www.enokiworld.com*

**1960s MONDRIAN-INSPIRED PRINT TUNIC AND SKIRT.** Printed nylon squares of chartreuse, brown, crimson, black, and white, zippered tunic and skirt, made by Personal, excellent condition. $80
*Courtesy of Enokiworld, www.enokiworld.com*

**1960s LUREX PANTSUIT.** Green, silver Lurex, with four-button top and matching belt, "Maurice Antaqa," excellent condition. $65
*Courtesy of The Fainting Couch, MA, www.faintingcouch.com*

**1960s JUMPSUIT.** Bouclé black wool, zippered front, metal trim, excellent condition. $250
*Courtesy of Vintage by Stacey Lee, White Plains, NY.*

## Dresses

**1960s HAWAIIAN SUNDRESS.** Spaghetti-strap sundress in bright Hawaiian floral pattern, excellent condition. $40
*Courtesy of Lynn Pastore, Avenue 13–5 and Dime Vintage, CO, www.510vintage.com*

**1960s HAWAIIAN SUNDRESS IN ABSTRACT PRINT.** Bright, bold abstract cotton print baby-doll mini dress in orange and white with pink and lime accents, scoop neck front and back, "Miss Hawaii," very good condition. $42
*Courtesy of www.fashiondig.com*

**1960s MINI SHIFT DRESS.** Polyester with wide flower border at hem, very good condition. $60
*Courtesy of www.fashiondig.com*

**1960s RED WOOL "LADYLIKE" DRESS.** Pencil-thin black trim with bow at waist, stand-up collar, long sleeves with cuffs, mint condition. $230
*Courtesy of www.fashiondig.com*

**1960s LIBERTY OF LONDON DAY DRESS.** Classic Liberty of London cotton print, front button opening, two side seam pockets, belted, Peter Pan collar, excellent condition. $48
*Courtesy of Karen Augusta, Antique Lace & Fashion, www.antique-fashion.com*

1960S LILLI ANN DRESS. Black wool knit, geometric white stripes, mint condition. $250
*Courtesy of Vintage by Stacey Lee, White Plains, NY.*

## Party Wear

1960S OLEG CASSINI COCKTAIL DRESS. Elegant, dress-length strips of fabric hang from front and back, label: "Oleg Cassini," retailer label: "Neusteters Department Store," excellent condition. $150
*Courtesy of Lynn Pastore, Avenue 13–5 and Dime Vintage, CO, www.510vintage.com*

1960S HOT RED CHIFFON COCKTAIL DRESS. Full skirt, scoop neck, "Miss Elliette" (used in the Kevin Costner film, *13 Days*), excellent condition. $95
*Courtesy of Art & Janene Fawcett, Vintage Silhouettes, CA, www.vintagesilhouettes.com*

1960S FLORAL JERSEY DRESS. Vibrant yellow and multicolored floral pattern, front split skirt, zippered back, "Maurice by Crizza," mint condition. $150
*Courtesy of www.fashiondig.com*

1960S HALTER-TOP GOWN. Brown polka-dotted sheer cotton, trapeze back, white pin-on rose at bodice, matching shoulder stole, "Bianchi, Boston, New York," perfect condition. $150
*Courtesy of The Fainting Couch, MA, www.faintingcouch.com*

1960S BLACK CREPE GOWN. Black crepe sleeveless polyester gown with black sequined waist inserts, label: "Stephan O'Grady," excellent condition. $75
*Courtesy of Art & Janene Fawcett, Vintage Silhouettes, CA, www.vintagesilhouettes.com*

1960S LACE COCKTAIL DRESS. Black cotton rose lace over dark taupe taffeta, sleeveless, features faux scoop-neck collar with black satin rosette, Princess seams, excellent condition. $65
*Courtesy of Art & Janene Fawcett, Vintage Silhouettes, CA, www.vintagesilhouettes.com*

1960S SLEEVELESS MINT GREEN EVENING GOWN. Bodice of silk polyester lining covered with veil of georgette, round ruffled collar, four-tiered skirt with curled edges (filament inserts), ribbon belt with jeweled and faux emeralds on round rhinestone buckle, excellent condition. $150
*Courtesy of The Fainting Couch, MA, www.faintingcouch.com*

**1960s SEQUIN AND BEADED MINI DRESS.** Brightly colored sequins and glass beads all over, silk shell, rayon lining, "Made in China," very good condition. $95
*Courtesy of The Fainting Couch, MA, www.faintingcouch.com*

**1960s–1970s COCKTAIL MINI DRESS.** Rhinestone buckle and satin ribbon, excellent condition. $40
*Courtesy of Lynn Pastore, Avenue 13–5 and Dime Vintage, CO, www.510vintage.com*

**1960s DRESS.** Beaded and sequined floral pink silk, cap sleeves, chiffon lining, pristine condition. $200
*Courtesy of Mary Troncale, Branford, CT.*

## Designer Dresses

**ANDRÉ COURRÈGES WOOL KNIT DRESS.** Cream wool knit, pieced and welted seams, metal zipper, two white plastic buttons, acetate lining, woven label: "Courrèges, Paris, Taille C, modèle deposé, made in France," excellent condition. $245
*Courtesy of Karen Augusta, Antique Lace & Fashion, www.antique-fashion.com*

**1960s GIORGIO DI SANT'ANGELO LONG JERSEY DRESS.** Ankle-length printed Lycra dress with fitted bodice and deep surplice neckline, gathered skirt, gypsy-inspired; cherry background with Matisse-inspired vases, overflowing with lemon and cobalt flowers, solid bands of black, white, and cherry at waist with white at wrists; bottom stitched in lettuce edge, excellent condition. $605
*Courtesy of Enokiworld, wwwenokiworld.com*

**1960s WILROY RUSSET BELTED DRESS.** Flaming russet floral print, colored Banlon in tangerine, burgundy, lime, banana, and black, modified bateau neckline, matching thin sash belt, excellent condition. $80
*Courtesy of Enokiworld, www.enokiworld.com*

**1960s EMILIO PUCCI SURPLICE DRESS.** Surplice bodice with taupe, pink, pale peach, and white flowers with swags, zippered back, excellent condition. $505
*Courtesy of Enokiworld, www.enokiworld.com*

**1960s CARLYE LITTLE BLACK COCKTAIL DRESS.** High slash neckline on black silk crepe, cap sleeves slit along outside of shoulder, open back with fitted underlayer, visible through divide, wide satin sash belt with flat bow, scalloped hem with 5" border of beaded passementerie, skirt with black silk satin lining, excellent condition. $130
*Courtesy of Enokiworld, www.enokiworld.com*

**1960S ABSTRACT SQUIGGLED SHIFT.** Mod shift covered with primary-hued splashes and squiggles of strong color, middle-weight cotton twill, partially zippered front, hips detailed with big round pockets, flawless condition. $50
*Courtesy of Enokiworld, www.enokiworld.com*

**1960S CHRISTIAN DIOR WOOL SHIFT WITH DAISIES.** Gray wool felt shift with exquisite construction, edged in daisies individually applied around the collar, sleeves and scalloped hem, modified Empire waist, short sleeves, gray silk crepe lining, flawless condition. $510
*Courtesy of Enokiworld, www.enokiworld.com*

**1960S GEOFFREY BEENE VOILE HALTER GOWN.** Dotted swiss organdy semi-sheer, halter neckline adorned with huge flat bow, nude silk lining, excellent condition. $845
*Courtesy of Enokiworld, www.enokiworld.com*

**1960S JO COPELAND MAGENTA SATIN GOWN WITH TASSELS.** Deep magenta silk satin gown with black silk tassels, deeply scalloped neckline and hem add defined edge to waves of gathered silk through-out skirt, inverted pleats at waist form a sort of apron through skirt, which stands away from body toward hem, wine silk crepe lining, made for Lisa Meril, excellent condition. $260
*Courtesy of Enokiworld, www.enokiworld.com*

**1960S EMILIO PUCCI SCALLOP PRINT SILK DRESS.** Radiating from waistband are scallops in pastel colors—lavender, shell pink, pale peach, silver, and cocoa, outlined in black, deep V neckline, slightly Empire waist, long sleeves, made for Lord & Taylor, excellent condition. $510
*Courtesy of Enokiworld, www.enokiworld.com*

**1960S PAULINE TRIGÈRE METALLIC "DAISY" GOWN.** Navy silk tulle embroidered with silver weaving lines resembling stylized chain links, bodice of metallic silver and gold daisy lace, high stand-up scalloped neckline, lining of nude silk crepe, unlined sheer sleeves, faceted rhinestone buttons at back, one slit back of knee, excellent condition. $645
*Courtesy of Enokiworld, www.enokiworld.com*

**1960S TEAL TRAINA LITTLE BLACK DRESS.** Black wool jersey, sleeves, grosgrain banded neckline, waist trimmed in ribbon, inverted pleats throughout skirt, grosgrain band 4" from hemline, small flat bow on back, excellent condition. $180
*Courtesy of Enokiworld, www.enokiworld.com*

**1960s DRESS WITH ULTRASUEDE BULL'S-EYES.** Forest green wool gabardine with Ultrasuede bull's-eyes, in rust, mocha, cream, and black encircling hem, each punctuated with single grommet, wide belt, ends in single Ultrasuede target, emerald green silk crepe lining, made in France for Iby, flawless condition. $195
*Courtesy of Enokiworld, www.enokiworld.com*

**1960s OSCAR DE LA RENTA FLORAL CHIFFON DRESS.** Bright floral silk chiffon, edged in lime green grosgrain, full billowing sleeves, baby doll waist, lined bodice and skirt, sheer sleeves, flawless condition. $90
*Courtesy of Enokiworld, www.enokiworld.com*

**1960s REVERSIBLE SILK JERSEY DRESS.** Muted celadon becomes ultimate little black dress, drawstring neckline has long tie which pulls in to form small drape of neckline and back, like modified cowl, celadon side is slightly shorter than the black, leaving slice of black at hem, Walter Bass, nearly excellent condition. $145
*Courtesy of Enokiworld, www.enokiworld.com*

## Suits

**1960s WOOL TWEED SUIT WITH BEAVER COLLAR.** Boxy double-breasted jacket with two columns of chunky black buttons, classic sixties low-positioned faux pocket flaps and modified stand-away portrait collar, zippered side slim skirt, black silk crepe lining, made by Monarch with the original hangtags and price, dated March 1965, flawless condition. $260
*Courtesy of Enokiworld, www.enokiworld.com*

**1960s SAFARI TWILL PANTSUIT.** Saks Fifth Avenue "Young Dimensions" cotton twill duo, button chest, epaulets, hip pockets, slim-legged pants flared at hem, excellent condition. $130
*Courtesy of Enokiworld, www.enokiworld.com*

**1960s GEOMETRIC PRINT DRESS AND MATCHING COAT.** Rayon crepe, Op Art print in red, white, and blue, zippered back, faux pocket flaps at hips, raglan sleeves, matching coat buttons with a row of chunky navy buttons, self-belt at back, made by Robert Leonard, excellent condition. $135
*Courtesy of Enokiworld, www.enokiworld.com*

**1960s ORANGE AND PINK KNOTTED SUIT.** Wool and silk blend crocheted suit in pale pink, cherry red, and tangerine, boxy with coral and

gilt buttons, strawberry-hued silk crepe lining, made in Portugal for Christele Ann, a Parisian firm, excellent condition. $215
*Courtesy of Enokiworld, www.enokiworld.com*

**1960s NAVY SHEATH WITH MATCHING JACKET.** Navy Thai silk woven with pink, changes colors with movement, two pink and violet organza bands at neck, navy and pink Harlequin lining through bodice, and elbow-sleeved boxy jacket, three opalescent purple buttons, inseam hip pockets, made by Decker's, flawless condition. $90
*Courtesy of Enokiworld, www.enokiworld.com*

**1960s SUMMER SUIT WITH EYELET.** Beige and ivory cotton, forming alternating bands of crochet and oversized eyelet, V-neck jacket, two large matte white buttons at diaphragm, formfitting skirt, tiered layers, scalloped edges, made by Saks Fifth Avenue, silk crepe lining, backed by cotton batiste, excellent condition. $105
*Courtesy of Enokiworld, www.enokiworld.com*

**1960s OSCAR DE LA RENTA BRIGHT CHECKED SILK SUIT.** Lime green and lemon checkerboard print, bursts of pale peach roses and blue foliage, silk jersey top button-down, sleeveless, tucks into gathered skirt, matching placket encircled at waist with matching belt, gilt metal buckle, excellent condition. $120
*Courtesy of Enokiworld, www.enokiworld.com*

**1960s DAVIDOW STRIPED WOOL SUIT.** Ivory and navy Irish wool tweed, slim skirt, single-breasted jacket, gilt metal dome buttons, white silk crepe lining, excellent condition. $305
*Courtesy of Enokiworld, www.enokiworld.com*

**1960s LILLI ANN FAUX SHANTUNG SUIT.** Synthetic shantung, in deep cocoa, silk lined in red, copper, and navy, tuck-pleated pockets, deep V pleat centered in front of skirt, excellent condition. $85
*Courtesy of Enokiworld, www.enokiworld.com*

**1960s JO COPELAND GRAY FLANNEL COCKTAIL SUIT.** Slightly shaped, collarless, eight rhinestone buttons, silk crêpe de chine lining, excellent condition. $245
*Courtesy of Enokiworld, www.enokiworld.com*

**1960s ORIGINALA NAVY WOOL SUIT.** Double-breasted jacket, in double rows of polished gilt metal buttons, high-buttoned collar, skirt zippered on diagonal, inside pocket, navy silk crêpe de chine lining, excellent condition. $235
*Courtesy of Enokiworld, www.enokiworld.com*

## Outerwear

1960s FLOCKED COAT. Reds, greens, grays, yellows, and golds in flocked floral on black ground, single-button closure at neck, round collar, A-line, three-quarter-length sleeve, black silk lining, excellent condition. $175
*Courtesy of Amy Smith.*

1960s WOOL COAT. Black and white diamond pattern, "Grace's Nashville," excellent condition. $375
*Courtesy of From Around the World Vintage, New York, NY.*

1960s LILLI ANN COAT. Black wool with three-quarter-length sleeves, multicolored satin lining, perfect condition. $200
*Courtesy of Lynn Pastore, Avenue 13–5 and Dime Vintage, CO, www.510vintage.com*

1960s ORIGINALA "GRAPE NEHI" WOOL COAT. Grape Nehi–hued with enameled purple buttons, crossed in gold, double-breasted, cuffed patch pockets low at each hip and split cuffs, plum silk crepe lining, flawless condition. $155
*Courtesy of Enokiworld, www.enokiworld.com*

1960s TRICOLOR MINK AND LEATHER COAT. Diamond patterns of mink outlined by dark brown leather, matching sash belt, collar is all vanilla; rayon satin lining in abstract marigold, cocoa, and white print, made by Spritzer Furs, excellent condition. $430
*Courtesy of Enokiworld, www.enokiworld.com*

1960s UNISEX LEATHER JACKET. Red with black trim, very good condition. $275
*Courtesy of Screaming Mimi's, New York, NY.*

1960s JACKET. Black patent leather, double-breasted, red wool zippered lining, excellent condition. $250
*Courtesy of Vintage by Stacey Lee, White Plains, NY.*

1960s ORIGINALA HOODED WALKING COAT. Beige and off-white twist wool, thigh length, short arm, large framing hood, slash pockets, taupe crepe lining, flawless condition. $160
*Courtesy of Enokiworld, www.enokiworld.com*

1960s BONNIE CASHIN SUEDE THREE QUARTER COAT WITH FUR. Tobacco colored, possum collar, back vent held shut with strap attached to lining, deep pockets with flaps, signature brass turning closures at hip, lined in greige acrylic pile, made for Sils, excellent condition. $625
*Courtesy of Enokiworld, www.enokiworld.com*

**1960s Pierre Cardin Suede Jacket with Circles.** Double-breasted, cropped suede, two silver lozenge buttons, leather belt ending in quilted circles, small round pocket, caramel rayon crepe lining, excellent condition. $405
*Courtesy of Enokiworld, www.enokiworld.com*

**1960s Belted Plaid Wool Tweed Coat.** Double-breasted Tartan plaid, glossy black buttons, "belted" wrists, inseam pockets, matching sash belt, forest green silk satin lining, plaid stripe at hip, made by Women's Haberdashers, excellent condition. $280
*Courtesy of Enokiworld, www.enokiworld.com*

**1960s "Bonwit Teller" All-Weather Coat.** Full raccoon lining, excellent condition. $275
*Courtesy of Linda Ames, Vintage Textile, www.vintagetextile.com*

**1960s Eton Buffalo Plaid Jacket.** Brown and cream wool, double-breasted, two side slit pockets, button sleeves, "Made in Austria," excellent condition. $75
*Courtesy of The Fainting Couch, MA, www.faintingcouch.com*

**1960s Geoffrey Beene Mink Coat.** Casual cuffed sleeves, deep patched pockets, "Lord & Taylor, New York," excellent condition. $600
*Courtesy of Linda Ames, Vintage Textile, www.vintagetextile.com*

**1960s Pedro Rodriquez Coat.** Gray wool tweed, asymmetrical design, front closes diagonally on bias, one diagonal pocket, unevenly spaced buttons, gray and white plaid lining of soft brushed wool, excellent condition. $375
*Courtesy of Linda Ames, Vintage Textile, www.vintagetextile.com*

**1960's Red Leather Mod Coat.** Fox fur cuffs and collar, label: "Dan Di Modes," excellent condition. $200
*Courtesy of Lynn Pastore, Avenue 13–5 and Dime, CO, www.510vintage.com*

**1960s Pink Leather Faux Fur Coat.** Pale pink leather, fur lapel, collar, and sleeves, excellent condition. $150
*Courtesy of Lynn Pastore, Avenue 13–5 and Dime, CO, www.510vintage.com*

**1960s Mod Fur Jacket.** Leather and fox fur coat, unusual geometric design, very Hollywood, excellent condition. $200
*Courtesy of Lynn Pastore, Avenue 13–5 and Dime, CO, www.510vintage.com*

**1960s Floral Ski Jacket.** Rug-like fabric, excellent condition. $80
*Courtesy of Lynn Pastore, Avenue 13–5 and Dime, CO, www.510vintage.com*

1960s–1970s Mod Leather Coat. Double-breasted dark brown leather coat, hip "Euro" design, very good condition. $70
*Courtesy of Lynn Pastore, Avenue 13–5 and Dime, CO, www.510vintage.com*

1960s Coat with Mink Collar. A-line, black bouclé, pale cream mink collar, three-quarter-length sleeves, slash pockets, six covered buttons, black silk lining, "Vanity Frocks Irvington," excellent condition. $95
*Courtesy of Amy Smith.*

## Accessories

1960s Floral Brocade Heels. Trimmed with bronze-colored leather, bronze 3" leather heel, "Johanson Bon Marché," size 7B, very good condition. $40
*Courtesy of Art & Janene Fawcett, Vintage Silhouettes, CA, www.vintagesilhouettes.com*

1960s Silver and Rhinestone Sandals. Silver heels, two rhinestone studded straps across top, silver halter strap at heel, by Fiammante, size 5M, 4¼" spiked heel, excellent condition. $40
*Courtesy of Enokiworld, www.enokiworld.com*

1960s Triple Snakeskin Stilettos. Colored snakeskin in whiskey, emerald, and vanilla, pointy toes, skinny heels, piped in gold, made by Julianelli, size 7B, 3¾" heel, excellent condition. $145
*Courtesy of Enokiworld, www.enokiworld.com*

1960s Evins Faux Cobra Heeled Loafers. High-throated vamp resembling men's leather slipper, heel and body of printed leather, size 7½A, 2½" heel, excellent condition. $65
*Courtesy of Enokiworld, www.enokiworld.com*

1960 Herbert Levine Silver Sandals with Rhinestones. Clear vinyl uppers, diagonal rhinestone accent, blunt toe, asymmetrical heel straps, Herbert Levine, size 9½AA, 3½" heel, excellent condition. $70
*Courtesy of Enokiworld, www.enokiworld.com*

1960s Roger Vivier Fuchsia Satin Pumps with "Tassels." Little rhinestone-encrusted icicles suspended from strap across top, (stationary but moved into position by bending attached satin-wrapped wire), rounded toe, size 7N, 3" heel, excellent condition. $260
*Courtesy of Enokiworld, www.enokiworld.com*

1960s Saks Alligator Pumps. Pointed toe, skinny heel, from the Young Elite shop Saks Fifth Avenue, size 6A, 3¼" heel, excellent condition. $125
*Courtesy of Enokiworld, www.enokiworld.com*

1960s CHARLES JOURDAN MOD SNAKESKIN LOAFERS. Burgundy snakeskin, cabernet-hued leather detail at toes, original box, size 6B, stacked wooden 3″ heel, excellent condition. $45
*Courtesy of Enokiworld, www.enokiworld.com*

1960s BONNIE CASHIN FOR COACH, BLACK LEATHER BAG. Long thin leather straps, snap pockets on each side with central open compartment, signature striped cotton lining, protective feet, 8½″ h × 5½″ w × 4½″ d, double 18″ handles, Bonnie Cashin for Coach, excellent condition. $305
*Courtesy of Enokiworld, www.enokiworld.com*

1960s GUCCI BLACK LUNCHBOX PURSE. Black calfskin, domed, lacquered bamboo handle, polished gilt metal hardware stamped "Gucci," one patch pocket, fine leather interior lining, 6¾″ h × 8½″ w with 3½″ handle, excellent condition. $485
*Courtesy of Enokiworld, www.enokiworld.com*

1960s BEADED SHELL BAG. White shimmy, small oyster shell–shaped beads attached to seed bead loops, foundation of iridescent mermaid sequins, white silk satin interior, one patch pocket, gilt metal chain handle tucks inside for convertible clutch, made by Stylecraft–Miami, 5½″ h × 7″ w with single 5½″ handle, excellent condition. $110
*Courtesy of Enokiworld, www.enokiworld.com*

1960s SWIRLED CANVAS OVERNIGHT BAG. Deep taupe and black scrolled print, black vinyl texture and trim, jumbo bowling bag shape, exterior patch and zippered pockets on each side; waterproof interior with one large zippered pocket, made by Lark, 13″ h × 15¾″ w × 6½″ d with double 6″ handles, excellent condition. $190
*Courtesy of Enokiworld, www.enokiworld.com*

1960s BONNIE CASHIN FOR COACH ORANGE MINI TOTE. Mandarin orange leather, small snap pocket on front, white contrast stitching along the handles, signature striped cotton lining, 8″ h × 9½″ w with double 6½″ handles, excellent condition. $275
*Courtesy of Enokiworld, www.enokiworld.com*

1960s GEOMETRIC VELOUR SHOULDER BAG. Silver, brown, and black print, slightly rounded bottom, flap in front, black rayon faille lining with patch pocket, 10″ h × 9½″ w with single 13″ strap, excellent condition. $65
*Courtesy of Enokiworld, www.enokiworld.com*

1960s KORET FAKE-CROCODILE HANDBAG. Highly textured embossed black leather, combination gilt and silver hardware, adjustable strap,

black leather lining, two interior pockets outlined in yellow with turquoise rayon faille lining, 8¼" h × 9" w with single 6" handle, excellent condition. $130
*Courtesy of Enokiworld, www.enokiworld.com*

**1960s KORET TEXTURED PLEATHER BAG.** Little clasp, adjustable strap, brass feet, signature embossed Koret lining, one patch and one zippered pocket, cherry rayon faille lining, 7" h × 9½" w with strap extension to 12", excellent condition. $65
*Courtesy of Enokiworld, www.enokiworld.com*

**1960s TURQUOISE PATENT HANDBAG.** Interior black faille lining, zippered pocket, made by Theodor, 9½" h × 11¼" w with single 6" handle, excellent condition. $45
*Courtesy of Enokiworld, www.enokiworld.com*

**1960s LUCILLE DE PARIS BLOND OSTRICH BAG.** Delicate clasp of braided gold wires bent into a Queen Anne curve, four interior pockets, just over 7" h × 9" w with single 4½" handle, excellent condition. $360
*Courtesy of Enokiworld, www.enokiworld.com*

**1960s MARIMEKKO FLORAL CLUTCH.** Indigo, brown, black, wine, and cherry printed cotton, gilt metal frame, 8" h × 8" w, excellent condition. $70
*Courtesy of Enokiworld, www.enokiworld.com*

**1960s BIG LEOPARD PURSE.** Black leather bag with panel of tiny leopard print pony-hair, cutout handle, divided main compartment, zippered pocket, 13½" h × 12½" w, in excellent condition. $185
*Courtesy of Enokiworld, www.enokiworld.com*

## Menswear

**1960s STOVEPIPES.** Light green, 34" × 30", never worn, excellent condition. $50
*Courtesy of Lynn Pastore, Avenue 13–5 and Dime Vintage, CO, www.510vintage.com*

**1960s JANTZEN SURF TRUNKS.** Early Jantzen Surf Wear, geometric pattern, 100% cotton, excellent condition, $18
*Courtesy of Lynn Pastore, Avenue 13–5 and Dime Vintage, CO, www.510vintage.com*

**1960s BOWLING SHIRT.** Shiny gold and black synthetic, very wild and unusual, excellent condition. $70

*Courtesy of Lynn Pastore, Avenue 13–5 and Dime Vintage, CO,*
*www.510vintage.com*

**1960S MEN'S SINGLE-BREASTED SUIT.** Three-button, olive and blue
sharkskin, "Ro Craft," size 44S, excellent condition. $210
*Courtesy of Art & Janene Fawcett, Vintage Silhouettes, CA,*
*www.vintagesilhouettes.com*

**1960S MEN'S SINGLE-BREASTED SUIT.** Three-button, blue/gray
sharkskin, "Hart Schaffner & Marx," size 44S, excellent condition. $210
*Courtesy of Art & Janene Fawcett, Vintage Silhouettes, CA,*
*www.vintagesilhouettes.com*

**1960S MEN'S SPORTS JACKET.** Single-breasted, three-button, gray,
black, cream, and mauve, size 39R, excellent condition. $64
*Courtesy of Art & Janene Fawcett, Vintage Silhouettes, CA,*
*www.vintagesilhouettes.com*

Bill Gibb's Skirt and Jacket. *Courtesy of Enokiworld,
www.enokiworld.com. Photograph by Madeline Meyerowitz.*

# *Choices and Change*

Two trends prevailed in the seventies; one in answer to the riotous sixties and the other a classic conservatism. As fashion historian Valerie Steele observed in her book, *Fifty Years of Fashion: New Look to Now,* "Tired of fashions excesses, yet sympathetic to the hippies' creed of dressing to suit oneself, many people adopted a modernized version of the classics for work, and sportswear separates (especially jeans) for leisure." (p.87)

In the early part of the decade women went from elephant bells to midis to hot pants, often designed in daring fabrics and bold colors. Incredibly high chunky platform shoes for both men and women were shown with flared jeans—a symbol for the decade in later years. Finally when women entered the workforce in even greater numbers they rejected many of these earlier styles. The fashion model of the moment was now Lauren Hutton, whose natural makeup, blow-dry hairstyle, and simple gold chain jewelry typified the natural look. Women chose classic natural styles in tailored pants and pantsuits. The women's pinstripe or vested pantsuit, styled after men's fashions, was a practical and courageous statement for the times. It was the first time that trousers were considered acceptable dress for women in the workplace. Women even adopted the men's tuxedo for evening. It was also a time when dressing meant prominently displaying the logos of four or five designers on clothing and accessories. Fashion houses with logos of Gucci, Chanel, Perry Ellis, and Calvin Klein vied for the fashion market.

In 1977, Ralph Lauren dressed Diane Keaton in a vest, tuxedo, shirt, hacking jacket, and fedora for the movie *Annie Hall.* Women chose to dress in easy-to-wear, masculine-style clothing. Natural fabrics like silk, wool, and cotton returned. The interest in ecology led to the prevalent use of earth tones in every aspect of designing, from home decorating to clothing. Leather returned as a popular material for handbags, briefcases, and shoes. Even underwear introduced by Gossard/Lily of France had the natural "glossy" look.

In 1971, the Coty Fashions Critics Award went to Levi Strauss & Co. for their famous jeans. This was seen as symbolic of the change occurring in the lifestyles of men and women to a more independent and unisex style of dress. Jeans became available in a variety of styles—bleached, faded, shrunk, stonewashed, or brushed. For the classic woman dresser, Calvin Klein introduced designer jeans at the end of the decade that were soon to become a fashion statement in the eighties. They were snug-fitting and acceptable for even dressy occasions, often worn with a blazer. The blazer, made popular by Bill Blass, was a staple in the wardrobe as was the cotton jersey T-shirt. The long evening skirt in black, especially black velvet, as well as tartan plaid remained popular throughout the decade. Sometimes a blazer was added to create an evening suit.

Exercise was popular and the leotard appeared originally for workouts, and later in clothing designs worn with pants and skirts. The string bikini was a new swimsuit addition. Disco dressing was a fashion phenomenon replacing the earlier flashier styles. Mini skirts and even micro minis were worn with Lurex tube tops and high-heeled sandals. Shiny fabrics like satin, velvet, and PVC were used. In 1977 the movie, *Saturday Night Fever,* showed John Travolta in a formfitting white Dacron leisure suit with flared trousers, a black Quiana nylon shirt and platform shoes; polyester clothing soon became synonymous with the disco scene.

Calvin Klein received three Coty Awards in the seventies for his separates, all based on finely tailored silhouettes. Ethnic fashion was also a trend. In 1976, Yves Saint Laurent created "Russian" fashions, followed by his Chinese collection inspired by President Richard Nixon's trip to China. Japanese designer, Kenzo Takada, added to Western dress accents like kimono sleeves, shawls, and layered looks. Giorgio di Sant'Angelo designed clothing with ethnic influences, such as the peasant-style caftan. Stephen Burrows designed collections influenced by African-American popular dance. Dashikis, headcloths, and the Afro hairstyle were in vogue. Ralph Lauren showed the "prairie look" toward the end of the decade. Laura Ashley began designing textiles for the home and later developed an English country dress style reminiscent of Victorian and Edwardian dress with fitted bodices, high necks, and long skirts.

Boutiques in department stores featured the labels of less expensive designers, and couture was obviously not the only influence on styles. Millinery and couture departments closed. Women had their own ideas about dress and personal choice prevailed. Fashion designers such as Zandra Rhodes showed punk designs that helped make an antifashion style fashionable. Ready-to-wear manufacturers were able to produce a variety of clothing that met women's fashion needs. Another factor in the decreasing role of couturiers was that many of the great early designers such as Chanel, Balenciaga, Schiaparelli, Vionnet, and Norell died in the seventies, leaving serious voids along with their legacies.

Women were creating their own personal style of dress. "Retro" mania created interest in vintage clothing and auction houses began selling antique and vintage clothing. The platform cork espadrille was one "retro" item rediscovered for women.

In the early seventies, men's fashions went wide, especially lapels and ties. Ties reached a record five inches across. Flowered and psychedelic ties and bow ties in cotton fabrics were favorites. Bold striped or patterned dress shirts with long pointed collars were worn with polyester knit suits. Knit trousers were also very popular, with back-buckled Western-wear pockets and flared pants. Blunt, chunky-heeled, square-toed shoes or Frye boots accentuated fitted and flared trousers. Men wore their hair long with big sideburns. Long, straight hair was now fashionable for both sexes and unisex clothing like body-tight, ribbed turtlenecks, and flared pants were the trend. African-American influences on fashion were seen in high-heeled boots, black turtlenecks, and leather coats. The turtleneck worn under jackets was popularized in movies and became a fashion statement for men in the seventies.

Italian designer Armani was one of the only couture designers who first designed men's fashions, followed by a collection for women. He designed soft clothing and was known for tweeds on tweeds. Other designers like Pierre Cardin and Ralph Lauren designed for men as well. At the close of the seventies, men's fashions evolved to a more individualized mode of dress.

## Signature Fabrics of the 1970s

Cottons, linen, wool, silk for the return of natural fabrics for separates and dresswear

Wool doubleknit, wool jersey, silk jersey, wool crepe for dresses, skirts

Cotton cheesecloth for hippy dresses

Velvets for dresses

Suede for suits, jackets, and handbags

Corduroy for flares

Synthetic blends for cotton rayon, nylon jersey for dresses

Synthetics:

    Lycra used for leotards, seamless underwear

Polyesters used in men's leisure suits and men's and women's shirts and pantsuits

Acrilan for sweaters

Faux fur for coats, trims, clothing

Ultrasuede used in dresses and pantsuits; a favorite of the fashion designer Halston

Viscose rayon for gowns

Nylon for lingerie

## Important Designers and Manufacturers of the 1970s

**ADOLFO:** In the seventies, Adolfo featured clean-lined knit designs, such as crocheted halter dresses and Chanel-inspired suits in bouclé yarns.

**GIORGIO ARMANI:** Armani began his career as a menswear designer. He is, perhaps, most famous for his men's suits; however, his later designs for women share the same understated style of these suits. One of his most influential designs of the seventies was his loose-cut blazers.

**LAURA ASHLEY:** In the 1970s, Ashley began to use an Edwardian style with high collars and leg-of-mutton sleeves. Most of her fabrics were floral motifs inspired by textile designs of the eighteenth and nineteenth centuries.

**GEOFFREY BEENE:** Beene's designs of the early seventies were similar to his wool dresses with collars and cuffs from the sixties. In the late seventies, he showed a generous, skirted look on pants, jumpsuits, and pajamas. In addition to his couture line, Beene had less expensive collections under the names Beene Bazaar, Beene Boutique, and Beene Bag.

**LAURA BIAGIOTTI:** Biagiotti opened her own design studio in Florence, Italy, in 1972. Having taken over a knitwear company, she showed practical, low-maintenance cashmere dresses. Biagiotti was able to design the "transseasonal" wardrobe with casual but elegant classic separates.

**BILL BLASS:** Bill Blass's best-known design of the seventies was his single-breasted blazer with a single button. He showed these jackets with pants. Blassport was his less expensive line.

**DONALD BROOKS:** Brooks began designing under his own label in 1958. The following year he began a career as a costume designer for both theater and film. He is known for promoting the chemise and for his clean, unadorned dresses, coats, and stoles. Brooks's designs are styled in distinctive fabrics most of which are of his own design.

**STEPHEN BURROWS:** In the mid-seventies, Stephen Burrows was known for his daring fashion designs: leather clothes decorated with studded nails, disco fashions in matte jersey, and garments of jersey with zigzag stitching and lettuce edges.

**PIERRE CARDIN:** In 1970, Pierre Cardin's belted, cardigan suit for men helped promote a more casual suited look. His fashions for women were uncomplicated and bold with strong lines. He experimented with more fluid materials in the seventies like angora jersey.

**BONNIE CASHIN:** In the seventies, Cashin started the Knittery, which produced her handmade sweater designs. She showed short and long dresses, long skirts unbuttoned over pants, and tunics over leggings. She also designed leather purses.

**HOUSE OF CHANEL:** Suits, gilt-chained purses, and pearls.

**LIZ CLAIBORNE:** In the mid-seventies, when Liz Claiborne first began to design independently, she strived to meet the demands of working women who needed moderately priced clothing for work and leisure.

**OSSIE CLARK:** British designer Ossie Clark featured classic seventies styles: hot pants, maxi coats, handkerchief-point hemlines on long "Gypsy" dresses and skirts, and wraparound dresses which exposed part of the back. In 1975, Clark worked for the dress manufacturer, Radley, designing crepe and chiffon ready-to-wear evening attire.

**OSCAR DE LA RENTA:** Whether from his couture or ready-to-wear collections for women, Oscar de la Renta's day and evening designs were bright and upbeat in the seventies. As in the sixties, his most renowned designs were cocktail dresses and ball gowns. Many of these evening dresses had flounced skirts and fitted bodices with cummerbunds at the waist. He used a variety of fabrics in solids and prints, with patterns from Persian rug designs.

**FRYE:** The Frye Company was founded in 1863 by John Frye, a shoemaker from England. The company was family run until 1945. Frye boots have a long and interesting history. Frye boots were worn by Teddy Roosevelt and his Rough Riders, and during World War II thousands of servicemen ordered Frye's Wellingtons, called Jet Boots. Frye boots were used in most Hollywood westerns. In the 1960s Frye showed the Campus Boot based on the original 1860s boot—bulky toe and chunky heel that came to represent the styles and attitudes of the 1960s and 1970s. In 1971 and in 1975 Frye was awarded the American Shoe Designer Award by the Leather Industries of America.

**BILL GIBB:** A very admired designer in the seventies, Gibb created chiffon evening dresses and jersey dresses with appliqué and embroidery. In 1974, Gibb produced a successful knitwear collection. His firm closed in the late seventies.

**GUCCI:** In the seventies, Gucci accessories, especially purses and scarves, which appeared earlier were coveted by the label-conscious consumer.

**HALSTON:** Halston's most well-known seventies design was the halter-top dress that clung from the body to the ankles. He had several other dress designs in the seventies including cashmere dresses, loose-fitting caftan-style dresses, and strapless, long dresses with a sarong tying over the breasts. In 1972, he designed a "shirtwaister" in Ultrasuede which was copied by many.

**CATHY HARDWICK:** Cathy Hardwick was known in the seventies for her affordable separates, designed to coordinate with previous years' collections.

**BETSEY JOHNSON:** In the seventies, Betsey Johnson was best known for her stretchy designs of matte jersey for disco dancing. Other designs sported her signature spirit, including brightly colored knits, high-waisted, hip-hugger pants, and Princess-style dresses. She also created bathing suits, retro sundresses, and off-the-shoulder tops with leggings.

**NORMA KAMALI:** Norma Kamali first established herself in the seventies with her quilted coats of nylon and down. Her second-most popular collection used sweatshirt material for pants, jackets, shirts, and short cheerleader skirts. In the mid and late seventies, Kamali showed suits, silk dresses, and wrap bathing suits that were all one-piece.

**KENZO:** By 1972 Kenzo was known for his brilliantly colored designs in cotton. He produced many-layered styles including tunics, smocks, wide-legged pants, and garments in velvet. He also revolutionized designs in knitwear. He was able to combine Eastern and Western dress in contemporary styles.

**ANNE KLEIN:** In the seventies, Anne Klein was known for her sportswear designs, including wasp-waisted dresses, blazers, and battle jackets. Her separates with their well-cut lines were very popular throughout the decade: hooded blouson tops, jersey dresses, bodysuits with zipped-on miniskirts, kilts, and knickers,. In 1974, Anne Klein died and Donna Karan and Louis Dell'Olio took over the designing. Her house continues to create designs today.

**CALVIN KLEIN:** In the early seventies, Calvin Klein showed sportswear collections which included coatdresses, jumpsuits, his famous blazer pantsuits, tank tops, and shirt jackets. His sportswear was known for its clean lines and soft tailoring. In the late seventies, Klein's designs became increasingly sophisticated with slim-line coats, loosely cut jackets and blazers, and linen and silk designs. His designer jeans took off in the late seventies and remained very popular in the eighties.

**KRIZIA:** Krizia Company—Kriziamaglia—was founded in Milan, Italy, by Mariuccia Mandelli. Her lighthearted yet alluring designs were featured in knitwear and ready-to-wear fashions. In the 1970s she showed her signature animal motif on her garments. She is also known for her pleated eveningwear.

**RALPH LAUREN:** Ralph Lauren's seventies collections were inspired by English country fashion with hacking jackets and hunting clothes. His other collections included women's suits with men's-style tailoring, Fair Isle sweaters, pleated skirts, walking shorts, and trenchcoats. In 1974, he created the costume designs in linen for the movie *The Great Gatsby*. In the late seventies, Ralph Lauren came out with his "prairie look" design, denim skirt over a petticoat.

**KARL LAGERFELD FOR CHLOÉ:** In the mid-seventies, when designing for Chloé, Karl Lagerfeld showed shepherdess-style dresses with scarves tied around the torso and waist to form a bodice.

**BOB MACKIE:** In the seventies, Bob Mackie was best known for his floor-length evening dresses worn by Carol Burnett and Cher on their respective television shows.

**MARY MCFADDEN:** In the mid-seventies, Mary McFadden was established as an independent company. The house's first collection included charmeuse robes with one shoulder and quilted vests with Chinese decoration. Other collections included Fortuny-style silks for dresses with hand-painted or quilted patterns in international motifs. Throughout the decade, however, McFadden was best known for her quilted coats and jackets with Middle Eastern, oriental, or African designs.

**MISSONI:** Ottavio (Tai) Missoni and his wife Rosita Jelmini are the design team of Missoni. In the 1970s they produced knitwear, dresses, sweaters, suits, jackets, and coats, in bold designs with skillfully blended colors. They are most famous for their long cardigan sweaters and jackets.

**ISSEY MIYAKE:** In the seventies the Japanese designer Miyake developed his infamous layered and wrapped designs. He created his bold geometric fashions from the flow of the fabric, often also of his own design.

**ZANDRA RHODES:** In the seventies, Zandra Rhodes was known for her avant-garde designs. Rhodes's designs often used hand-screened chiffons and silks for interesting evening dresses with uneven hemlines. Rhodes used Art Deco motifs, zigzag patterns, as well as designing her own prints featuring large lipsticks or cacti. In the late seventies, she brought punk into high fashion with her pink dresses that featured gold pins and gold embroidered holes.

**YVES SAINT LAURENT:** In the early seventies, Yves Saint Laurent was best known for his signature blazers. In the mid-seventies, he showed peasant-inspired collections with bodices and long, full skirts, worn with boots. He also designed a line of tailored clothes for female executives.

**GIORGIO DI SANT' ANGELO:** In the seventies, Sant' Angelo designed innovative clothing of stretchy jersey. He showed leotards, bodysuits, and dresses with wrap skirts in this material with bright, bold-patterned prints. He created lines inspired by the Old West and Navajo and Gypsy cultures. Later, he designed more sophisticated lines for female executives.

**SCAASI:** During the seventies, Scaasi designed luxurious formal clothes, such as hand-painted crêpe de chine caftans. His specialty, however, continued to be evening dresses with small fitted waists and full skirts. Many of his designs used expensive bugle beading and some came with coordinating jewelry.

**GEORGE STAVROPOULOS:** In the sixties and seventies, Stavropoulos showed graceful, yet highly imaginative evening gowns.

**KENZO TAKADA:** Kenzo Takada brought exciting innovations to designers of the United States with his full, deep kimono-style sleeves and squared shoulders in his knitwear collection of separates and shawls.

**VALENTINO:** In the seventies, Valentino continued to design elegant clothes for evening, with dramatic details.

**DIANE VON FURSTENBERG:** Diane von Furstenberg's most popular design in the seventies was her mid-length wrap dress in geometric and floral printed jersey. Her wraparound dresses had long sleeves and closely fitted tops.

**KANSAI YAMAMOTO:** Yamamoto opened his design studio in 1971. He is known for his blending of traditional Japanese dress with that of Western daywear. His designs are seen as abstract and exotic.

## 1970s
## *Introduction Frontispiece*

1970S BILL GIBB'S SKIRT AND JACKET. Wrap-jacket embroidered with black and white ivy leaves, black and white ostrich feathers at neck and cuffs, batwing armhole, contrast stitching, five marbled polymer buttons, ivory silk crepe, white silk crepe de chine lining, excellent condition. $875 (See photograph on page 196)
*Courtesy of Enokiworld.*

## VINTAGE FASHIONS OF THE SEVENTIES

Halston Silk Dress. *Courtesy of
Enokiworld, www.enokiworld.com.
Photograph by Madeline Meyerowitz.*

1970s HALSTON SILK DRESS. Black silk crêpe de chine, tornado print
in orange and red on blouson top, gathered skirt, matching long sash
wraps at waist, matching shawl, excellent condition. $485
*Courtesy of Enokiworld.*

*The Ultimate in 1970s Evening Fashion.*

1973 Halston orange nylon knit evening dress. *Courtesy of Philadelphia Museum of Art. Gift of the Arons Family Foundation in memory of Edna S. Beron.* 1980s Salvatore Ferragamo leather evening sandals in gold. *Courtesy of Philadelphia Museum of Art. Gift of Mrs. Louis C. Madeira.* 1970 Kenneth Jay Lane gold-plated earrings with satin finish. *Courtesy of Philadelphia Museum of Art. Collection of the designer. All objects are accessioned and part of the permanent collection.*

Givenchy Sable Fur Coat. *Courtesy of Isadora's, WA,*
*www.isadoras.com. Photograph by Jennifer A. Ledda.*

1970s GIVENCHY SABLE FUR COAT. Deep rounded collar with slight
points in front, scalloped hem, full silk lining, made for I. Magnin,
"Givenchy for Alixandre," pristine condition. $7,775
*Courtesy of Isadora's, WA.*

Ossie Clark Halter Dress. *Courtesy of Enokiworld, www.enokiworld.com. Photograph by Madeline Meyerowitz.*

**1970s Ossie Clark Halter Dress.** Two-piece dress, fire engine red moss crepe, wide parted collar, halter, peplum waist, long fitted skirt, flared hem, "Ossie Clark for Radley," excellent condition. $695
*Courtesy of Enokiworld*

*Detail of Emilio Pucci Dress:* Pucci print. *Photograph by Linda Ames.*

Emilio Pucci Dress. *Courtesy of Linda Ames, Vintage Textile, www.vintagetextile.com. Photograph by Linda Ames.*

**1970S EMILIO PUCCI DRESS.** Silk jersey, one-piece with printed top, formfitting, deep V neckline, skirt with deep soft pleats in front and back, zippered back, label: "Emilio Pucci—Made in Italy for Lord & Taylor," signed "Emilio" throughout the print, very good condition. $325 *Courtesy of Linda Ames, Vintage Textile.*

*Detail of Gown:* Trompe l'oeil necklace. *Photograph by Deborah Burke.*

Bob Mackie Gown. *Courtesy of Deborah Burke,*
*Antique & Vintage Dress Gallery,*
*www.antiquedress.com. Photograph by Deborah Burke.*

LATE 1970S BOB MACKIE GOWN. Silver, copper, gold, and white, allover beading, Egyptian-inspired, sheer brown net, bugle beads, rhinestones, trompe l'oeil necklace and twisted bead "rope," sheer beaded
sleeves, brown silk crepe removable lining, limited production, excellent
condition. $5,000
*Courtesy of Deborah Burke, Antique & Vintage Dress Gallery.*

Diane von Furstenburg Wrap Dress. *Courtesy of Darlene Dull and Jennifer Parker-Stanton, Cookie's Closet, www.cookiescloset.com. Photograph by Sanders Stanton.*

**1970s ORIGINAL DIANE VON FURSTENBURG WRAP DRESS.** Red jersey, white swirl design, easy to wear, very good condition. $195
*Courtesy of Darlene Dull and Jennifer Parker-Stanton, Cookie's Closet.*

1970s Ultrasuede Trenchcoat. *Courtesy of Darlene Dull and Jennifer Parker-Stanton, Cookie's Closet, www.cookiescloset.com. Photograph by Sanders Stanton.*

Lanvin of Paris Shirtwaist Dress. *Courtesy of Darlene Dull and Jennifer Parker-Stanton, Cookie's Closet, www.cookiescloset.com. Photograph by Sanders Stanton.*

**1970s Ultrasuede Trenchcoat.** Deep burgundy, belted, for I. Magnin by Haire for Friedrick's, very good condition. $98
*Courtesy of Darlene Dull and Jennifer Parker-Stanton, Cookie's Closet.*

**1970s Lanvin of Paris Shirtwaist Dress.** Italian end-paper design in pinks and greens, self-tie belt, very good condition. $75
*Courtesy of Darlene Dull and Jennifer Parker-Stanton, Cookie's Closet.*

*1920s Summer Chemise Dress.* Sunshine yellow organdy, hand-embroidered flowers, lace hem, no slip attached, excellent condition. $300.
*Courtesy of Mary Troncale, CT. Photograph by Tom Amico.*

*1920s Wire-Frame Hat.* Lace crown, wide silk brim with hand stitching, decorated with bouquet of silk roses, perfect. $425. *Courtesy of Linda Ames, Vintage Textile, www.vintagetextile.com. Photograph by Linda Ames.*

*1920s Opera Coat.* Orange velvet, metallic gold thread, oriental motif with coral and pink beadwork, jet beads, full sleeves, excellent condition. $900. *Courtesy of Mary Troncale, CT. Photograph by Tom Amico.*

*1920s Chemise Dress.* Black silk floral chiffon, border print neckline, shirring in sleeve and center front, pleated skirt, rhinestone belt buckle, covered buttons on cuff, no slip, excellent condition. $275. *Courtesy of Mary Troncale, CT. Photograph by Tom Amico.*

*1930s Silk Chiffon Dress.* Netted trim, square neckline, design of brightly colored flowers, pristine condition. $625. *Courtesy of Isadora's, WA, www.isadoras.com. Photograph by Jennifer A. Ledda.*

*1930s Evening Dress.* Halter top, green and pink sequins on brown silk chiffon, backless, mint condition. $900. *Courtesy of Mary Troncale, CT. Photograph by Tom Amico.*

*1930s Chiffon Dress.* Floral chiffon, rose corsage, excellent condition. $250. *Courtesy of Mary Troncale, CT. Photograph by Tom Amico.*

*1940s Three-Piece Ensemble.* Suit with matching coat, brown wool, contrasting forest green top stitching on jacket and coat, fully lined, exceptional detailing, covered buttons, mint condition. $375. *Courtesy of Pepper, NY. Photograph by Tom Amico.*

*1940s Sequined Dress.* Black crepe skirt, white top with black sequins, accented with a sequined stemmed red rose, short-sleeve, mint condition. $250. *Courtesy of Mary Troncale, CT. Photograph by Tom Amico.*

*1940s Rayon Dress.* "Face and bird print," side drape at hip, side closure, excellent condition. $200. *Courtesy of Mary Troncale, CT. Photograph by Tom Amico.*

*1950s Cocktail Dress.* "New Look," crepe top, taffeta plaid skirt, slim belt, "New York Creation," excellent condition. $225.
*Courtesy of Gisele Ferari.*
*Photograph by Tom Amico.*

*1950s Ben Reig Dress.* Two-piece, navy silk, buttons front and hips, "New Look," excellent condition. $395. *Courtesy of Patina, NY. Photograph by Tom Amico.*

*1960s Roberta di Camerino Handbags.* "Made in Italy" all in mint condition with signature "R". Small cranberry velvet with blue stripe, leather interior. $350. Rectangular cranberry flocked velvet, leather interior with three compartments. $500. Blue cut-velvet, satin-lined pouch. $450.
*Courtesy of Vintage by Stacey Lee, NY.*
*Photograph by Tom Amico.*

*1960s Pierre Cardin Dress.* Tomato red, double-knit shift, vinyl polka dots, vinyl trim, excellent condition. $1,200. *Courtesy of Resurrection, NY. Photograph by Tom Amico.*

*1960s Guy Laroche Cocktail Suit.* Wool and gold metallic thread, silk lining, covered buttons, "Made in France for Jordan Marsh," mint condition. $325. *Courtesy of Patina, NY. Photograph by Tom Amico.*

*1960s Ken Scott Dress.* Nylon shift, red-and-yellow geometric print, patch pocket, perfect condition. $275. *Courtesy of Patina, NY. Photograph by Tom Amico.*

*c.1960s Cocktail Dress.* Cherry red, beaded silk, sweetheart neckline, silk chiffon overblouse; skirt, gathered at waist, front panel with pulled tulip hem, excellent condition. $550. *Courtesy of Mary Troncale, CT. Photograph by Tom Amico.*

*1970s Shoes.*
*(Left)*
Loafers—leather,
platform soles, black
piping edges to brown patches,
leather laces, 3.5-inch heels, "Made in Greece." $64.
*(Middle)* Wooden-soled mules with plastic cherries clip—
raffia woven upper, painted carving in heels. $85.
*(Right)* Kid leather mules, holed overtoes, wedged heels with
holed overlay, "Capobianco, Paris." $85. *All Courtesy of Atomic*
*Passion, NY. Photograph by Tom Amico.*

*1970s Halter Dress.* Purple cut rayon velvet with
dewdrop pattern, "Estaban," excellent condition. $60.
*Courtesy of Atomic Passion, NY. Photograph by Tom Amico.*

*1970s Polyester Dress.* Multicolored floral,
contrasting bodice and skirt, elastic bands at waist
and neckline, "Goldworm brand, made in Italy,"
"Saks Fifth Avenue," excellent condition. $60.
*Courtesy of Atomic Passion, NY. Photograph by Tom Amico.*

*1970s George Stavropoulos Chiffon Dress.* Pink chiffon, tiers of sheer petals, surplice bodice of triple-layered chiffon backed with cherry silk crepe, high neckline, sheer sleeves, ruffled, matching scarf, excellent condition. $845. *Courtesy of Enokiworld, www.enokiworld.com. Photograph by Madeline Meyerowitz.*

*1970s Lizard Jacket.* Aqua lizard, lined, perfect condition. $450. *Courtesy of Patina, NY. Photograph by Tom Amico.*

*1970s Zandra Rhodes Cape.* Full-length, wool, "Henri Bendal Limited," pink and green patterning, mint green tassels at collar and cuffs, perfect condition $1,795. *Courtesy of Patina, NY. Photograph by Tom Amico.*

*1980s Skirt, Tube Top, and Matching Jacket.* Floral silk chiffon, modified polka-dot tube top with boning, silk corsage, gored skirt with handkerchief hem; matching jacket, purple chiffon lining, "Norma Waters New York," excellent condition. $200. *Courtesy of Author. Photograph by Tom Amico.*

*1990s Thierry Mugler Hot Pink Suit.* Side buckle, scalloped-edged jacket, mint. $350. *Courtesy of Pepper, NY. Photograph by Tom Amico.*

*1980s Smurf Dress.* Cotton, excellent condition. $145. *Courtesy of Enokiworld, www.enokiworld.com. Photograph by Madeline Meyerowitz.*

*1980s Carolina Herrera Cocktail Dress.* Blue satin with gold scrolled embellishment, excellent condition. $275. *Courtesy of Pepper, NY. Photograph by Tom Amico.*

*1980s Lanvin Velvet Two-Piece.* Green and red velvet pin-tucked stretch top, pin-pleated skirt, mint condition. $375. *Courtesy of Patina, NY. Photograph by Tom Amico.*

Nina Platform Pumps. *Courtesy of Enokiworld, www.enokiworld.com. Photograph by Madeline Meyerowitz.*

Missoni Silk Knit Top. *Courtesy of Enokiworld, www.enokiworld.com. Photograph by Madeline Meyerowitz.*

**1970s Missoni Silk Knit Top.** Zigzag silk knit in pink, pale peach, slate blue, and navy, contrasting weave around deeply slashed neckline, made for Bloomingdale's, excellent condition. $215
*Courtesy of Enokiworld.*

**1970s Nina Platform Pumps.** All-leather, having 2½″ platform and 5½″ heel, excellent condition. $205
*Courtesy of Enokiworld.*

1970s Lovable Bells. *Courtesy of Darlene Dull & Jennifer Parker-Stanton, Cookie's Closet, www.cookiescloset.com. Photograph by Sanders Stanton.*

**1970s LOVABLE BELLS.** Navy and white cotton, bell-bottoms, "lovable" print, excellent condition. $65
*Courtesy of Darlene Dull and Jennifer Parker-Stanton, Cookie's Closet.*

Yves Saint Laurent Jacket. *Courtesy of Linda Ames, Vintage Textile, www.vintage textile.com. Photograph by Linda Ames.*

Guy Laroche Jacket. *Courtesy of The Way We Wore, Cookie's Closet, www.cookiescloset.com. Photograph by Sanders Stanton.*

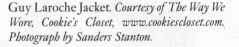

**1970s YVES SAINT LAURENT JACKET.** Beaded burgundy wool and black velvet short jacket, black velvet appliqué outlining center panel decorated with jet beads and black cording, edges of jacket and cuffs outlined with black braid piping, black satin lining, excellent condition. $285
*Courtesy of Linda Ames, Vintage Textile.*

**1970s GUY LAROCHE JACKET.** Printed plush velvet cotton, tailored fit, no vents, double-breasted lapel, excellent condition. $150

Magazine Pocketbook. *Courtesy of Screaming Mimi's, New York, NY. Photograph by Tom Amico.*

1970S MAGAZINE POCKETBOOK. "Jours de France" made to look like a rolled magazine, excellent condition. $200
*Courtesy of Screaming Mimi's, NY.*

Shirts. *Courtesy of From Around the World Vintage, New York, NY. Photograph by Tom Amico.*

Print Blouses. *Courtesy of Screaming Mimi's, New York, NY. Photograph by Tom Amico.*

**1970s SHIRT.** Polyester multi-stripe, zippered front, "Miss Holly," excellent condition. $50

**1970s SHIRT.** Polyester paisley and floral print, fitted, "Aileen," excellent condition. $45
*Both Courtesy of From Around the World Vintage, NY.*

**1970s PRINT BLOUSES.** Nylon, excellent condition, multi $38, cream $35
*Both Courtesy of Screaming Mimi's, New York, NY.*

1970s Jeans Jacket. *Courtesy of Atomic Passion, NY. Photograph by Tom Amico.*

**1970S JEANS JACKET.** Patches and embroidery, "Sears Roebuck hand-done patches" flannel lined, excellent condition. $78
*Courtesy of Atomic Passion, NY.*

Shirts. *Courtesy of From Around the World Vintage, New York, NY. Photograph by Tom Amico.*

Western Shirt. *Courtesy of From Around the World Vintage, New York, NY. Photograph by Tom Amico.*

**1970S SHIRT.** Men's polyester, orange with flocked dots, manufacturer: "Lilly Daché," excellent condition. $75

**1970S SHIRT.** Men's nylon acetate, psychedelic design in blues and oranges, "Mickey Mouse," excellent condition. $100

**1970S SHIRT.** Men's polyester, in style of Robin Hood, "No Fade for Anthony's," excellent condition. $100

*All Courtesy of From Around the World Vintage, NY.*

**1970S WESTERN SHIRT.** Men's black polyester, embroidered, nylon fringe, "H Bar C Ranchwear," mint condition. $250
*Courtesy of From Around the World Vintage, New York, NY.*

Athletic Jackets.
*Courtesy of From
Around the World
Vintage, New York,
NY. Photograph by
Tom Amico.*

Suits. *Courtesy of
Screaming Mimi's,
New York, NY.
Photograph by Tom
Amico.*

1970s MEN'S ATHLETIC JACKETS. Double-knit, both in very good condition, "JC Penney the Fox." $75; "Safari Sportswear." $150
*Both Courtesy of From Around the World Vintage, NY.*

1970s MEN'S SUITS. Both "New Old Stock," brown polyester, plaid trim, bell-bottoms, "Valdenti." $110
Green plaid polyester, plaid trim, bell-bottoms. $150
*Both Courtesy of Screaming Mimi's, NY*

## MARKET TRENDS FOR THE SEVENTIES

### Lingerie

**1970s MINI HALF-SLIP.** In tropical sherbert hues, scallop-edged hem, nylon, by Vanity Fair, excellent condition. $30
*Courtesy of Enokiworld, www.enokiworld.com*

### Swimwear

**1970s DANSKIN SWIMSUIT AND MATCHING WRAP SKIRT.** Strapless maillot, stylized pheasant feather print in cerulean blue, magenta, pink, and indigo on deep violet background, button strap option, built-in shelf bra, excellent condition. $125
*Courtesy of Enokiworld, www.enokiworld.com*

### Separates

**1970s FLORAL PRINT POLYESTER BLOUSE.** Navy blue floral print, white ground, large pointed collar, long sleeves, "JC Penney," excellent condition. $45
*Courtesy of www.fashiondig.com*

**1970s VERA COTTON BUTTON-DOWN BLOUSE.** Brushed cotton, big dots soften the bold geometry of two blue angular brush strokes, excellent condition. $45
*Courtesy of Enokiworld, www.enokiworld.com*

**1970s WOMAN'S BELL-BOTTOM PANTS.** Zippered front, shiny copper penny color faux fur, excellent condition. $65
*Courtesy of Lynn Pastore, Avenue 13–5 and Dime Vintage, www.510vintage.com*

**1970s LEVI'S BELL-BOTTOM JEANS.** Flared more than belled, original 1970s Levi's, 100% cotton but very soft (almost velvety), "New Old Stock," excellent condition. $50
*Courtesy of Lynn Pastore, Avenue 13–5 and Dime Vintage, www.510vintage.com*

**1970s LEE BELL-BOTTOM JEANS.** Medium blue, very hard to find Lee bells, excellent condition. $50
*Courtesy of Lynn Pastore, Avenue 13–5 and Dime Vintage, www.510vintage.com*

**1970s JEANS.** Cotton, lace trimmed, flower patches, label: "Petit Fors," excellent condition, $125
*Courtesy of From Around The World Vintage, New York, NY.*

**1970s DENIM CULOTTES.** Multi-stitched striping, excellent condition. $55
*Courtesy of Screaming Mimi's, New York, NY.*

**1970s VEST.** Black suede, white crochet and embroidery, crocheted buttons, "JGEE," excellent condition. $45
*Courtesy of Screaming Mimi's, New York, NY.*

**1970s VEST.** Rust suede, crochet and embroidery, excellent condition. $45
*Courtesy of Screaming Mimi's, New York, NY.*

**1970s CHERRY CASHMERE SWEATER WITH BUTTON SHOULDER.** Gathered shoulders, four pearly red buttons over left shoulder, made for Lord & Taylor, excellent condition. $70
*Courtesy of Enokiworld, www.enokiworld.com*

**1970s SONIA RYKIEL "FLOWER" SWEATER.** Black lambswool, flat "flower" detail along neckline, each cluster centered with one clear rhinestone, nape has wool ribbon tying in small bow, deeply ribbed cuffs, hip-length, excellent condition. $105
*Courtesy of Enokiworld, www.enokiworld.com*

**1970s LILLY PULITZER HYACINTH PRINT SKIRT.** Pink, cotton and acrylic blend, purple iris and hyacinth print with turquoise foliage and deep pink blossoms, cotton lace appliqué down the center, pocket on right, white lining, bar and tab closure, zippered back, excellent condition. $75
*Courtesy of Enokiworld, www.enokiworld.com*

**1970s PINK WOOL PLAID FLOOR-LENGTH SKIRT.** Pink tartan plaid with kelly green and sage undertones, accordion pleated through hips, flared at hem, made by Kelita, excellent condition. $175
*Courtesy of Enokiworld, www.enokiworld.com*

**1970s GUCCI SUEDE SKIRT.** Forest green, wide waistband, front inverted pleat, gilt metal chains with tiny plaques that say "Gucci"; moss green silk crepe lining is printed "Gucci," excellent condition. $315
*Courtesy of Enokiworld, www.enokiworld.com*

**1970s YSL RIVE GAUCHE LEATHER PANTS.** Lambskin, pleated front, slash pockets, wide leg, two back button pockets, fire engine red acetate lining, 1½" belt loops, flawless condition. $475
*Courtesy of Enokiworld, www.enokiworld.com*

**1970s DONALD BROOKS QUILTED SILK PAISLEY JACKET.** Burgundy with emerald, cherry, lemon, and white, no buttons, meant to be worn open, shawl collar, cantaloupe-hued silk crepe lining, excellent condition. $260
*Courtesy of Enokiworld, www.enokiworld.com*

**1970S BAGATELLE BELTED SUEDE SHIRTJACKET.** Wine colored, matching sash belt, raglan sleeves, subtle pleating along shoulder, chunky marbled buttons along placket, curved pockets at hip, split hem, excellent condition. $85
*Courtesy of Enokiworld, www.enokiworld.com*

**1970S ANNE KLEIN CHARCOAL WOOL JERSEY FLOOR-LENGTH SKIRT.** Slim through hips, black silk crêpe de chine lining, flawless condition. $195
*Courtesy of Enokiworld, www.enokiworld.com*

**1970S CATHY HARDWICK SEQUINED SWEATER AND SKIRT.** Magenta wool, wool and nylon blend, fuchsia and cherry red sequins on both, clear and red bugle beads on sweater between the bands of pink and red emphasizing the horizontal line, cap sleeves, excellent condition. $225
*Courtesy of Enokiworld, www.enokiworld.com*

**1970S ANDRÉS COURRÈGES JUMPSUIT.** Blue velvet, zippered front, drawstring waist and sleeves, nylon lining, label: "Made in France," excellent condition. $650
*Courtesy of Vintage by Stacey Lee, White Plains, NY.*

**1970S JUMPSUIT.** Burnt orange, label: "Bon Jour," excellent condition. $75
*Courtesy of Atomic Passion, New York, NY.*

## Dresses

**1970S LILLY PULITZER HALTER DRESS.** Rose print in bright green and pink, signature cotton lace trim, cotton and polyester blend, excellent condition. $160
*Courtesy of Enokiworld, www.enokiworld.com*

**1970S GEOFFREY BEENE PEASANT DRESS.** Gossamer raw silk, pale celadon, low-tie front neckline, meticulous details, cartridge pleats along scooped back, matching elastic braided belt, flawless condition. $515
*Courtesy of Enokiworld, www.enokiworld.com*

**1970S ULTRASUEDE DRESS.** Cerulean blue, jewel neckline, dropped yoke waist, sash belt, blue silk crepe lining, "Count Romi," excellent condition. $95
*Courtesy of Enokiworld, www.enokiworld.com*

**1970S SWEATER DRESS.** Bronze metallic, polyester, and acrylic knit, pointelle details at neckline and cuffs, cowl neck, ribbed waist, ribbed sleeves, pointelle flowers at bodice and hem, "Wenjilli," excellent condition. $60
*Courtesy of Atomic Passion, New York, NY.*

**1970S LANVIN BELTED SHIRTDRESS.** Scalloped green and white stripe, nylon jersey, placket has retro daises in navy and red, extra-wide sash, excellent condition. $205
*Courtesy of Enokiworld, www.enokiworld.com*

**1970S DONNA KARAN AND ANNE KLEIN WOOL WRAP DRESS.** Chocolate wool and cashmere jersey, fixed wrap, zippered back, surplice bodice, draped skirt, cocoa silk crepe lining, excellent condition. $345
*Courtesy of Enokiworld, www.enokiworld.com*

**1970S YVES SAINT LAURENT THREE-PIECE PEASANT DRESS.** Sage wool crepe skirt with accents of caramel, lavender, and olive, matching silk crepe blouse, asymmetrical buttons, waist sash, long attached neck scarf, "Yves Saint Laurent Rive Gauche," flawless condition. $245
*Courtesy of Enokiworld, www.enokiworld.com*

**1970S PIERRE CARDIN DRESS.** 1930s-inspired, polyester crepe, gently elasticized waist, inseam pockets, white charmeuse lining, labels: "Neiman Marcus" and "Pierre Cardin Paris," excellent condition. $165
*Courtesy of Enokiworld, www.enokiworld.com*

**1970S LILLY PULITZER RUFFLED SCOOP HALTER.** Spider mums print in lemon, lime, and raspberry, high Empire waist, pleated ruffle hemline, cotton polyester blend, 58″ length, excellent condition. $145
*Courtesy of Enokiworld, www.enokiworld.com*

**1970S LANVIN BELTED ANKLE-LENGTH SHIRTDRESS.** Polyester crepe, stylized flowers print, midnight blue, emerald green, and navy, white ground, matching wide-sash belt, wide-pointed collar, double-button barrel cuffs, covered buttons from neck to hem, excellent condition. $295
*Courtesy of Enokiworld, www.enokiworld.com*

**1970S LANVIN AZTEC PRINT BELTED SHIRTDRESS.** Matte nylon jersey, predominantly red, white, green, midnight blue, and yellow across center, pointed collar, matching wide-sash belt, excellent condition. $245
*Courtesy of Enokiworld, www.enokiworld.com*

**1970S GUSTAVE TASSELL FOR NORELL SILK DRESS.** Black silk jersey asymmetrically draped at shoulder, gathered over hip, elegant simplicity, excellent condition. $810
*Courtesy of Enokiworld, www.enokiworld.com*

**1970S DONALD BROOKS TWO-PIECE PEASANT WENCH DRESS.** Printed cotton seersucker, striped corset blouse with front lacing, flared peplum, long floral skirt with matching long scarf, cherry silk crepe lining top, excellent condition. $260
*Courtesy of Enokiworld, www.enokiworld.com*

1970S HALSTON ULTRASUEDE APRON DRESS. Pink-tinged Ultrasuede, buttons underneath at waist, ties back, simple, excellent condition. $310
*Courtesy of Enokiworld, www.enokiworld.com*

1970S MARIMEKKO PINK AND ORANGE SHIRTDRESS WITH TINY
POCKETS. Bright cerise, orange polka dots, five tiny patch pockets
placed randomly along bodice placket, polished stainless-steel buttons,
excellent condition. $190
*Courtesy of Enokiworld, www.enokiworld.com*

1970S BIBA COLUMN DRESS WITH RED LACE. Black synthetic satin,
cherry red lace banding at midriff, upper thigh, and hem, zippered side,
slit to knee on one side, excellent condition. $205
*Courtesy of Enokiworld, www.enokiworld.com*

1970S PAULINE TRIGÈRE RED WOOL DRESS. Red heavyweight wool
jersey, line of diagonally set pleats across abdomen, slightly high neckline, long, fitted sleeves, cherry silk crêpe de chine bodice, excellent condition. $170
*Courtesy of Enokiworld, www.enokiworld.com*

1970S JOHN BATES LEATHER BATWING DRESS. Band collar fastens at throat leaves the chest open, gentle pleating flanking sides of
placket, enormous batwing sleeves from waist to shoulder with arm
extension, belted waist, inseam pockets, black silk crepe lining, excellent condition. $1,150
*Courtesy of Enokiworld, www.enokiworld.com*

1970S HALSTON CASHMERE TWO-PIECE DRESS. Deep purple cashmere, draped batwing sleeves, boatneck collar high on the neck, purple
silk waistband with attached purple silk half-slip, black lace trim, two
inseam pockets, flawless condition. $325
*Courtesy of Enokiworld, www.enokiworld.com*

1970S ALBERT CAPRARO WOOL SHIRTDRESS. Lightweight wool
serge, collarless, autumn shade of heather brick, matching belt, double
silver belt loops, flawless condition. $85
*Courtesy of Enokiworld, www.enokiworld.com*

1970S DIANE VON FURSTENBERG BLACK AND WHITE WRAP
DRESS. Cotton and rayon jersey, abstract print in zebra-like stripes,
décolletage, pointed French cuffs, made in Italy, excellent condition. $260
*Courtesy of Enokiworld, www.enokiworld.com*

1970S LEONARD CAP SLEEVE DRESS. Medium-weight silk jersey,
chemise, slightly squared neckline, hem, silk print palm frond and

anemone, green, indigo, and lilac, with blue and pink accents, cap sleeves lined in black, matching tie belt, hanging fobs stamped "Leonard," excellent condition. $165
*Courtesy of Enokiworld, www.enokiworld.com*

**1970s EMILIO PUCCI SILK QUEEN ANNE'S LACE DRESS.** Peacock blue, violet, and white Queen Anne's lace print on black, pointed collar, plunging neckline, 57″ l, excellent condition. $985
*Courtesy of Enokiworld, www.enokiworld.com*

**1970s VIOLET CREPE COWL.** Draped neckline with deeper cowl at back, Grecian-inspired, tulip hemline higher in front with cleft revealing knees, skirt of two layers semi-sheer crepe, "Made by The Gilberts for Tally," flawless condition. $260
*Courtesy of Enokiworld, www.enokiworld.com*

**1970s OSSIE CLARK SPANGLED GOWN.** Viscose, spangled ruby gown, tiny swirling clusters of sparkling cerise allover, column turns around from front to stunning back, five satin buttons at back of neck, made for Lady Corina Frost, model for Ossie Clark, and wife of talk show host, David Frost, label: "Ossie Clark," flawless condition. $725
*Courtesy of Enokiworld, www.enokiworld.com*

**1970s HALSTON WOOL DRESS WITH MATCHING SHAWL.** Black wool knit with a diagonal band of wine and royal blue sleeve, matching massive triangular shawl, echoing bands of wine and blue at one corner, medium-weight wool jersey, excellent condition. $265
*Courtesy of Enokiworld, www.enokiworld.com*

**1970s GEOFFREY BEENE SWEATER DRESS.** Camel-hued knit, welted pleats along slash neckline with thin attached ties, wide sleeves, inseam pockets at each hip, excellent condition. $210
*Courtesy of Enokiworld, www.enokiworld.com*

**1970s RALPH LAUREN PRAIRIE SUNDRESS.** Pale pink cotton, allover tiny blue flowers with yellow highlights on mauve stems, fitted bodice, thin straps crisscross at back, full gathered skirt, hidden hip pockets, excellent condition. $170
*Courtesy of Enokiworld, www.enokiworld.com*

**1970s OSCAR DE LA RENTA VELVET PEASANT DRESS.** Black silk velvet, ruching at shoulders, full sleeves, pair of silk button and loop closures at wrist, row of silk buttons at neck, small slits at sides of hem, inseam pockets, black silk crepe lining, excellent condition. $135
*Courtesy of Enokiworld, www.enokiworld.com*

**1970s LANVIN IVY-PRINTED BELTED SHIRTDRESS.** Nylon crepe, teal, royal blue, and cherry, black and white foundation, tailored button placket, wide-pointed collar, matching covered buttons, wide sash belt, machine washable and air dry, excellent condition. $215
*Courtesy of Enokiworld, www.enokiworld.com*

**1970s OP ART DAISY.** Soft cotton, concentric circles, black and white with magenta centers, form Op Art daisies, wide-spread collar, low-slung ring belt, black cherry buttons, excellent condition. $105
*Courtesy of Enokiworld, www.enokiworld.com*

**1970s DONALD BROOKS LEOPARD SILK SHIRTDRESS.** Supple silk leopard print, buttoning to the waist with a row of matching covered buttons, black silk lining, matching long wide sash, inseam pockets at each hip, flawless condition. $305
*Courtesy of Enokiworld, www.enokiworld.com*

**1970s MOLLIE PARNIS BOUTIQUE COWL NECK AND WRAP SKIRT.** Purple wool, silk, and angora, modified cowl neckline, zippered back, thin-ribbed allover, ankle-length wrap skirt, inverted pleats at waistband and inseam pockets, designed by Morty Sussman for Mollie Parnis Boutique, excellent condition. $135
*Courtesy of Enokiworld, www.enokiworld.com*

**1970s RUFFLED CHIFFON HALTER DRESS.** Turquoise chiffon print, peach and beige flowers, ruffle dips onto shoulders, ties at back of neck, lightweight nude muslin lining, "Made by Denise l. for Saks Fifth Avenue's Young Dimensions Boutique," excellent condition. $80
*Courtesy of Enokiworld, www.enokiworld.com*

**1970s BLACK GABARDINE DRESS WITH SUPER SLIT.** Acetate/nylon gabardine, squared neckline, moderately scooped back, thigh-high slit on left side, designed by Pierany Paris, excellent condition. $185
*Courtesy of Enokiworld, www.enokiworld.com*

**LANVIN IVY PRINT DRESS.** Nylon knit, fuchsia, violet, and lime ivy on black and white, ankle-length, stand-up neckline dips revealing cleavage, matching sash belt, washable, flawless condition. $195
*Courtesy of Enokiworld, www.enokiworld.com*

**1970s DONALD BROOKS LEOPARD GOWN WITH JEWELED BUCKLE.** Black spots on bronze brown background resembles fur, stand-up band collar, covered buttons, matching silk belt with Art Deco–inspired jeweled buckle, black silk crêpe de chine lining, flawless condition. $340
*Courtesy of Enokiworld, www.enokiworld.com*

**1970s HOLLY HARP SPIRAL CHIFFON DRESS.** Pale pink silk chiffon, shoulders sheer, dress becomes opaque with layered chiffon, 1930s-inspired, white silk crepe lining, excellent condition. $310
*Courtesy of Enokiworld, www.enokiworld.com*

**1970s MISSONI TWO-PIECE SET.** Gossamer rayon and metallic floral knit, gold, gray, and black, skirt 4″ yoke very full, V-neck top, shoulder yoke, striped rib-knit cuffs and waistband, excellent condition. $250
*Courtesy of Karen Augusta, Antique Lace & Fashion, www.antique-fashion.com*

**1970s VICTOR COSTA DRESS.** Polyester/jersey, full-length, navy, green, and yellow "Pucci-inspired" print, "Romantica by Victor Costa," excellent condition. $80
*Courtesy of www.fashiondig.com*

**1970s LEOPARD PRINT GOWN.** Polyester blend, wide-pointed collar, full front buttoning with gold-colored buttons, side splits, original belt, very good condition. $115
*Courtesy of www.fashiondig.com*

**1970s "GRANNY" DRESS.** Multicolored geometric print, 100% acetate knit, "Young Miss Morton," excellent condition. $120
*Courtesy of www.fashiondig.com*

## Evening Dresses

**1970s BILL BLASS RED SILK CHIFFON EVENING DRESS.** Bias-cut, with bodice flounce repeated around hem and edges of triangular matching stole, excellent condition. $695
*Courtesy of Linda Ames, Vintage Textile, www.vintagetextile.com*

**1970s CAROLYNE ROEHM EVENING DRESS.** Black and white corded silk, large bodice bow, long skirt softly pleated below hipline, excellent condition. $455
*Courtesy of Linda Ames, Vintage Textile, www.vintagetextile.com*

**1970s MOLLIE PARNIS, EVENING DRESS.** Black silk layered chiffon ending in ruffles at hem, rhinestone-studded bodice with narrow straps, self-bow at hip, very good condition. $685
*Courtesy of Linda Ames, Vintage Textile, www.vintagetextile.com*

**LAMÉ TUNIC OVER HAREM PANTS.** French cuffs, silk chiffon lining, "Yves Saint Laurent—Paris, numbered 39080," excellent condition. $1,135
*Courtesy of Linda Ames, Vintage Textile, www.vintagetextile.com*

**1970S BILL BLASS RAINBOW SILK EVENING DRESS.** Skirt with three layers of blue silk chiffon underneath rainbow-colored top layer, stole, excellent condition. $785
*Courtesy of Linda Ames, Vintage Textile, www.vintagetextile.com*

**LATE 1970S TWO-PIECE VELVET EVENING SET.** Silver gray panne velvet jacket and skirt, pleated jacket with plunging neckline, nipped waist, long sleeves, gathered skirt, "Saint Laurent Rive Gauche," excellent condition. $225
*Courtesy of fashiondig.com*

**1970S BILL BLASS BIAS-CUT EVENING GOWN.** Cream matte silk jersey, silk organza ruffles swirling diagonally to hem, bodice cut with single shoulder ruffle, no sleeve, excellent condition. $350
*Courtesy of www.fashiondig.com*

**1970S HANAE MORI PAINTED SILK CAFTAN.** Floating layer of painted chiffon over silk sheath underdress with same painting, satin cord back tie, excellent condition. $545
*Courtesy of Linda Ames, Vintage Textile, www.vintagetextile.com*

## Suits

**1970S MISSONI ROSEBUD SUIT.** Acetate blend, rose print, shades of chartreuse, magenta, and emerald, wide-pointed collar, large Lucite button, "Made for Neiman Marcus," flawless condition. $275
*Courtesy of Enokiworld, www.enokiworld.com*

**1970S BAGATELLE RUST VELVET SUIT.** Single-breasted tailored blazer, patch pockets, back vent, tangerine satin lining, skirt slim through hips, flares at calf with slit at knee, designed by Nicola Pelly for Bagatelle, flawless condition. $90
*Courtesy of Enokiworld, www.enokiworld.com*

**1970S ANNE KLEIN UNCONSTRUCTED WOOL KNIT SUIT.** Deep red wool and acrylic medium-weight knit, subtle ribbing at waist forms banded waistline, delicately embossed brass buttons, made for Sadimara, excellent condition. $155
*Courtesy of Enokiworld, www.enokiworld.com*

**1970S HALSTON DOUBLE-FACED WOOL SUIT.** Reversible taupe wool to teal, shaped jacket, seamed with split button cuffs, one-button closure, matching brushed wool skirt, two inseam hidden pockets worked into front seams, mocha silk crepe lining, made in Italy, flawless condition. $240
*Courtesy of Enokiworld, www.enokiworld.com*

1970s ANNE KLEIN SUIT WITH SUEDE ELBOW PATCHES. Camel and deep mahogany herringbone weave, fitted curved blazer over prairie-type skirt, front inverted pleat, deep hip pockets, suede patches at elbow, woven leather buttons, milk chocolate silk crepe lining, excellent condition. $120
*Courtesy of Enokiworld, www.enokiworld.com*

## Outerwear

c. 1970s GEOFFREY BEENE CROPPED JACKET. Double-breasted navy wool with military styling, oversized lapels, button-cuff sleeves, excellent condition. $150
*Courtesy of www.fashiondig.com*

1970s JILL THRAVES 1970s PATCHWORK JACKET. Wide lapels, high quality, satin lining, excellent condition. $75
*Courtesy of Lynn Pastore, Avenue 13–5 and Dime Vintage, CO,*
*www.510vintage.com*

1970s FUNKY TWEED JACKET. Tweed, black rabbit fur cuffs and collar, excellent condition. $65
*Courtesy of Lynn Pastore, Avenue 13–5 and Dime Vintage, CO,*
*www.510vintage.com*

1970s FAUX FUR COAT. Leopard print full-length coat, vinyl trim, satin lining, made in France by Jean Louis, excellent condition. $120
*Courtesy of Lynn Pastore, Avenue 13–5 and Dime Vintage, CO,*
*www.510vintage.com*

1970s GREEN SUEDE COAT. Black leather trim and buttons, very well made, great details, Big Super Fly lapel, excellent condition. $85
*Courtesy of Lynn Pastore, Avenue 13–5 and Dime Vintage, CO,*
*www.510vintage.com*

1970s BURBERRY LINED TRENCHCOAT. Tailored, matching belt, leather buckle, lining in Burberry cotton plaid, no wool liner, Saks Fifth Avenue label, excellent condition. $260
*Courtesy of Enokiworld, www.enokiworld.com*

1970s PAULINE TRIGÈRE BROWN WOOL MELTON COAT. Cocoa brown robe coat, welted seams, stand-up wing collar, armholes detailed with wide welted seam echoed in vertical at back, brown silk crêpe de chine lining, one internal button and strap closure, matching sash belt, excellent condition. $345
*Courtesy of Enokiworld, www.enokiworld.com*

## *Accessories*

**1970s Snakeskin Clutch Bag.** Red snakeskin interior, three inside compartments, zippered compartment has antique beaded pull, antique belt buckle fashioned from cut steel beads, metal La Jeunesse's label, made by the specialty Madison Avenue bag shop, La Jeunesse, 11″ × 6″, mint condition. $425
*Courtesy of Linda Ames, Vintage Textile, www.vintagetextile.com*

**1970s Black Ultrasuede Hobo Bag.** Black sling, lined in natural twill with one zippered pocket, polished gold decorative tabs at ends of zipper, by Reva, 17″ w × 13″ h, with 11″ handle, excellent condition. $125
*Courtesy of Enokiworld, www.enokiworld.com*

**1970s Pierre Cardin Blond Logo Clutch.** Taupe logo canvas, leather trimmed, envelope styling, cocoa pleather lining, measures 7½″ h × 10¼″ w, condition flawless outside, excellent inside. $45
*Courtesy of Enokiworld, www.enokiworld.com*

**1970s Roberta di Camarino Velvet "Lattice" Purse.** Café au lait velvet, brown and black "lattice print" with dual handles, three pockets—two patch and one zippered, dark brown leather lining, made in Italy, 7¼″ h × 11½″ w with single 13½″ strap, excellent condition. $510
*Courtesy of Enokiworld, www.enokiworld.com*

**1970s Gucci Suede "Gym" Bag.** Brown suede bowling bag style, green and red cotton webbing down front and back, brown leather trim, one zippered pocket, soft diamond-patterned cotton lining, 13½″ h × 14¼″ w with double 7″ handles, excellent condition. $295
*Courtesy of Enokiworld, www.enokiworld.com*

**1970s Purple Suede Shoulder Bag.** Grape Nehi–hued hacking suede, big brass rings, turning clasp on the flap over top of bag, interior zippered black vinyl pocket, made by Trio, 10¼″ h × 11½″ w with double 7½″ handles, excellent condition. $105
*Courtesy of Enokiworld, www.enokiworld.com*

**1970s Kenzo Leather Kiltie Bag.** Front flap resembles kiltie without fringe, perforated detail thin cognac strap, 5½″ h × 8½″ w with strap of 2″, excellent condition. $65
*Courtesy of Enokiworld, www.enokiworld.com*

**1970s Christian Dior Chain-Handle Purse.** Bordeaux calfskin, polished gloss, Dior logo gilt metal chain handle, a big "CD" on front

flap, optional clutch, interior contrast stitching, double compartments with one patch and two yellow zippered pockets, yellow faille lining, 7½" h × 10½" w with single 13" handle, excellent condition. $230
*Courtesy of Enokiworld, www.enokiworld.com*

**1970s CHARLES JOURDAN PERFORATED SUEDE BAG.** Gray suede and leather, saddlebag shape, zippered top, tiny perforations on front and back, inset with tiny mirrors, long shoulder straps, 9¼" h × 11" w, single, nonadjustable 21" strap, excellent condition. $110
*Courtesy of Enokiworld, www.enokiworld.com*

**1970s RED LEATHER "GG" BAG.** Oversized, closure strap over top of bag, handle continuous piece of cherry leather knotting around plated hoops, gilt metal plates run down sides, black vinyl lining, 10½" h × 15" w with double 10" handles, excellent condition. $245
*Courtesy of Enokiworld, www.enokiworld.com*

**1970s SCULPTURED PLATFORM SANDALS.** Brown leather platform, sand leather upper, sculpted through the heel, curved, seriously high, made by the Wild Pair, 6" back end 2" front, size 9M, flawless condition. $205
*Courtesy of Enokiworld, www.enokiworld.com*

**1970s CHARLES JOURDAN CALF LACE SANDALS.** Glossy strips of camel leather perforated along entire length and woven across top, chiseled square toe, brushed aluminum razorback heel, size 9M, 20½" l straps, 4" heel, flawless condition. $205
*Courtesy of Enokiworld, www.enokiworld.com*

**1970s RED BOOTS WITH ANKLE STRAPS.** Red leather with mod profile higher in front than in back, thin strap around each ankle attached to polished gold "T" on outer ankle, stitched detail on vamp. Made by SJA in Spain, size 8½N, 2½" heel, excellent condition. $125
*Courtesy of Enokiworld, www.enokiworld.com*

**1970s GUCCI EMBROIDERED SUEDE BOOTS.** Single embroidered floral detail in mocha on outside, soft leather lining, stacked wooden heel 2¼", no zippers, 18" h, excellent condition. $285
*Courtesy of Enokiworld, www.enokiworld.com*

**1970s NINA MID-SHAFT BLACK LEATHER BOOTS.** Rounded, slightly pointed toe, thin heels, vent at top, slim strap wrapping around boot, ending in gold buckle, size 8½M, 3¼" heel and measuring 13½" from floor to top, excellent condition. $165
*Courtesy of Enokiworld, www.enokiworld.com*

**1970S CHARLES JOURDAN PERFORATED OPEN-TOE PUMPS.**
Supple calfskin, resembles woven leather, peep-toe in the front, perfo-
rated heels, size 10M, 3½" heel, excellent condition. $115
*Courtesy of Enokiworld, www.enokiworld.com*

**1970S SLINGBACKS WITH GOLD MIRRORED HEELS.** Black and gold
Lurex uppers, delicate ankle straps, polished gold mirrored heels, "Made
for Saks Fifth Avenue," size 6B, 3¾" heel, excellent condition. $130
*Courtesy of Enokiworld, www.enokiworld.com*

**1970S XAVIER DANAUD STILETTO BOOTS.** Black leather, slightly
pointed toe, round heel, running zipper inside leg, emerald green leather
lining, made in Paris, size 6B, 18" from heel to top, 4" heel, excellent
condition. $360
*Courtesy of Enokiworld, www.enokiworld.com*

**1970S WALTER STEIGER SUEDE AND PATENT LEATHER OXFORDS.**
Black, gilded kidskin lining on breasted Louis heel, size 5½B, 2¼" heel,
excellent condition. $80
*Courtesy of Enokiworld, www.enokiworld.com*

## Menswear

**1970S VINTAGE POLYESTER SHIRT.** Photo-collage shirt, 1970s summer beach and sunset theme, butterfly collar, excellent condition. $40
*Courtesy of Lynn Pastore, Avenue 13–5 and Dime Vintage, CO*
*www.510vintage.com*

**1970S BANLON SHIRT.** Black, never worn, New Old Stock. $30
*Courtesy of Lynn Pastore, Avenue 13–5 and Dime Vintage, CO*
*www.510vintage.com*

**1970S OCEAN PACIFIC CORDUROY SHORTS.** Purple, classic OP style,
excellent condition. $12
*Courtesy of Lynn Pastore, Avenue 13–5 and Dime Vintage, CO*
*www.510vintage.com*

**1970S WESTERN SHIRT.** Polyester, peach colored, embroidered dice
and cards, embroidered riverboat on back, pearl snaps, "Gaucho," excellent condition. $55
*Courtesy of Screaming Mimi's, New York, NY.*

Pauline Trigère Suit. *Courtesy of Isadora's, Seattle, WA,*
*www.isadoras.com. Photograph by Jennifer A. Ledda.*

# Affluence and Attitude

Conspicuous consumption abounded in the eighties. It became popular to own and wear luxury items like Rolex watches, Hermès silk scarves, and Armani suits. The emergence of the "Yuppies" (young urban professionals) led to affluent lifestyles and the attitude that anything was affordable. Young designers moved to the forefront of fashion. New fabrics as well as luxury fabrics were part of almost every collection. In the mid-eighties padding shoulders was one way power defined dressing. Television shows like *Dynasty* and *Dallas* personified wealthy lifestyles. In contrast Donna Karan offered functional seasonless clothing for the working woman. The strong interest in physical fitness inspired body-conscious clothing: Lycra leggings, biking shorts, and aerobic wear. Catalog shopping became popular. Cotton T-shirts and jogging suits were worn for everyday. Boxy jackets, oversized sweaters, knit evening sweaters, black leather skirts, pants, coats, and full-length Blackgama mink coats were all fashions of the eighties. Bathing suits were Hollywood-inspired; they were shown in animal skin prints or metallic skin-tight maillots. In 1985, the Designer of the Year Award went to Azzedine Alaïa for his finely fitted fashions, labeling him "The King of Cling."

Japanese designers were on the cutting edge of fashion. Designers like Issey Miyake, Rei Kawakubo, and Yohji Yamamoto created highly individualized fashions. Rei Kawakubo first showed her work in Paris in 1981. Her designs appeared as abstract shapes, often in black, and were fashioned from unusual textiles. Fashion historian Valerie Mendes suggests that Rei Kawakubo was the woman who deleted color from fashion. The color black, once regarded as antifashion, was now freely worn.

The desire for status symbols and big spending brought excess back in fashion but it also brought more choices. In 1986, Christian Lacroix designed extravagant dress styles featuring bustles and hoops and the infamous "pouf" cocktail dress. Other designers spared nothing in their retro-historic styles or by bringing punk and streetwear styles to haute couture designs. Some designers like Ralph Lauren even offered whole lifestyles along with their clothing. The craze for colorful and well-made mass clothing was also well established in the eighties.

The Armani suit for men, expensive but casual, reestablished the suit. The power of pinstripes popularized by Michael Douglas in the movie, *Wall Street*, made "power dressing" symbolic of the decade. Savile Row returned to style menswear. Hollywood redefined men's clothing styles with the movie, *American Gigolo*. Actor Richard Gere's interest in his wardrobe led men to a new interest in dressing. Gere gave men's clothing a sense of glamour by wearing designer suits, new styled shirts, and showing a powerful upper body physique. Ties became important accessories as well, whether they were interpreted for designer suits or for stylish daywear. Boxer shorts featured the innovative designs of "Joe Boxer."

## Signature Fabrics of the 1980s

Wool used in both men's and women's fashions

Linen and linen chambray for women's separates

Satin for underwear as outerwear

Luxury fabrics of silks, satins, cashmere jersey, taffeta for gowns, evening-wear, and separates

Cotton for T-shirts

Chino for trousers

Synthetics:

> Lycra and Lycra blended with wool, silk, cotton. Lycra took over when fitness was popular in the eighties and was used for formfitting styles. It was endorsed by Prada, Ozbek, Armani, Betty Jackson, Nicole Farhi, Karl Lagerfeld, Gianni Versace, Donna Karan, and Norma Kamali. Donna Karan's bodysuits and leggings are examples of Lycra, and lingerie is another.

> Nylon for sportwear, gym wear

> Acetate taffeta for dinner dresses

## Designers and Manufacturers of the 1980s

GIORGIO ARMANI: Armani was thought to be the most influential designer of the eighties. He showed suits for women with very wide shoulders resulting in the power suit style of the decade. By mid-decade his designs became more relaxed and sleek for both men and women. His designs were styled in muted colors.

**AZZEDINE ALAÏA:** Alaïa's first collection was shown in 1981. His early designs were created to hug the body and were made in soft leathers, jersey, and silk, giving him the title, "The King of Cling." He frequently experimented with fabrics, particularly Lycra and wool. He is also famous for incorporating his signature zips in his designs.

**DIRK BIKKEMBERGS:** Bikkembergs has been designing menswear since 1986 and is known for his unisex designs.

**BODY MAP:** Body Map catered to the youth market and was known for its monochromatic tubular garments in offbeat colored knits.

**JOE BOXER:** Novelty boxer shorts were first introduced by Joe Boxer in 1985. The designs in the 1980s and 1990s were made in yarn dye flannel/poplin and "vintage washed" soft fabrications.

**CAROLINE CHARLES:** In the 1970s, Caroline Charles's designs were long and flowing. In the 1980s she continued these designs using luxurious fabrics in prints and patterned motifs. Her collections are based on a working wardrobe. In the 1980s she designed for Diana, Princess of Wales, creating the clothing she wore for royal tours and special occasions.

**SCOTT CROLLA:** Crolla, designer of menswear, in the eighties was known for his multi-patterned prints.

**CHANEL:** In 1983, Karl Lagerfeld took over as head designer of Chanel redefining the House with more modern fashions. In 1984, he continued to work under the Chanel name, but also started designing under his own name.

**HOUSE OF DIOR:** The Fashion Industry's Foundation Award went to the House of Dior in 1990.

**DOC MARTENS:** A popular utilitarian boot style of the 1960s that was redefined for the 1980s.

**DOLCE & GABBANA:** Dolce & Gabbana is the design firm of Domenico Dolce & Stefano Gabbana which opened in 1982. Early clothing designs featured unstructured clothing with highly involved clothing fastenings. In 1987, Dolce and Gabbana came out with a romantic collection with full skirts, shawls of lace, and ruffled blouses. Their later collections included some of their signature styles: gangster trouser suits in pinstripes, black suits, and corset dresses to name a few.

**PERRY ELLIS:** Ellis was known in the eighties for his knitwear collections.

**FENDI:** The Fendi Company is a family run business founded in 1918. They are primarily known for their fur collections.

**JOHN GALLIANO:** Galliano's first collection, "Les Incroyables," was influenced by eighteenth century dress and was an immediate success. His designs are highly creative and inventive. Galliano prefers his designs to be derived from historical fashions. His collections include such titles as "Afghanistan Repudiates Western Ideals," "Fallen Angels," "Princess Lucretia," etc. He is also known for his tailoring techniques that included a scissors dress cut to form a basque at the hip, a disappearing lapel on a jacket, and a "winking seam" which opens to reveal parts of the skin. His work is often seen as theatrical.

**JEAN-PAUL GAULTIER:** In 1982, Gaultier created the "corset dress" establishing the corset as outerwear; reminiscent of the sweater girl of 1950, the design was interpreted as power dressing. In 1990 he designed the costumes for Madonna's "Blonde Ambition" tour. He is known for his eclectic style, which influences are that of streetwear and punk style. In 1984 Gaultier started designing menswear; reinventing classic styles and introducing skirts for men.

**HUBERT DE GIVENCHY:** Givenchy is known for his designs for Audrey Hepburn both on- and offscreen. He retired in 1988 but continued to work for the company until 1996.

**CHARLES JOURDAN:** A shoe firm that makes shoes for Pierre Cardin and Xavier Danaud as well as having its own line.

**DONNA KARAN:** Karan launched her first collection on her own in 1985. Karan believed a wardrobe should be able to go from morning to night and from season to season. She is inspired by the pace of New Yorkers and the busy lives of women who work. Her signature styles include Lycra bodysuits, black cashmere, and bodywrap garments.

**REI KAWAKUBO:** The Japanese designer Kawakubo received her fame for her designs in the eighties which redefined women's clothing in the East and West. Her shapeless styles often had a randomness of trimmings and were torn or crumbled. Her knitwear was equally distressed but her designs had a great influence on rethinking dress design in the eighties.

**MARTIN KIDMAN:** Designer for Joseph Tricot, Kidman created various fashions including chunky sweaters.

**KENZO:** In 1983, Kenzo added menswear to his collection, calling the collection, "Around the World in Eighty Days." Kenzo is known for including many ethnic styles from around the world in his designs. In 1984, his designs incorporated fashion styles from North Africa and India.

**CHRISTIAN LACROIX:** The couture house of Christian Lacroix opened in

1987. Lacroix created extravagant designs featuring such elements as embroidered brocades, fur, reembroidered lace, ethnic prints, asymmetrical draping, and baby-doll silhouettes. He is infamous for his styles displaying bustles and hoops and particularly for his "pouf" cocktail dress in 1986. His magnificent fashions draw many retro fashions and incorporate ideas from the theater, historical costume, his Provençal youth, and London street styles.

**RALPH LAUREN:** Lauren designs for the entire family—men, women, and children—as well as for their entire home. His styles are deeply rooted in American culture and feature classic lines and tailoring in high quality fabrics and materials. In 1980, he showed ruffled blouses in linen, hooded capes, and full skirts in his collection.

**JUDITH LEIBER:** Leiber began designing her signature handbags in 1963. In 1993 the company was sold to Time Products PLC. Leiber's handbags are famous for their unique styling. Her handbags are very whimsical and are of the finest workmanship and quality. Her jeweled minaudières are very collectible. She designed exclusive animal handbags for first ladies Barbara Bush and Hillary Clinton based on their pets.

**MARTIN MARGIELA:** Margiela showed his first Paris collection in 1989. His monochromatic creations display outside seams, a sense of ripped sleeving, uneven edgings, and linings that stand outside the garment.

**MISSONI** (Tai and Rosita): A husband and wife team that designed knits in the seventies. Missoni is famous for long cardigans and sweaters in unusually blended colors and designs.

**ISSEY MIYAKE:** Miyake continued to make his linear and geometric-shaped clothing in the eighties based on the line and flow of his fabrics. In 1988, he designed a collection called "Pleats Please Issey Miyake" to great acclaim.

**CLAUDE MONTANA:** In the eighties Montana showed heavily shoulder-padded dresses and leather coats with a military inspiration.

**THIERRY MUGLER:** In 1980 Mugler added menswear to his collections.

**JEAN MUIR:** Muir founded her own company in 1966. She designs classic garments and is famous for her tailoring and craftsmanship. Muir manipulates jersey and suede to make dresses, skirts, and tops.

**RIFAT OZBEK:** Rifat Ozbek showed his first collection in 1984. His clothes are influenced by the Far East and included designs such as brocade jackets and embroidered black cocktail suits. His clothing is often interpretations of ethnic clothing and has an exotic appeal.

**EDINA RONY:** Rony along with her partner Lena Stengard are known for their knitwear designs with Fair Isle patterns and bead decorations.

**SONIA RYKIEL:** Rykiel is well known for her knitwear.

**SAVILE ROW:** English tailors.

**GRAHAM SMITH:** Millinery designer for Diana, Princess of Wales, in the 1980s.

**STEPHEN SPROUSE:** Sprouse designed clothes for rock and roll stars in the 1970s and 1980s. In 1983 he showed his first collection. He favored fluorescent colors and was inspired by the styles of the sixties mini dresses and mini skirts.

**ANGELO TARLAZZI:** In the 1970s Tarlazzi was the artistic director of Patou. In 1978, he opened his own house in Paris. Tarlazzi designs uncommon clothing for the traditional woman. His fashions are crisp and sculptured with asymmetrical styling. Tarlazzi is also known for his knitwear and long cashmere cardigans.

**EMANUEL UNGARO:** In the eighties Ungaro showed shirred and pleated dresses that were audacious and sensual.

**GIANNI VERSACE:** Versace is considered one of the most influential designers in the eighties and nineties. His bold sense of color and use of styles like bias cuts were a credit to his keen technical abilities. His styles almost always wrapped the body and were often designed in new fabrics with unusual trimmings. Versace also designed for the theater and ballet.

**VIVENNE WESTWOOD:** In 1981, Westwood and her partner, Malcolm McLaren, renamed their clothing shop "World's End." Westwood showed her first influential collection, "Pirate," with shorts, breeches, and baggy flat-heeled boots. Her "Buffalo" collection followed, showing satin underwear as outerwear. Westwood's "Witches" collection featured graphic designs of Keith Haring. From 1983 Westwood began to show her own designs exclusively, incorporating historical fashions into contemporary styles.

**YOHJI YAMAMOTO:** Yamamoto blends traditional Japanese clothing with that of Western dress for his everyday wear. His designs are bold and dramatic.

**YVES SAINT LAURENT:** Yves Saint Laurent's collection in the eighties reflected his taste in fine art and the exotic elements of non-Western cultures. He continued to show fashions that defined his fine tailoring skills. Several styles in the eighties were based on his previous tuxedo suits.

**ADRIENNE VITTADINI:** Vittadini received the Coty American Fashions Critic Award in 1984. Vittadini began her career in 1979 as a knitwear designer. Her knit collections are unfussy with clean uncomplicated lines. Vittadini is known for her use of interesting textiles.

## VINTAGE FASHIONS OF THE EIGHTIES

*Detail of Chanel Boutique Dress:*
Beaded bodice with
black velvet ribbon.
*Photograph by Linda Ames.*

Chanel Boutique Dress.
*Courtesy of Linda Ames,*
*Vintage Textile,*
*www.vintagetextile.com.*
*Photograph by Linda Ames.*

**1980s CHANEL BOUTIQUE DRESS.** Black satin bodice with alternating rows of bugle beads and black velvet ribbon, silk taffeta skirt, black satin petticoat with finished hem ruffle, heavyweight black silk satin lining, excellent condition. $525
*Courtesy of Linda Ames, Vintage Textile.*

Judith Leiber with her exquisite and highly collectible handbags. *Courtesy of Judith Leiber.*

Evening Jacket and Evening Top. *Courtesy of Gladys Deitrich. Photograph by Tom Amico.*

Yves Saint Laurent Stretch Top. *Courtesy of Linda Ames, Vintage Textile, www.vintagetextile.com. Photograph by Linda Ames.*

**1980s EVENING JACKET AND EVENING TOP.** Silk, sequined designs, "Nite Line," excellent condition. $200 each
*Courtesy of Gladys Deitrich.*

**1980s YVES SAINT LAURENT STRETCH TOP.** Black stretch knit top, long tight sleeves with 4″ l zippers at cuffs, "Rive Gauche" label inside, very good condition.
*Courtesy of Linda Ames, Vintage Textile.*

Baseball Jacket. *Courtesy of Deborah Burke, Antique & Vintage Dress Gallery, www.antiquedress.com. Photograph by Deborah Burke.*

Emanuel Ungaro Dress. *Courtesy of The Way We Wore, Cookie's Closet, www.cookiescloset.com. Photograph by Sanders Stanton.*

**1980s BASEBALL JACKET.** Entirely encrusted with hologram silver sequins, fully lined, "attributed to Halston," store label: "L.A. Schulman, White Plains, N.Y.," mint condition. $295
*Courtesy of Deborah Burke, Antique & Vintage Dress Gallery.*

**1980s EMANUEL UNGARO DRESS.** Silk floral crepe jacquard, scoop cowl neckline, gathered peplum at hips, shoulder pads, box pleat, excellent condition. $250
*Courtesy of The Way We Wore, Cookie's Closet.*

Yves Saint Laurent Rive Gauche
Gown. *Courtesy of The Way We
Wore, Cookie's Closet,
www.cookiescloset.com. Photograph by
Sanders Stanton.*

**1980s YVES SAINT LAURENT RIVE GAUCHE GOWN.** Rayon crepe,
black and white print, slight dolman sleeves, zippered cuffs, high-
waisted, two hip pockets, very good condition. $600
*Courtesy of The Way We Wore, Cookie's Closet.*

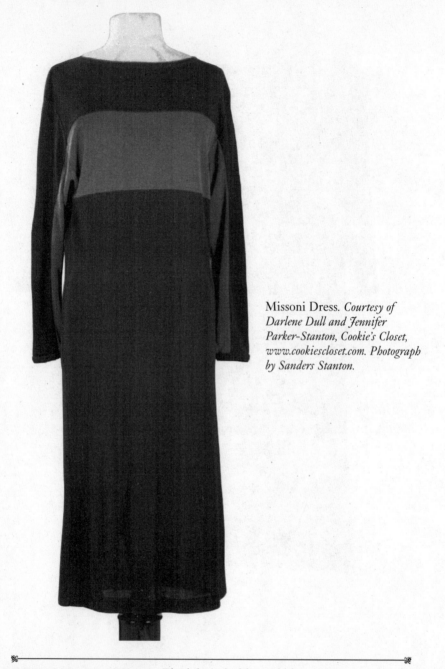

Missoni Dress. *Courtesy of Darlene Dull and Jennifer Parker-Stanton, Cookie's Closet, www.cookiescloset.com. Photograph by Sanders Stanton.*

**1980s MISSONI DRESS.** Black knit, bold royal blue stripe across bodice and down side of long sleeves, very good condition. $98
*Courtesy of Darlene Dull and Jennifer Parker-Stanton, Cookie's Closet.*

Issey Miyake Suit. *Courtesy of Linda Ames, Vintage Textile, www.vintagetextile.com. Photograph by Linda Ames.*

Galanos Suit. *Courtesy of Darlene Dull and Jennifer Parker-Stanton, Cookie's Closet, www.cookiescloset.com. Photograph by Sanders Stanton.*

**1980s ISSEY MIYAKE MINI SUIT.** Tropical weight wool plaid, unlined, from Miyake's ready-to-wear line, mint condition. $295
*Courtesy of Linda Ames, Vintage Textile.*

**1980s GALANOS SUIT.** Blue and white open weave plaid with black braiding decoration, Chanel-like, black buttons, delicate silk georgette crepe lining, excellent condition. $400
*Courtesy of Darlene Dull and Jennifer Parker-Stanton, Cookie's Closet.*

Gucci Dress. *Courtesy of Darlene Dull and Jennifer Parker-Stanton, Cookie's Closet, www.cookiescloset.com. Photograph by Sanders Stanton.*

**1980s GUCCI DRESS.** Black wool crepe, velvet collar and cuffs, button front, self-belt in back, diagonal pockets at hip, Gucci rayon lining, excellent condition. $250.

*Courtesy of Darlene Dull and Jennifer Parker-Stanton, Cookie's Closet.*

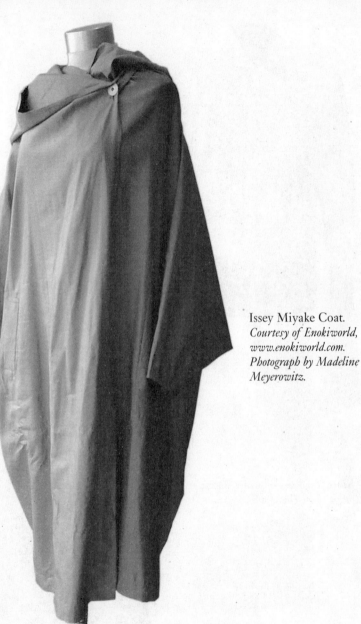

Issey Miyake Coat.
*Courtesy of Enokiworld,*
*www.enokiworld.com.*
*Photograph by Madeline*
*Meyerowitz.*

1980s Issey Miyake Coat. Crinkled nylon, lightweight, one-strap
neck closure with two carved shell buttons, one on each side of strap,
"wind coat" prototype, excellent condition. $1,050
*Courtesy of Enokiworld.*

Jacket. *Courtesy of Atomic Passion, New York, NY. Photograph by Tom Amico.*

T-Shirt. *Courtesy of Craig Smith, Photograph by Tom Amico.*

1980s JACKET. White leather, fringed, very good condition. $75
*Courtesy of Atomic Passion, NY.*

1980s T-SHIRT. "Wine Women Porsches not necessarily in that order," excellent condition. $20
*Courtesy of Craig Smith.*

*1980s*
## Introduction Frontispiece

**1980s PAULINE TRIGÈRE SUIT.** Black and white wool suit has one black vinyl button with a matching vinyl button on jacket, pleated skirt, full white silk lining, by Pauline Trigère for Gump's of San Francisco, pristine condition. $475 (See photograph on page 234)
*Courtesy of Isadora's, WA.*

# MARKET TRENDS FOR THE EIGHTIES

### Designer Separates

**1980s YVES SAINT LAURENT BLOUSE.** Silk, burgundy, bow tie, "Made in France," excellent condition. $225
*Courtesy of Vintage by Stacey Lee, White Plains, NY.*

**1980s GIVENCHY BLOUSE.** Black with blue polka dots, metallic fibers with "plastique" finish, excellent condition. $195
*Courtesy of Vintage by Stacey Lee, White Plains, NY.*

**1980s EMANUEL UNGARO CURVY CORAL JACKET.** Soft coral pink cotton, scooped neckline, split turn-back sleeves, peplum waist, coral rayon crepe lining, excellent condition. $80
*Courtesy of Enokiworld, www.enokiworld.com*

**1980s NORTH BEACH LEATHER TOGGLE VEST.** White leather, contrasting stitching, galosh turnings along placket and patch pockets, designed by Michael Hoban, flawless condition. $190
*Courtesy of Enokiworld, www.enokiworld.com*

**1980s MISSONI KNIT JACKET.** Trapeze-style in navy, royal blue, purple, and cocoa with little flecks of white, wool with nylon for durability, closes asymmetrically with one large purple textured button; stand-up neckline, purple trim along the edges, giant floral print lining, excellent condition. $160
*Courtesy of Enokiworld, www.enokiworld.com*

**1980s STEPHEN SPROUSE PINK SATIN SKIRT.** Simple fuchsia rayon satin skirt, small back vent, diagonal slash pockets over each hip, original price tag from Saks and pockets still basted shut, excellent condition. $145
*Courtesy of Enokiworld, www.enokiworld.com*

**1980s ISSEY MIYAKE LINEN SLOUCH SKIRT.** Black linen, drawstring waist hanging low on waist, slouch pockets at each hip, side slits at the hem, gathers erratically at the hem, excellent condition. $320
*Courtesy of Enokiworld, www.enokiworld.com*

1980s FUCHSIA SILK RHUMBA BLOUSE. Slightly iridescent, sleeves hang below elbow in a rampage of pink ruffles, button front, excellent condition. $115
*Courtesy of Enokiworld, www.enokiworld.com*

1980s VALENTINO RUFFLED SILK BLOUSE AND SKIRT. Abbreviated sleeve, ruffled shoulder, cuff, and base of neckline underneath collar, modified, gently pleated wrap, crêpe de chine skirt, fixed waistband, deep slit to top of thigh, pockets each hip, three opalescent buttons on back vent, white silk lining, excellent condition. $260
*Courtesy of Enokiworld, www.enokiworld.com*

1980s YVES SAINT LAURENT PISTACHIO FAILLE JACKET. Bellboy jacket, silk faille, breast pockets on both sides, squared black buttons along placket and wrist cuffs, pistachio crepe lining, designed for ready-to-wear Rive Gauche line, excellent condition. $160
*Courtesy of Enokiworld, www.enokiworld.com*

1980s TIE-DYE SUEDE PANTS. Deep cherry red and purple turn into blue here and there and then are brightened with spidery bursts of white, gently elasticized waist, deep patch pockets at both hips, slim legs slightly tapered, "Made by Therapy," excellent condition. $130
*Courtesy of Enokiworld, www.enokiworld.com*

1980s BETSEY JOHNSON PINK PORTRAIT JACKET. Synthetic moiré, double-breasted cut, wide sweeping collar, gathered sleeves, pink rayon satin lining, excellent condition. $105
*Courtesy of Enokiworld, www.enokiworld.com*

1980s STEPHEN SPROUSE "HARDCORE 1988" SKIRT. Grainy silkscreens of two snarling skinheads, urban camouflage background of neon green, hot pink, yellow, and black, cotton, flat waistband, pockets at each hip, excellent condition. $305
*Courtesy of Enokiworld, www.enokiworld.com*

## Dresses

1980s FENDI COAT DRESS. Navy cashmere with red zigzag topstitching, shoulder pads, small decorative buttons of red silk, closes with fabric-covered snaps, perfect condition. $325
*Courtesy of Linda Ames, Vintage Textile, www.vintagetextile.com*

1980s PIERRE BALMAIN WRAP DRESS. Wool gabardine, red pinstripes on ecru ground, square shoulders, stand-out pockets, unlined, excellent condition. $325
*Courtesy of Linda Ames, Vintage Textile, www.vintagetextile.com*

**1980S JEAN MUIR SILK DRESS.** Tomato silk printed with green pattern, gathered sleeves, self-ties at neck, yoked waistline, contrasting ribbon belt and crystal-clear Lucite buttons along placket, excellent condition. $240
*Courtesy of Enokiworld, www.enokiworld.com*

**1980S BETSEY JOHNSON JERSEY SNAP DRESS.** Early '80s, charcoal cotton, fitted bodice, full gathered skirt and dropped waistline, drooping pockets low at each hip, edged in black webbing, snaps shut with a row of tiny fasteners, excellent condition. $160
*Courtesy of Enokiworld, www.enokiworld.com*

**1980S STRAPLESS "DEBBIE HARRY" DRESS.** Reversible matte Lycra jersey, snap pea green on one side and black on other, back open at top, tying to form small bow, excellent condition. $110
*Courtesy of Enokiworld, www.enokiworld.com*

**1980S GRAFFITI PRINT SILK DRESS.** Neon lightning bolts in shades of yellow, green, pink, blue, and orange cut across bodice and hem, slit to knee on right side, excellent condition. $165
*Courtesy of Enokiworld, www.enokiworld.com*

**1980S SWEATER DRESS.** "John Richard" turquoise acrylic and nylon knit, angora flower accents, faux-pearl clusters on shoulders, excellent condition. $28
*Courtesy of Atomic Passion, New York, NY.*

## Suits

**1980S GEORGES RECH METALLIC VELVET SUIT.** Woven with metallic gold thread, looks like black lace over a nude background but is opaque, collarless neckline, piped in black silk satin along the placket, hem, and wrists, filigree buttons and double slim slash pockets over the right hip of the jacket, "Made by Georges Rech in Paris," black crepe lining, excellent condition. $160
*Courtesy of Enokiworld, www.enokiworld.com*

## Eveningwear

**1980S SILK BEADED DRESS.** Royal blue sheath, beaded, fully lined, zippered back, excellent condition. $125
*Courtesy of Deborah Burke, Antique & Vintage Dress Gallery, www.antiquedress.com*

**1980S PARTY DRESS WITH POUF SKIRT.** Stretch top, small shoulder pads, watered pink taffeta pouf skirt, wide gathered cummerbund, oversized bow at hip, "Morton Myles," excellent condition. $85
*Courtesy of Deborah Burke, Antique & Vintage Dress Gallery, www.antiquedress.com*

## Eveningwear (Designer)

**1980S MARY MCFADDEN SUIT.** Sea foam green, gold detailing, "Fortuny" pleated skirt, excellent condition. $350
*Courtesy of Pepper, NY.*

**1980S OSCAR DE LA RENTA BLACK TAFFETA EVENING DRESS.** Black silk taffeta dress ruffles, low décolletage, formfitting torso, ruched for texture, sleeves large and puffed, skirt opens below large hip bow exposing leg, excellent condition. $765
*Courtesy of Linda Ames, Vintage Textile, www.vintagetextile.com*

**1980S OSCAR DE LA RENTA SILK EVENING GOWN.** Silk organza, one-shouldered, floor-length, jeweled bodice, black silk organza skirt draping to large bow, cascading ruffles on left side, excellent condition. $875
*Courtesy of Linda Ames, Vintage Textile, www.vintagetextile.com*

**1980S CHANEL BOUTIQUE SILK CHIFFON PARTY DRESS.** Very low-cut, off-the-shoulder neckline with boned, stand-up ruffle, short off-the-shoulder sleeves, skirt, longer in the back, ruffled flounce just below hipline, excellent condition. $550
*Courtesy of Linda Ames, Vintage Textile, www.vintagetextile.com*

**1980S SWEE LO HAND-BEADED SILK DRESS.** Red silk chiffon, lavishly hand-beaded pattern formed from mixture of red beads, pink pearls, and pink sequins, free-hanging loops of beads on skirt echo shape of scalloped hem, excellent condition. $375
*Courtesy of Linda Ames, Vintage Textile, www.vintagetextile.com*

## Jackets and Coats

**1980S GIORGIO ARMANI JACKET.** Wool gabardine, excellent condition. $285
*Courtesy of Linda Ames, Vintage Textile, www.vintagetextile.com*

**1980S KARL LAGERFELD WOOL SWING COAT.** Unlined wool, bias-cut, self-faced front folding over to form collar and full-length lapel, excellent condition. $350
*Courtesy of Linda Ames, Vintage Textile, www.vintagetextile.com*

## *Accessories*

**1980s LOUIS VUITTON SADDLEBAG.** Excellent condition. $495
*Courtesy of Vintage by Stacey Lee, White Plains, NY.*

**1980s BIENAN DAVIS SMALL SNAKE HANDBAG.** Brown snake handbag, interior brown calf lining, small pocket for mirror, "Henri Bendel," mint condition. $285
*Courtesy of Linda Ames, Vintage Textile, www.vintagetextile.com*

**1980s PALOMA PICASSO SHOULDER BAG.** Black lamb stamped with the signature gilt metal X on front, ringed hardware, dual interior compartments, Paloma printed satin lining, closes in middle with magnetic snap closure, gently gathered silhouette, excellent condition. $105
*Courtesy of Enokiworld, www.enokiworld.com*

**1980s BOHEMIAN COTTON SHOULDER BAG.** Black and white cotton checkerboard, appliquéd flower and sequins, black fringe, long strap, cherry cotton faille lining, one interior patch pocket, hinged frame, padded, made by Alexa Hope, original tag still attached, excellent condition. $155
*Courtesy of Enokiworld, www.enokiworld.com*

**1980s CHARLES JOURDAN OPEN TOE LEATHER PUMPS.** Off-white, purchased in France, never worn, size 7B, excellent condition. $285
*Courtesy of Linda Ames, Vintage Textile, www.vintagetextile.com*

**1980s COMME DES GARÇONS RUBBER PUMPS.** High vamp, rounded toes, little kitten heel, all in bumpy rubber, size 8½, flawless condition. $230
*Courtesy of Enokiworld, www.enokiworld.com*

**1980s MAUD FRIZON WOVEN METALLIC SLINGBACKS.** Copper, gold, and silver leather, woven in herringbone pattern, open toes, straps, heel narrows at bottom before flaring out, size 5½, 4" heel, excellent condition. $165
*Courtesy of Enokiworld, www.enokiworld.com*

**1980s JUDITH LEIBER GOLD WAVE AND LIZARD BELT.** Sculpted, polished gilt metal buckle on wide band of buff-hued lizard; belt approximately 2" wide, because of signature Leiber adjustable back fits 29" to 35" waist; both belt and buckle signed, excellent condition. $160
*Courtesy of Enokiworld, www.enokiworld.com*

**1980s BROWN SUEDE SHOES.** Tufted wool cuff, very good condition. $80
*Courtesy of Atomic Passion, NY.*

Moschino Couture Suit. *Courtesy of Deborah Burke, Antique & Vintage Dress Gallery, www.antiquedress.com. Photograph by Deborah Burke.*

# THE 1990s
# Streetwear and Sophistication

The nineties answer to the affluent eighties was to pay less attention to the influence of designers; cultural influences predominated. As fashion historians Amy De La Haye and Valerie Mendes stated in their book, *20th Century Fashion,* "Authenticity became the new buzzword and subcultural style and ethnic clothing traditions entered fashion as major influences." (p. 252) Youth, music, African-American, streetstyle, ethnic, exotic, computer age, and technology all had a hand in creating the fashions of the nineties.

Grunge, a combination of hippie and punk styles, originated with rock bands and was immediately embraced by the youth. It was an example of a clothing style coming from outside the fashion realm that was adopted into mainstream designer collections. Deconstruction, monastic dressing, the sleek "pure" look of the millennium, all made fashion headlines. Linda Evangelista, Claudia Schiffer, Naomi Campbell, and Cindy Crawford were the "supermodels" of the decade. By mid-decade, dark red nails and spike heels became fashionable. Street influences like tattooing, body piercing, fetish dress, and leather clothing appeared. The suit for both men and women remained in fashion in the nineties. The Gap continued to come out with casual styles for men and women. Gene Meyer produced ties and fashions with a unique sense of color and contemporary styling. Retro fashions were interpreted for women by designers like John Galliano in exotic and innovative ways. The anticolor, black, continued to be fashionable. At the same time "high-tech" technology was also influencing fashion design. The sleek "high-tech" look of the millennium was inspired by new fabrics like Latex with wool or cotton, Tactel for sportswear, or Tencel, which can imitate many of the foremost fabrics used in clothing making.

## Signature Fabrics of the 1990s

Wool for Armani suits

Wool jersey, cashmere, wool velour, chenille

Satins for separates

Linen used in Armani separates

Synthetics:

Lycra by itself or combined with wool

Tactel is DuPont's ultrafine variation of nylon sportwear

Tencel is Courtauld's cellulose fiber that imitates velvet, corduroy, gabardine twill, jersey voile, lace, and crepe

Tyvek is DuPont's nonwoven paper-based material that can be used as fabric, particularly protective clothing

## Designers and Manufacturers of the 1990s

**GIORGIO ARMANI:** Armani was the most influential designer in menswear in the twentieth century. His designs in the nineties for both men and women were based on a well-tailored minimalist silhouette.

**MANOLO BLAHNIK:** Blahnik is known for his exotic shoes, often styled in colored leathers with a signature vamp. *Vogue* named him the "king of high-fashion shoes."

**JIMMY CHOO:** Jimmy Choo is a high-end shoe and handbag design company founded in 1996 by Tamara Yeardye; the creative director is Sandra Choi.

**COMME DES GARÇONS:** Designers Yohji Yamamoto and Rei Kawakubo head up this fashion company that uses deconstruction and new materials in their clothing designs.

**ANN DEMEULEMEESTER:** Demeulemeester's signature styles include asymmetrical suits, blouses falling off the shoulders, and low-slung trousers.

**DOC MARTENS:** Popular shoe and boot styles.

**DOLCE & GABBANA:** In the nineties the Italian design firm of Dolce & Gabbana was one of Italy's most successful ready-to-wear companies.

Lauren Sweder. "Fashion Illustration of the 1990s," March 2001.

They produced a rhinestone bodice in 1991, which was popularized by Madonna.

**JOHN GALLIANO:** In 1995, Galliano designed for Givenchy. In 1997 he left to design for the House of Dior. Galliano is known for his bias-cut gowns and historical-inspired clothing.

**JEAN-PAUL GAULTIER:** Gaultier's foremost contribution to fashion in the eighties and nineties was focused on the bustline. Gaultier designed for Madonna's world tours in the late 1980s and early 1990s. His work often demonstrates his keen sense of technical ability.

**GIVENCHY:** John Galliano became director of the house in 1996. Galliano introduced "fantasy" fashions. Alexander McQueen replaced Galliano as director in 1997.

**GUCCI:** Gucci is famous for leather purses, handbags, belts, and shoes, often displaying a stirrup or horse bit design.

**TOMMY HILFIGER:** Hilfiger strives for classics, collegiate looks in menswear. His clothing sports his logo and in the 1990s had a "Main Line" appeal.

**MARC JACOBS:** Jacobs previous work was for Perry Ellis. By 1994 he was designing under his own name. Jacobs favors soft and sensuous fabrics like angora, cashmere, and mohair. His designs also include styles incorporating a new use of fabrics like rubber for separates and laminated jeans.

**DONNA KARAN:** Karan is known for her "body wrapping" styles but also in the nineties for her beautifully designed eveningwear.

**CALVIN KLEIN:** A designer in the minimalist tradition, Klein offers pared-down unisex styles in muted tones that appeal to both sexes. In the 1990s his underwear was an international success story.

**MICHAEL KORS:** Kors started his own designs in 1981. Known for his minimalist styles, Kors designs are body-hugging, often seen paired with a more classic jacket. He has done jackets which also work as shirts.

**KRIZIA:** In the nineties, Krizia showed knitwear with an emphasis on textures—cashmere, wool, kid mohair. Skirts were asymmetrical with uneven hems; dresses had diagonal slits and openings.

**KARL LAGERFELD:** Lagerfeld has been known to move streetwear styles to the forefront of haute couture with his design elements. He had a great influence on design in the eighties and nineties.

**HELMUT LANG:** A deconstructionist, Lang's styles incorporate well-tailored clothing with quirky details. He also experiments with new fabrics.

**RALPH LAUREN:** Ralph Lauren's styles incorporate very American elements. Lauren uses traditional fabrics to create a gentrified elegance to his clothing.

**MARTIN MARGIELA:** Margiela's first collection appeared in 1989. Known for his deconstruction styles, he uses unusual fabrics and often works in red, black, and white. Hermès hired him in 1997 as a future-minded designer for their line.

**STELLA MCCARTNEY:** McCartney was appointed head of House of Chloé in 1997. Her styles are long and flowing, echoing Chloé's design philosophy.

**ALEXANDER MCQUEEN:** In 1996, McQueen was appointed head designer of Givenchy. His previous work included such garments as "bumster trousers" slashed clothing, laminated lace dresses, and a Princess-style dress out of riveted vinyl.

**GENE MEYER:** In the nineties, Gene Meyer designed fashion accessories—women's scarves and handbags, and men's ties and boxers. In 1994, Meyer designed a men's collection with his signature-style accessories. His designs are well known for their unique color combinations and contemporary styling.

**ISSEY MIYAKE:** Miyake worked as a design assistant to Guy Laroche and for Givenchy in the sixties. He established his own studio in 1970. His bold designs incorporate Eastern influences. In the nineties, he incorporated tattooing into his bodysuits and tights and designed with irregularly pleated fabrics. He is a very innovative designer and visionary.

**ISAAC MIZRAHI:** Mizrahi started designing under his own name in 1987. Mizrahi designs reflect a keen sense of color and use luxurious fabrics. His signature styles include baby-doll dresses, evening jumpsuits, and tube dresses.

**FRANCO MOSCHINO:** Moschino's clothing often incorporates whimsical elements. His flattering clothing is thought to be highly provocative. His signature designs include the "polka dot" Minnie Mouse dress, black satin evening dress, and printed waistcoats.

**THIERRY MUGLER:** Mugler has been designing under his own name since 1973. His designs are theatrical and body-conscious. Mugler incorporates many elements into his styles, like Hollywood glamour, science fiction, and industrial design.

**RIFAT OZBEK:** Ozbek shows very exotic and highly sophisticated clothing in his collections. In the nineties he created separates mostly in white, which were inspired by "The New Age." He is known for working ethnic designs into fashion.

**MIUCCIA PRADA:** Prada is known for elegant and sleek clothing. Often traditional articles are given a modern look by adding elements such as trimming; nylon parkas with mink are one example. The Prada Sport line was first produced in 1998.

*The Incredible in Fabric Technology in the Nineties.*

1994 Issey Miyake "Flying Saucer" Dress made from heat-set polyester and paper lanterns. *Courtesy of Philadelphia Museum of Art. Gift of Issey Miyake. This object is accessioned and part of the permanent collection.*

**SONIA RYKIEL:** Famous for her knitwear and sailor-motif jumper, Rykiel also showed long knitted jackets and wide trousers in the nineties.

**JIL SANDER:** Sander's signature minimalist style is popular in the international market. She uses luxury fabrics with clothing inspired by menswear.

**KATE SPADE:** Spade is an accessory designer known for her non-fussy understated styles reflecting her taste for a clean look. Her handbags are designed in interesting fabrics like nylon, silk-satin, tweed, and madras in subtle or bright colors.

**ANNA SUI:** Sui started designing in the 1980s, but became well known in the nineties for her modern versions of retro styles: Baby Doll, Flapper, and the 1960s. She also designs accessories.

**PHILIP TRACEY:** Tracey, a milliner, designed for both Chanel and Givenchy in the 1990s.

**RICHARD TYLER:** In the nineties, Tyler worked as head designer for Anne Klein, and in 1996 for Byblos. Tyler's fashions show fine men's tailoring techniques such as in his signature-style jackets lined with silk.

**GIANNI VERSACE:** Versace was famous for his strong sense of color and texture and the way in which he would wrap the female form. His designs were often executed in leather and newer fabrics, and reflected the theater and historical references.

**ADRIENNE VITTADINI:** Knits, knits, knits.

**VIVIENNE WESTWOOD:** Westwood is infamous for designing clothing that shocks. In the nineties she reinvented traditional garments in new and unheard-of ways. Her work was very influential in the last two decades of the century.

## 1990s
## Introduction Frontispiece

**1990S MOSCHINO COUTURE SUIT.** Multicolored ethnic print, in shiny plush fabric. The suit came from the television series *The Nanny* with Fran Drescher, excellent condition. $895 (See photograph on page 256)
*Courtesy of Deborah Burke, Antique & Vintage Dress Gallery.*

# VINTAGE FASHIONS OF THE NINETIES

Geoffrey Beene Evening Gown (front and back).
*Courtesy of Deborah Burke, Antique & Vintage Dress Gallery,*
*www.antiquedress.com. Photographs by Deborah Burke.*

**1990S GEOFFREY BEENE EVENING GOWN.** Navy light wool jersey, low back with diagonal lace detail, excellent condition. $385
*Courtesy of Deborah Burke, Antique & Vintage Dress Gallery.*

Gown. *Courtesy of Deborah Burke, Antique &*
*Vintage Dress Gallery, www.antiquedress.com.*
*Photograph by Deborah Burke.*

**1990s Gown.** Princess Diana–inspired evening gown, black lightweight
knit with sparkly metallic threads, low-draped back, excellent condition. $145
*Courtesy of Deborah Burke, Antique & Vintage Dress Gallery.*

AJ Bari Sarong Dress. *Courtesy of Deborah Burke, Antique & Vintage Dress Gallery, www.antiquedress.com. Photograph by Deborah Burke.*

**1990s AJ Bari Sarong Dress.** Extremely vibrant, multicolored design, silk, excellent condition. $95
*Courtesy of Deborah Burke, Antique & Vintage Dress Gallery.*

Banu Paris Suit.
*Courtesy of Deborah
Burke, Antique &
Vintage Gallery,
www.antiquedress.com.
Photograph by
Deborah Burke.*

1990s BANU PARIS SUIT. Gray floral, unique off-the-shoulder detail,
removable shoulder straps, never worn, original tag, fully lined, mint
condition. $148
*Courtesy of Deborah Burke, Antique & Vintage Dress Gallery.*

Yves Saint Laurent
Suit. *Courtesy of
Deborah Burke,
Antique & Vintage
Dress Gallery,
www.antiquedress.com.
Photograph by
Deborah Burke.*

**1990s YVES SAINT LAURENT SUIT.** Tiger print, shiny plush faux fur fabric, the suit from the set of the television series, *The Nanny,* excellent condition. $895
*Courtesy of Deborah Burke, Antique & Vintage Dress Gallery.*

## MARKET TRENDS FOR THE NINETIES

### *Dresses and Gowns*

**1990s OSCAR DE LA RENTA BALL GOWN.** Silver and gold sequined and beaded jacket, chocolate satin, green gathered full-length skirt, excellent condition. $600
*Courtesy of Pepper, NY.*

**1990s DONNA KARAN BACKLESS GOWN.** Black stretch jersey, rayon, and Spandex, gold signature label, excellent condition. $245
*Courtesy of Deborah Burke, Antique & Vintage Dress Gallery,*
*www.antiquedress.com*

**1990s BLACK CREPE COCKTAIL DRESS.** Nearly backless, double bows on back with rhinestone circles on bows, "Lloyd Williams," excellent condition. $95
*Courtesy of Deborah Burke, Antique & Vintage Dress Gallery,*
*www.antiquedress.com*

**1990s DANA BUCHMAN DRESS.** Black velvet torso, sweetheart bustline, black silk chiffon, three-layered skirt, excellent condition. $145
*Courtesy of Deborah Burke, Antique & Vintage Dress Gallery,*
*www.antiquedress.com*

**1990s BLACK CREPE AND BLACK VELVET DRESS.** Cut-out bodice design, short skirt, "Kathyn Dianos," excellent condition. $95
*Courtesy of Deborah Burke, Antique & Vintage Dress Gallery,*
*www.antiquedress.com*

**1990s EMANUEL UNGARO PARALLELE SILK DRESS.** Bodice, gathered at midpoint with bow; skirt, three layers of two short ruffled chiffon over straight longer underskirt; waist, sarong-wrapped, tying with bow; four zippers, at side, upper back, and on each sleeve; made in Italy, excellent condition. $195
*Courtesy of Deborah Burke, Antique & Vintage Dress Gallery,*
*www.antiquedress.com*

**1990s GIORGIO ARMANI SUIT(S) "LE COLLEZIONE."** Jacket and skirt (matching pants), pure white silk, "made in Italy," pristine condition. $1,800
*Courtesy of Susan Viniar.*

1880–1900 Silk Zardozi Wedding Shawl from India. *Courtesy of Vintage Textiles, www.vintagetextiles.com. Photograph by Amadeus Guy.*

*Detail of Wedding Shawl:* Zardozi work.
*Photograph by Amadeus Guy.*

# Special Interests

## SELECTIONS FROM THE NINETEENTH CENTURY (1850–1900)

In 1856, Charles Frederick Worth began his career as the first Parisian couturier, designing for the two foremost women of the time, Queen Empress Victoria of Great Britain and Empress Eugénie of France. Worth's magnificent gowns with outstanding detail and luscious fabrics were in constant demand and were imitated throughout the Victorian period of 1850–1900 in both Europe and America. Worth changed the craft of dressmaking into the art of the designer and was therefore credited with laying the basis for haute couture in the twentieth century.

To Victorian women, dress was very important. In the introduction to the Cincinnati Art Museum's exhibition catalog, *With Grace & Favour*, fashion historian, Otto Charles Theime, stated that women of this period as well as at the turn of the century, believed that "chaste and correct appearance through dress that was tasteful, dress that was correct, and dress that was appropriate exerted a resulting positive moral influence on her husband, her family, and community." (p. vii) Thus, a woman's dress was seen as a reflection of her morality and of the propriety of her family and lifestyle. Fashion was a serious endeavor and women pored over magazines like *Godey's Lady Book*, *Peterson's*, and *Harper's Bazaar*, learning the proper attire, accessories, and latest Parisian styling and trim.

However, before the nineteenth century woman could consider her outward appearance, she had to contend with the many layers of underclothes that were *de rigueur* for the fashionably dressed lady. The proper dress required undervests, drawers, a tightly laced corset, a chemise, petticoats (sometimes with cage or crinoline), an additional bustle, when fashion dictated, and stockings. On top of these underclothes were her outer garments of heavy cloth, usually a skirt and bodice. Gloves, high-laced boots, an ornamented hat, and a beaded mantle completed the outfit. Patricia Cunningham, a fashion historian, estimated that such an ensemble weighed about twenty pounds.

The gowns most highly prized in the last three decades of the nineteenth century were of Parisian design. Women who could not afford to shop in Paris could order patterns or ready-mades from department stores, which often required the assistance of family members or a dressmaker to complete the garment. The making of such clothing was a time-consuming occupation. Various styles came and went and women would remake many of their clothes into the new styles whenever possible. Only the very affluent were able to save dresses in their original design instead of remaking them.

The dress of 1850 had a very full hoop or crinoline with a round, full skirt. Dresses in mid-century usually had a pagoda sleeve which widened at the wrist over an undersleeve of lace. This style of sleeve was used in even larger proportions throughout the 1860s. Also during this period, dressmakers experimented with the bishop sleeve, which had a gathered shoulder and closer cuff at the wrist. The coat sleeve, a slim sleeve that curved out at the elbow using two seams, was the ensuing style, used until 1890.

Dresses were usually two pieces, skirt and bodice. In the 1850s, bodices ended at the waist and were worn with full skirts. A major fashion change of the time was the bodice, which fastened in the front and flared out over the skirt, eliminating a waist seam. Later, dresses also came with slightly longer, pointed bodices over triangular-shaped skirts. Various types of pleating were used on skirts to accommodate the varieties of skirt shapes to reduce the bulk at the waist and hips. As bodices were designed to be even longer-waisted, skirts were designed with gored panels in front to accommodate the bodices. These gored, paneled skirts drew attention to the back of the skirt; around the 1870s, this emphasis resulted in dress designs with trains.

In the late 1870s, the déshabillés were first introduced. These highly decorated, loose gowns, worn in the home to receive guests, were later known as tea gowns, the one relief women had from the highly constricted fashions of the time.

In the mid-1870s, dresses had a back-swept silhouette with a large drape of fabric across the front from the waist, drawn toward the back, and up to the tournure. Skirts had a great deal of pleating, shirring, and tucking. In 1880, a renewed style brought further emphasis to the hips, where fabric was used in swags, called panniers. A bodice that came down well over the hips, called the cuirass bodice, was designed in the mid-1870s and started the style for the slim silhouette that was fashionable for many years to come.

By the 1890s, working girls wore leg-of-mutton or gigot-sleeved blouses with unadorned gored skirts that were worn with a bustle. Increasingly larger sleeves were popular until 1895, when they were modified. These styles led to the hourglass silhouette of the long-sleeved, tight-fitting blouse with high collar worn over a gently flaring gored skirt; a dress style that was captured in the illustrations of Charles Dana Gibson. This look remained stylish until there was a change of corseting at the turn of the century.

Other Parisian couturiers, such as Jacques Doucet, Madame Leferrière, Émile Pingat, and Redfern were soon producing equally fine fashion designs such as Worth's. In addition Worth and the other couturiers also did much to improve the textile industry. Worth ordered great quantities of silks and velvets to be made in Lyon, France, a leader in textile manufacturing. The industry became known for their extravagant and beautifully made fabrics, The increased demand for these fabrics as well as other printed cottons and silks for daily use led to swatch services which mailed out fabric samples to subscribers, enabling them to order fabric without going to Paris.

Victorian women wore "confections" which were shawls, cloaks, and mantles. They loved the trims, ribbons, and fans of point de gaze lace with ivory sticks that were imported from France. Buttons in black jet, carved ivory, porcelain, fabric, and cut steel were ornaments in themselves.

Men also had a code of dress. Proper clothing had to be worn for every occasion. Change in men's clothing was more subtle than women's and was usually seen in a detail like a change in lapel width. The frock coat in either single- or double-breasted design was the standard garment throughout the century. The sack suit was the other common choice in dress. Clothes reflected the formality of the fabrics used and the accessories that came with them. Until about 1860, embroidered vests called waistcoats were made of rich silk and brocade. Malacca walking sticks, gloves, and high button shoes were standard dress. Silk scarves, cravats with stickpins, white linen shirts fastened in front with buttons or shirt studs, and silk top hats were part of men's dress. The tail coat, derived from the eighteenth century riding coat, was a formal coat worn in the evenings and made in wool of black or a dark blue.

By 1880, men's clothing had a more modern appearance. The dress lounge coat, which sported silk lapels, was the forerunner to the tuxedo.

The Norfolk jacket of the late nineteenth century was the country or sporting jacket, worn with knickerbockers. Bowlers, boaters, and Homburgs were the choices for hats.

Adaptations of dress styles and fashions occurred in the nineteenth century. Changing times required different dress. Women left their homes to go to work and everyone was encouraged to participate in athletics. However, the attention given to detail and the use of rich and beautifully made fabrics was still of primary concern and is what makes nineteenth century fashions collectible today.

## Important Designers and Manufacturers of the Victorian Era

**BROOKS BROTHERS:** Brooks Brothers first opened in 1818 as a manufacturer of ready-to-wear men's clothing. Many of their designs were adaptations of garments worn by men in Great Britain. In 1896, they introduced the button-down-collar shirt, which was copied from English polo players. Other such adaptations of the late nineteenth and early twentieth centuries included the foulard tie, madras plaid, Harris tweeds from Scotland, and Shetland sweaters.

**DUVELLEROY:** Duvelleroy designed and produced fans.

**MADAME A. LEFERRIÈRE:** Mme. Leferrière was known for her fine silks and lingerie in the Victorian era, as well as for everyday fashions.

**LIBERTY & CO:** Founded by Arthur Lazenby in 1875, Liberty & Co. imported silks from the Orient, solids, and Indian or Japanese prints. They were known for their beautiful Art Nouveau textiles.

**CHRISTOPHE-PHILIPPE OBERKAMPF:** A textile mill of the nineteenth century, Oberkampf was known for its French provincial style prints with realistic, colored flowers on dark backgrounds.

**ÉMILE PINGAT:** In the 1860s, Pingat designed women's clothing, ready-to-wear, and custom-made. He sold fabrics to be made into clothing, designed day dresses, ball gowns, and courtly clothing. Pingat's formal eveningwear of the 1860s survives today thanks to this careful selection of silks which were hardier than those of many of his contemporary dressmakers. He trimmed his fancy gowns with laces, chenille fringe, and metallic-wrapped threads. In the 1870s, Pingat designed three-piece day dresses that still show the designer's extreme devotion to detail. By 1880, Pingat was famous for his gorgeous outerwear, often worn over matching dresses.

**REDFERN:** One of Redfern's first designs for women was the "Jersey Lily," which was the 1879 costume worn by Lillie Langtry. He also did tailored serge outfits for the active lady of this era. Since Redfern's design studio was in an English port city, his next well-known designs were 1885 women's yachting suits, traveling suits, and riding habits. In 1888, Redfern was selected as dressmaker for Queen Victoria, which ensured a high profile for his Victorian designs. Redfern was heralded as a merchandising genius, with his advertisements appearing in magazines. He offered to send design sketches and samples to women unable to travel to Paris.

CHARLES FREDERICK WORTH: In 1850, Worth opened a department store in Paris, having moved from England. In France he was a favorite designer of Empress Eugénie. In the 1860s, Worth's tunic dresses, knee-length tunics over long skirts, were popular. In 1864, he made yet another change to the popular silhouette by abandoning crinolines in favor of a shorter skirt and long back train. In 1869, Worth changed fashion by the waistlines on his designs and adding bustles. His designs were favorites with European royalty and international actresses. Most famous for his beautiful evening gowns, he also did more conservative traveling ensembles. He was the first designer to show his fashions on live models instead of on mannequins.

JEAN-PHILLIPE WORTH: Jean Phillipe Worth was the son of Charles Worth (see previous reference) and also designed for his father's House of Worth.

## Nineteenth-Century Introduction Frontispiece

1880–1900 SILK ZARDOZI WEDDING SHAWL FROM INDIA. Zardozi work is gold couching with gold tubular beads, hand applied to a silk field. This decorative technique dates back hundreds of years, employing an entire family for many generations. A wedding shawl with heavy zardozi work can weigh as much as 7 to 10 pounds Valued at $2,500 or greater, depending on age, condition, complexity of design, and metal content. (See photograph on page 270)
*Courtesy of Vintage Textiles.*

# MARKET TRENDS FOR THE NINETEENTH CENTURY

## Corsets

1870–1880 STRIPED CORSET. Gold and black cotton sateen stripe, beige cotton canvas lining, laces replaced, name of original owner written in ink inside, very good condition. $765
*Courtesy of Linda Ames, Vintage Textiles, www.vintagetextile.com*

Worth/Boberg Ensemble. *Courtesy of Sothebys.com. Photograph by Monica Anchin.*

**1860S CHARLES FREDERICK WORTH AND OTTO BOBERG DAY ENSEMBLE.** Deep rust faille, two-piece, high-waisted Princess-cut bodice, lavishly embellished with ribbon work at yoke, front and cuffs, ivory silk lining, skirt is embellished with ribbon work, flounces, bows, and passementerie, fragile. $9,625
*Courtesy of Sothebys.com*

1870–80 CORSET WITH HAND EMBROIDERY. Beige, heavy cotton sateen with hand-embroidered trim, feather and satin stitches decorate seams, original laces, label: "Baleine," purchased in France, excellent condition. $785
*Courtesy of Linda Ames, Vintage Textile, www.vintagetextile.com*

## Waists

1898–1902 EMBROIDERED LINEN WAIST. Natural linen, mother-of-pearl buttons, hand-done cotton embroidery in olive green, brass hooks, excellent condition. $175
*Courtesy of Karen Augusta, Antique Lace & Fashion, www.antique-fashion.com*

c. 1893 WAIST WITH GLASS BUTTONS. Brown cotton sateen with white dots, silk cord, glass buttons, cotton lining, excellent condition. $145
*Courtesy of Karen Augusta, Antique Lace & Fashion, www.antique-fashions.com*

## Bodice

1890s VICTORIAN BODICE. Black net over cream silk satin, overbodice and sleeves of black net on net (probably made in Brussels), adorned with black sequins, black beads, and jet beads; sleeves fold gently at elbow, secured with flat black velvet bow, décolleté neckline with larger black velvet rose bow, ivory needle-lace undersleeves trimmed with deep Carrickmacross lace border, nine bones, ornamented, black silk cummerbund with black velvet trim, brass hooks in back, large velvet rose back bow, label: "A. & M. Kilroy, importers, 108 East 30th Street, New York," excellent condition. $375
*Courtesy of Amy Ferrante.*

## Skirts and Dresses

1890s VICTORIAN SKIRT. Heavy cotton, gored, set waistband, five tiny mother-of-pearl buttons, 26″ waist, excellent condition. $135
*Courtesy of Miss Kitty & Calico Jack, The Cat's Pajamas, PA, www.catspajamas.com*

1890s FLOWERED VICTORIAN DRESS. Bodice and skirt, tiny red flowers on white ground, buttoned bodice, leg-of-mutton sleeves, excellent condition. $245
*Courtesy of Miss Kitty & Calico Jack, The Cat's Pajamas, PA, www.catspajamas.com*

**1892–1895 TWO-PIECE DAY DRESS.** Red and white piqué cotton, all hand-done cotton tambour embroidery, tight-fitting undersleeve with fully gathered oversleeve, eight bone buttons, brown muslin lining, excellent condition. $625
*Courtesy of Karen Augusta, Antique Lace & Fashion, www.antique-fashion.com*

**1870s BLUE-STRIPE DRESS AND JACKET OUTFIT.** Boned bodice completely lined with white polished cotton, hooks in back, jacket is unlined, revealing dress, jacket, bodice, and swagged overskirt trimmed with rows of pleated cream-colored organdy with heavier woven stripe of bright blue, very good to excellent condition. $865
*Courtesy of Linda Ames, Vintage Textile, www.vintagetextile.com*

**1850s FLORAL SILK DRESS.** Silk satin damask weave in floral pattern of red, green, light blue, and off-white, burgundy satin floats in weaving, boned bodice with pointed front, narrow corded piping outlines the neckline, hemmed armholes and bodice, handsewn, ecru polished cotton lining, very good condition. $95
*Courtesy of Linda Ames, Vintage Textile, www.vintagetextile.com*

**1880s LAVENDER BUSTLE DRESS.** Two-piece, lavender silk faille, decorated with black velvet ribbon and bows, framed neckline with ecru handmade lace, bands of ruching decorate bell-shaped sleeves and lower skirt, boned bodice, white cotton lining, buttoned front, very good condition. $675
*Courtesy of Linda Ames, Vintage Textile, www.vintagetextile.com*

**c. 1869 PROMENADE DRESS IN GRAPHIC DESIGN.** Light sheer cotton stripe dress, two-layered, back-draped skirt, unboned and mostly unlined for summer wear, bodice, sloped shoulder cut, narrow corded piping around armhole, handmade buttonholes, pewter buttons, very good condition. $850
*Courtesy of Linda Ames, Vintage Textile, www.vintagetextile.com*

## Gowns

**c. 1895 ROBIN'S EGG BLUE MORNING GOWN.** Silk faille, China silk, embroidered cotton net lace collar and sleeve, waist sash with large rosette, Watteau back and train, known provenance, very good condition. $925
*Courtesy of Karen Augusta, Antique Lace & Fashion, www.antique-fashion.com*

**c. 1897 LILAC AFTERNOON GOWN.** Stiffened organdy-like cotton gauze fabric woven with white stripes gradually increasing in width, over this woven cloth is printed an intricate marbleized swirling pattern in

"The Season." from *Peterson's*, August 1890. *Courtesy of Irene Lewisohn Costume Reference Library, The Metropolitan Museum of Art.*
*Left:* Dress of light woolen stuff with draped skirt, full gathered bodice, ribbon accents. *Right:* Zephyr dress, guipure embroidery, bows as trimming, large straw hat with velvet and wildflowers. Child's pinafore dress, upper part of bodice and cuffs are smocked.

lilac, silk bobbin lace, brass hooks and eyes, known provenance, excellent condition. $775
*Courtesy of Karen Augusta, Antique Lace & Fashion, www.antique-fashion.com*

1890–1892 LACE TEA GOWN. Fine linen cambric with Broderie Anglaise lace, Mechlin lace, four whalebone stays in bodice, silk faille lining, windowpane buckram, brass and steel hooks and eyes, silk lining has narrow pleated silk ruffle with band of Broderie Anglaise lace sewn on top, silk front ruffle lined with 15″ band of pleated and lace-trimmed buckram, label: "Miss Slattery 16 Boylston St. Boston," known provenance, near-perfect condition. $2,000
*Courtesy of Karen Augusta, Antique Lace & Fashion, www.antique-fashion.com*

LATE 1890s GRAPHIC BLACK AND WHITE GOWN. Beaded black net on ecru silk satin lining in graphic black and white design, two-piece, boned bodice and trained skirt, back closes with hooks, waist finished with black taffeta cummerbund, very good condition. $1,250
*Courtesy of Linda Ames, Vintage Textile, www.vintagetextile.com*

c. 1890 BLACK VELVET BEADED GOWN. Black sequined bodice, beaded mesh sleeves, trained skirt, back with allover pattern of roses and ribbons formed from black jet beads and black sequins, ending in long tail of beaded tassels, neckline outlined with ecru lace, black taffeta lining, attached black taffeta petticoat, label: "Mrs. Dunstan—6 East 30th Street, New York," perfect condition. $1,685
*Courtesy of Linda Ames, Vintage Textile, www.vintagetextile.com*

## Shawls

1850s HAND-EMBROIDERED TRIANGULAR SHAWL. Sheer cotton batiste, scalloped edges, wide ruffled border exquisitely hand-embroidered with padded satin stitch, 104″ l at center back, 47″ w, excellent condition. $325
*Courtesy of Linda Ames, Vintage Textile, www.vintagetextile.com*

VICTORIAN IVORY SILK CHINESE SHAWL. Heavyweight ivory crepe, lavishly hand-embroidered with flowers, silk floss, edged with 26″ wide border of hand-knotted silk fringe, excellent condition. $785
*Courtesy of Linda Ames, Vintage Textile, www.vintagetextile.com*

## Jackets, Coats, and Capes

1890s VELVET CUT-AWAY-STYLE JACKET. Black satin velvet jacket with black jet beading, lapels and cuffs bordered with black silk faille,

ecru satin built-in vest decorated with hand-embroidered and hand-made needle-lace appliqué, hooks in front, light blue figured silk lining, excellent condition. $835
*Courtesy of Linda Ames, Vintage Textile, www.vintagetextile.com*

1890S LINEN COAT WITH GRAPHIC DETAIL. Intricately cut coat, dark brown piping outlining double cape collar, pockets, wide cuffs, and seams, pleated back skirt, excellent condition. $455
*Courtesy of Linda Ames, Vintage Textile, wwwvintagetextile.com*

1890S LINEN DUSTER. Leg-of-mutton sleeve, mother-of-pearl buttons, interesting pocket and sleeve detail, excellent condition. $265
*Courtesy of Miss Kitty & Calico Jack, The Cat's Pajamas, PA, wwwcatspajamas.com*

1880 VELVET CAPE LINED IN PURPLE SILK PLAID. Full circle–cut cape, lavishly decorated with foliate appliqué pattern, appliquéd black suede cloth outlined with black jet beads and black sequins, hem and collar trimmed with fur, purple silk plaid taffeta lining, very good condition. $765
*Courtesy of Linda Ames, Vintage Textile, www.vintagetextile.com*

"Les Modes Parisienne," *Peterson's,* April 1890. *Courtesy of Irene Lewisohn Costume Reference Library, The Metropolitan Museum of Art.*

TAILOR-MADE.

Ch. Drecoll. "Tailor-made," from *Peterson's*, 1896.
*Courtesy of Irene Lewisohn Costume Reference Library, The Metropolitan Museum of Art.*

**1890s BEADED VELVET COAT.** Decorated with pattern of interlocking bands of soutache and beaded appliqué collar edged with ruched band of velvet, back train ends in point, full-sleeved, ecru satin damask lining, interlined for warmth, very good condition. $685
*Courtesy of Linda Ames, Vintage Textile, www.vintagetextile.com*

## Accessories

**VICTORIAN DAFFODILS PURSE.** Brown leather, hand-tooled daffodils, turnlock mechanism on frame, leather whipstitched strap, "Reedcraft" suede lining, excellent condition. $145
*Courtesy of Miss Kitty & Calico Jack, The Cat's Pajamas, PA, www.catspajamas.com*

**1870s GLASS BEADED PURSE.** Glass beads, brass beads, silk floss, cotton thread, gray silk crepe-lined purse, hand-knit beadwork, crocheted

top with matching color cording for the drawstring, opalescent white background beads, very good to excellent condition. $295
*Courtesy of Karen Augusta, Antique Lace & Fashion, www.antique-fashion.com*

**1840–1860 CREWEL RETICULE.** Burgundy silk satin, silk-covered cotton cord, wool, cut steel beads, silk taffeta lining, known provenance, very good condition. $155
*Courtesy of Karen Augusta, Antique Lace & Fashion, www.antique-fashion.com*

**1870s MISER PURSE.** Cotton yarn, cut steel beads and ring, hand-knit, excellent condition. $225
*Courtesy of Karen Augusta, Antique Lace & Fashion, www.antique-fashion.com*

**c. 1880 MILLINERY ADVERTISING FAN.** "Summer 1880 C.A. Browning & Co. Boston," wooden guards and sticks, printed paper leaf, metal loop signed by printer, "Donaldson Brothers Five Points, NY," the straw hat styles pictured are all named, excellent condition. $850
*Courtesy of Karen Augusta, Antique Lace & Fashion, www.antique-fashion.com*

**c. 1870 PIERCED LINEN FAN.** Beech wood, linen, gilt paper, mother-of-pearl, excellent condition. $225
*Courtesy of Karen Augusta, Antique Lace & Fashion, www.antique-fashion.com*

## *Menswear*

**1850s MEN'S BLUE SILK DAMASK DRESS VEST.** Men's size 40, excellent condition. $195
*Courtesy of Deborah Burke, Antique & Vintage Dress Gallery, www.antiquedress.com*

**LATE 1800s MEN'S VELVET SMOKING JACKET.** Green velvet, black satin quilted trim, heavy braided frog closure, size 40R, near-mint. $395
*Courtesy of Deborah Burke, Antique & Vintage Dress Gallery, www.antiquedress.com*

# CHILDREN'S FASHIONS

Children's clothing is a favorite collectible of many collectors. Baby bonnets, christening gowns, small shoes, and special-occasion clothing are usually so treasured in a family that they are passed down to succeeding generations to be used again or perhaps to be framed and admired.

Early nineteenth century christening robes and bonnets were beautifully ornamented with embroidered lace. They came in a variety of styles, including the Empire style that became the favored twentieth century dress design for such robes. Victorian heirlooms featured lace, tucks, and embroi-

"Tailleurs et Robes d'enfant, de Jeanne Lanvin" from *Gazette du Bon Ton*, 1920.
*Courtesy of Irene Lewisohn Costume Reference Library, The Metropolitan Museum of Art.*

dery on the yoke. Silk underslips and bonnets with rosettes and fine ribbon
ties were made to match the robes. Family members often made baby bonnets with tatting, lace, or embroidery.

A variety of suit styles was designed for boys and girls in the nineteenth
and early twentieth centuries. Probably the best known is the sailor suit;
sailor caps worn with matching overblouses with pants or skirts, made popular by the British royal family. Another popular suit for boys which is often
captured in photographs is the Lord Fauntleroy suit featuring a velvet

tunic, wide lace collar and cuffs, and a wide sash tied over knickerbockers. Hair was long and curled, and feathered hats completed the outfit. In some photographs, young boys were shown in skirts, which was considered acceptable dress into the early 1900s.

The Eton suit, a popular turn-of-the-century style for boys, had a Norfolk jacket, high starched shirt, and wide black bow at the neck; it was worn with knickerbockers and kneesocks. Victorian girls were equally well dressed in pantaloons that showed under their pinafored skirts. Kate Greenaway, an English author and illustrator, captured these styles, reminiscent of eighteenth-century dress, in her book illustrations of the time. Empire waists, smocks, ruffled yokes, and big collars were also typical Kate Greenaway illustrations; these designs were later revived in the 1940s.

The long-waisted dress of broderie anglaise, with ribbon sashes at the hips and beautifully created bonnets, were especially typical of the fancy clothing of the Edwardians at the beginning of the century. Clothing was made from starched white cotton, lawn, and cotton piqué.

Twentieth-century children's clothing gradually became simpler, mirroring changing adult fashions and attitudes. Jeanne Lanvin made "Lanvin Blue" popular in 1914 when she began designing clothing for her daughter. Lanvin favored layered taffetas and embroidered silk velvets for her designs. In the 1920s, appliqué work was featured on dresses. In the 1930s, Shirley Temple popularized the "Shirley Temple" dress sporting a yoke and short, full-puffed sleeves with an above-the-knee-length skirt. Her coat had matching velvet cuffs, buttons, and collar. The ensembles were worn with patent leather buckled shoes and white gloves. Hand-knitted cardigans and polo-neck sweaters came into vogue for children in the 1930s as well. The "Margaret Rose" dress, a knitted dress with roses was made popular by the English Princesses Elizabeth and Margaret also in the 1930s.

In the late thirties and forties, previous party wear was dressed up by adding lace collars and cuffs. Little girls started wearing smocked dresses. Formal party dresses featured full skirts of taffeta or velveteen. Ribbons, ruching, and embroidery, as well as the well-known petticoat, were additional trimming for girls' dresses in the late 1940s and 1950s. Upscale simple but elegant designs were included in Florence Eiseman Collections beginning in the 1940s. Long party dresses and the Princess style of dress came into vogue with the 1950s "New Look." Summer dresses at this time were made in crisp washable cotton prints. Sunsuits and sundresses were other popular styles for dress for girls. For boys, tartan plaids and short pants with high socks returned.

In the past, straw hats with streamers or floral trims were fashion accessories for girls. Poke bonnets gave way to wide brims in the 1930s. Assorted berets and felt hats were also worn. In the seventies, old-fashioned sunbonnets and hats with wide brims and flowers were revitalized in fashions for children. The ubiquitous baseball cap in the eighties was worn by all and like the T-shirt could sport any logo; but the coolest boys wore their caps backwards.

In the late sixties and early seventies when the youth culture began dictating fashion, children's clothing styles became more similar to those of adult clothing. Little Orphan Annie styles, miniskirts and turtleneck sweaters prevailed. By the mid-seventies, fashions changed again and many styles were interpreted for the young with romantic and Edwardian looks. In the late seventies, Petit Bateau from France revolutionized infant wear with their footed, knitted cotton suits.

Several clothing designers created styles for children as well as for women. Claire McCardell designed baby and junior fashions in the forties and fifties. Her Baby McCardells proved to be more expensive to make than originally thought and there was a limited market for them. However, her Junior Editions in the 1950s were very successful and featured such classic McCardell design elements as her signature metal closures, long sashes, and wool jersey. Betsey Johnson designed clothing for children in the seventies. Laura Ashley offered clothing for mothers and daughters in simple country prints in natural fabrics in the seventies, eighties, and nineties.

During the last two decades of the century there was a wide selection of children's clothing to choose from. Manufacturers such as the United Colors of Benetton brought well-made and colorful clothing to children's wear. The Baby Gap brought casual, youth-minded clothing designs to the very young. Many fashion designers included lines of children's clothing in their collections. The market for children's clothing was never greater with designs as varied as those for adults. "Special occasion" styles had many interpretations from casual to elegant.

Collecting children's clothing is often about beautiful materials, handwork, uniqueness of style and a great amount of nostalgia. Photographs take on new meaning and life events are personalized by the clothing that was worn.

## Important Designers and Manufacturers of Children's Fashions

LAURA ASHLEY: Laura Ashley was established in 1968 offering simple nostalgic designs in country cotton floral prints. Her signature styles included pinafores and ankle-length jumpers in the 1960s and Edwardian dress styles in the 1970s. Her line of children's fashions reflected the same romantic feeling as her clothing for women. In the 1980s, aside from her signature cottons, cotton corduroys and jerseys were included in her collections. The company is still producing women's and children's clothing.

**BABY LULU, INC.:** The designer Erin Murphy started creating hand-painted overalls in 1993 in Los Angeles. From this she developed a line of styles for infants, toddlers, and children that utilize vintage fabrics and denims. Murphy also developed her own prints based on hand-painted flowers. She is best known for incorporating vintage fabric into her designs. In 1997, Baby Lulu won the girls/infant/toddler casual award. Their layette boy's line is called Pepper Toes and features such motifs as trucks, beach days, and puppies.

**BEST & CO.:** In the 1870s, Best & Co. was one of the fashionable department stores on Broadway that made up the so-called "Ladies Mile." The department store gained recognition for their infants' and children's wear in the late nineteenth century up to and including the 1960s when it was bought out.

**BETSEY JOHNSON:** In 1975 Betsey Johnson designed children's and maternity clothing.

**LAURA BIAGIOTTI:** The Italian designer opened her own design business in Florence in 1972. She designed a white linen batiste dress for her daughter and included it in her 1980s private collection.

**FLORENCE EISEMAN:** Florence Eiseman began her career as a dressmaker in the 1930s. To supplement her income she started making children's clothing to give as gifts. The clothing became so popular that in 1945 she designed a small group of pinafores for her husband to take to Marshall Field's where 3,000 were ordered on the spot. By the 1940s, department stores and children's specialty shops were buying her designs. In 1955 Neiman Marcus awarded Florence Eiseman a fashion award for her contribution to fashion. She was the first children's designer to receive the award. Her fashions in the early years included brother and sister fashions. In 1959 she added knitted turtlenecks to go with her back-to-school jumpers and from this developed a line of Florence Eiseman knits. In 1961 swimsuits were added to the collection, incorporating the new stretch nylon of the time, Helenca. Five years later Lycra was the material used for the stretch suits which are still manufactured today. Eiseman continued to design clothing for infants, girls to age ten, and boys to age four throughout the seventies and eighties. In 1985 the Denver Art Museum held a retrospective of her designs. Florence Eiseman died in 1988. The company was sold in 1989 but was reopened by her son, Lawrence, in 1999 as Eiseman, Inc. They continue to make boys' and girls' clothing, swimwear, and knits with the Eiseman quality designs. Florence Eiseman designs are upscale, well made, elegantly simple clothing in bright, clear colors often with appliqué work.

KRIZIA: This company—Kriziamaglia—was founded in 1954 in Milan, Italy, by Mariuccia Mandelli. She has been designing for children since 1969. Her designs are known to be festive and lighthearted.

JEANNE LANVIN: Lanvin began designing clothing for her younger sister and daughter in the early twentieth century. Her styles became so popular that she opened her own couture house and became famous for her mother and daughter fashions in the teens.

CLAIRE MCCARDELL: McCardell introduced her children's line known as "Baby McCardells" in 1956. She followed this with a line for teens, called "Junior Editions." The Junior fashions included her signature styles such as the use of wool jersey, long sashes, and metal closures.

NANETTE: Manufacturer of infants' dress wear, popular in the 1950s.

PETIT BATEAU: A French manufacturer known for its fine soft cotton since 1893.

POLLY FLINDERS: A popular manufacturer of smocked dresses for infants and children in the 1940s through the 1970s.

## MARKET TRENDS FOR CHILDREN'S FASHIONS

### Infants

EDWARDIAN BONNET. Fine batiste, fancy front lappets, hand-embroidered, lavishly decorated with tiny tucks, lace, and bows, excellent condition. $215
*Courtesy of Linda Ames, Vintage Textile, www.vintagetextile.com*

c. 1860 CHRISTENING GOWN. Fine white cotton lawn, cotton, and linen thread, all handsewn, exquisite embroidery, excellent condition. $565
*Courtesy of Karen Augusta, Antique Lace & Fashion, www.antique-fashion.com*

1860–1880 CHRISTENING BONNET. Cotton muslin, cotton thread, Valenciennes lace, lavishly embroidered large trumpet flowers, hand-sewn, perfect condition. $200.
*Courtesy of Karen Augusta, Antique Lace & Fashion, www.antique-fashion.com*

1940s INFANT SHIRT AND SHORT PANTS. Cotton, tiny red and white polka-dot shirt with rickrack-trimmed white Peter Pan collar, mother-of-pearl buttons, short white pants attached by buttons, belt loops, "Bob & Betty Shop White Plains, NY," excellent condition. $55
*Courtesy of Ann & Bruce Benedict.*

Child's Dress. *Courtesy of Mary Troncale, Branford, CT. Photograph by Tom Amico.*

Child's Dress. *Courtesy of Mary Troncale, Branford, CT, Photograph by Tom Amico.*

Chenille Robe. *Courtesy of Vintage by Stacey Lee, White Plains, NY. Photograph by Tom Amico.*

c. 1900 CHILD'S DRESS. Needle lace, ecru, pristine condition. $250
*Courtesy of Mary Troncale, Branford, CT.*

c. 1900 CHILD'S DRESS. Linen, beige, and white, ribbon sash, mother-of-pearl buttons, pristine condition, $175
*Courtesy of Mary Troncale, Branford, CT.*

1950s CHENILLE ROBE. Pink, excellent condition. $60
*Courtesy of Vintage by Stacey Lee, NY.*

**1940s INFANT SHIRT AND SHORT PANTS.** White dotted-swiss short-sleeved shirt, needle-run embroidered, Peter Pan collar, needle-embroidered trim, mother-of-pearl buttons, short white polished cotton shorts, belt loops and belt cover attaching shirt and pants buttons, "B. Altman & Co. Fifth Avenue New York, the Mason Line," excellent condition. $85
*Courtesy of Ann and Bruce Benedict.*

**1990s BABY LULU GIRL'S ALL-IN-ONE SUIT.** Cotton, floral with pink magnolia blossoms, pale chartreuse ground, cap sleeves, accented with bands of cutwork, pink-tinged satin bow at neck, large yellow and green buttons, long pants with snap crotch, very good condition. $45
*Courtesy of Annie Wilson.*

## Girls

**1890–1905 GIRL'S PARTY DRESS.** Cotton lawn, chemical lace, silk ribbon, pin tucks and rows of hand-embroidered feather stitching, drop waist, original ribbon rosettes, mother-of-pearl buttons, excellent condition. $425
*Courtesy of Karen Augusta, Antique Lace & Fashion, www.antique-fashion.com*

**1915–1920 GIRL'S PARTY DRESS.** Cotton gauze, Irish crocheted lace, silk ribbon rosettes, fabric-covered buttons, excellent condition. $295
*Courtesy of Karen Augusta, Antique Lace & Fashion, www.antique-fashion.com*

**1850s CALICO DRESS.** Brown and cream cotton, calico muslin lining in sleeves, handsewn, brass hooks and eyes, excellent condition. $235
*Courtesy of Karen Augusta, Antique Lace & Fashion, www.antique-fashion.com*

**C. 1905 PLAID DRESS.** Red, white, and black plaid cotton, tan flannel lining in back of bodice, handsewn, five mother–of–pearl buttons, in excellent condition. $125
*Courtesy of Karen Augusta, Antique Lace & Fashion, www.antique-fashion.com*

**1970s CHILD'S DRESS.** Cotton, deep purple floral, lace trim, "Gunne Sax by Jessica," excellent condition. $85
*Courtesy of Laura Smith.*

**1970s FLORENCE EISEMAN BELLS, HALTER TOP, AND MINI SKIRT.** Blue and white checked gingham, yellow and orange daisy appliquéd accents, mint condition. $125
*Courtesy of Kylie Nelson and Catherine Cooney.*

**1970s FLORENCE EISEMAN SWISS-STYLED DRESS.** Lightweight wool blend, pleated closed high on shoulders, opening to box pleats at

hem, pointed collar, long sleeves, snap cuffs, navy short vest with appliquéd hearts and flowers, ribbon trim, excellent condition. $85
*Courtesy of Kylie Nelson & Catherine Cooney.*

**1970s FLORENCE EISEMAN JUMPER WITH MATCHING SCARF.** Red and green wool plaid, matching scarf fringed in red, excellent condition. $45
*Courtesy of Kylie Nelson & Catherine Cooney.*

## Boys

**1920s TWEED SUIT.** Three-piece herringbone wool, jacket, vest, and full-length knickers buttoning at ankle, steel buckles on knickers, purple, tan, and cream, vegetable plastic buttons, original handkerchief with nursery rhyme included, very good condition. $200
*Courtesy of Karen Augusta, Antique Lace & Fashion, www.antique-fashion.com*

**c. 1940 BOY'S JACKET.** Heavy cotton duck cloth, mother-of-pearl buttons, label: "Palm Beach Jacket," very good condition. $48
*Courtesy of Karen Augusta, Antique Lace & Fashion, www.antique-fashion.com*

# BRIDAL DESIGNS

Bridal dress is often reflected by current trends in fashion as well as by the styles of royal weddings or those of prominent personalities of the time. According to bridal historian, Maria McBride-Mellinger, the bride who most influenced the bridal design of the twentieth century was Queen Victoria (1819–1901). Admired for her sense of morality and loyalty to family, Victoria's wedding in 1840 to her cousin Albert was a sensation. Queen Victoria's white satin wedding dress with white veil led the way for the distinctive white wedding gowns that followed.

In 1900, the proper wedding outfit included dresses made from white or ivory organdy, cotton, sheer linen, lawn, or silk. The full-front bodice was ornamented in great detail with tucks, ribbons, eyelets, and lace, characteristic of Edwardian fashion. Lace fans were part of the bride's attire as was the Victorian addition of the white veil of purity. Veils were often embroidered and trains accompanied the gowns. The bride's trousseau was equally brimming with lace and embroidery.

By 1915, wedding gowns had a straighter skirt and a more natural shape. The underclothing of the bride had also changed. Without severe corseting, gowns were simpler—high-waisted with straight lines. In the mid-1920s, the low-waisted gown with a short skirt, just below the knee, was in vogue. This was worn with a cloche cap with a floor-length veil and/or

Edwardian Wedding Dress. *Courtesy of Isadora's, WA, www.isadoras.com. Photograph by Jennifer A. Ledda.*

c. 1915 EDWARDIAN WEDDING DRESS. Fabulous lace work and netting at neck, high Edwardian neckline flowing into skirt and back puddle train, sleeves fall to top of hand in slight point, pristine condition. $2,400

*Courtesy of Isadora's, WA.*

train. The bridesmaids of the 1920s, in contrast, often wore full-length dresses.

Brides of the thirties, influenced by Hollywood fashions, demanded the elegance of a full-length or unevenly hemmed gown and yards of tulle. The beautiful bias-cut silk gown worn by Claudette Colbert in the movie, *It Happened One Night*, is a lovely example of the style worn by a bride in the thirties. A black satin wedding gown made a brief appearance in this decade, with the bride carrying a calla lily.

Wartime restrictions on the use of clothing materials made the wedding gown an exception in the forties. Hollywood designers dressed Katharine Hepburn in a classic forties gown with shoulder pads and cummerbund for the 1942 movie, *Woman of the Year*. However, more often wedding gowns were borrowed or rented as silk and satin were unavailable to make the traditional white wedding gown in the forties. The suit was often the alternative attire.

The wedding dress of Britain's Queen Elizabeth II in 1947 was designed by Norman Hartnell, the dressmaker of the royal family. He was noted for his lavish use of embroidery, satin, tulle, and trimmings on his wedding dresses. His designs were very influential on royal dress standards in the following decades.

The 1950s typified the "New Look." It was a time of affluence, and even a modest gown had regality with beautiful lace or embroidery. The wedding of the decade was that of Princess Grace of Monaco, whose gown, designed by Hollywood's Helen Rose, is in the costume collection of the Philadelphia Museum of Art. It was the most extravagant of any bridal gown of the time, with petticoats, Valenciennes lace, and pearls. Tiered, strapless gowns were also part of the fifties fashion. Some gowns had feather boning and Elizabethan collars. Many were ballerina-length made from organdy, point d'esprit, or nylon lace worn over crinolines; some brides wore tiaras. Later in the decade, and into the sixties, the sheath influenced the design of the wedding dress.

In the sixties, bridal fashions were most influenced by the style of Jackie Kennedy; a Princess-line sleeveless gown with pillbox headpiece was the style of the decade. The paper wedding dress was a fad of the times and the mini-skirted wedding gown was the exception. Often, the new nylon fabric, Quiana, was used to give the illusion of silk. Hairpieces and wigs often took the place of headpieces.

The seventies saw many types of wedding gowns as women began to look for individual expression in choosing wedding apparel. The most popular look was the romantic dress complete with picture hat. Ethnic wedding dresses like those made from Mexican cotton were another popular trend.

The royal marriage of Diana, Princess of Wales, in the eighties encouraged many brides to consider a more elaborate and traditional wedding dress than they had in the previous two decades. Princess Diana's gown was designed by David and Elizabeth Emanuel. They created an off-the-shoulder-styled gown with a bouffant silk taffeta skirt accented with tulle and velvet, having pearl and sequin trimmings, a tight bodice, and a sensationally long train. Throughout the affluent eighties, therefore, formal weddings were prevalent.

Dress trends in the nineties looked toward the millennium and influenced many brides to choose a minimalist style of wedding gown. Carolyn Bessette Kennedy's sleeveless, pearl-colored, floor-length, silk crepe gown was designed by Narciso Rodriguez for Nino Cerruti. The bride wore silk elbow-length gloves and a veil of hand-rolled silk tulle also by Rodriguez. The wedding was described as one of "understated elegance."

Designer bridal gowns reflect any number of fashion periods in history as well as unadorned contemporary styling. There are always brides who favor wearing an heirloom gown or veil. Although the modern bride of the eighties and nineties had more choices than at any other time, the twentieth century bride traditionally still favored a white or ivory dress, formal in nature, with hat, hair ornament, or veil.

## Important Designers and Manufacturers of Bridal Designs

CAROLINA HERRERA: Herrera established herself in the 1980s with bridal fashions that were highly feminine and classically elegant. Herrara enjoys designing with tulle and incorporating details in her gowns that have meaning to the bride. In 1986, she designed Caroline Kennedy's wedding dress embroidered with shamrocks.

JEANNE LANVIN: Lanvin began her career as a dressmaker and milliner in the 1890s. During the early twentieth century she created several signature designs for her couture house such as the "robe de style" based on eighteenth century designs, romantic "picture" dresses, exotic eveningwear and the infamous 1920s chemise dress, as well as children's dresses. Wedding gowns were a special addition to her collections. For these she took inspiration from historic costume designs and fashion plates which she collected.

PRISCILLA OF BOSTON: Priscilla Kidder opened her first Bridal Shop in Boston in 1945. Five years later, Priscilla designed the bridesmaid dresses for the wedding of Grace Kelly and Prince Rainier of Monaco. Priscilla continued to create fashionable wedding gowns through the sixties and seventies including the gowns for the White House brides, Luci Johnson, and Julie and Tricia Nixon. Priscilla of Boston continues to design gowns today in the contemporary styles of the decades. Her gowns reflect the finest fabrics: silks, satins, organdy, and detailed lace, her trademark.

VERA WANG: Wang worked as a senior fashion editor of *Vogue* and as design director for Ralph Lauren before showing her own collection of bridal fashions in 1990 at a salon at the Carlyle Hotel in New York. Her sophisticated contemporary designs emphasize luxurious fabrics and exquisite detailing. Although Wang originally designed for brides, her fashions have also included eveningwear for the stars at the Academy Awards.

JESSICA McCLINTOCK: Jessica McClintock has been designing since the 1960s beginning with her popular Gunne Sax label. The business name was eventually changed to Jessica McClintock and encompasses a wide range of special-occasion fashions. Hillary Clinton chose a Jessica McClintock dress for her wedding. McClintock's bridal gowns are based on her belief in fantasy and romance. She won the Retailers' Choice Award for Special Occasion and Bridal in 1996 and 1997.

## MARKET TRENDS FOR BRIDAL DESIGNS

1930s WEDDING DRESS. Champagne satin with lace bodice, cowl neck, pointed midriff, long sleeves ending in point, hemmed with satin piping, sweeping satin skirt, smooth over hip, excellent condition. $585
*Courtesy of Linda Ames, Vintage Textile, www.vintagetextile.com*

c. 1880 WEDDING GOWN. White-figured muslin, woven with small six-pointed stars, needle-run embroidered lace, seven whalebone stays, moiré silk ribbon, wax flowers and faux pearl buttons, full bustle on the back of gown, excellent condition. $1,375
*Courtesy of Karen Augusta, Antique Lace & Fashion, www.antique-fashion.com*

c. 1885 WEDDING SHOES. Ivory silk satin, leather sole, kidskin and cotton lining, satin rosettes, pristine condition. $295
*Courtesy of Karen Augusta, Antique Lace & Fashion, www.antique-fashion.com*

c. 1911 BRIDESMAID'S GOWN. Gold silk netting of outer layer, ecru satin underlayer, satin skirt with flannel lining holds shape of train, shaped and boned waistband, neckline, sleeves, and skirt edges trimmed with gold silk balls, spray of silk roses across one shoulder, known provenance, excellent condition. $895
*Courtesy of Linda Ames, Vintage Textile, www.vinagetextile.com*

EARLY 20TH CENTURY WEDDING SHAWL. Hand-embroidered, ivory on ivory silk, Chinese shawl, overall pattern of twining leaves and small flowers, large embroidered flower decorates each corner, embroidered

Charles Frederick Worth
Two-Piece Evening
Gown or Bridal Gown.
*Courtesy of Sotheby's.com.*
*Photograph by Monica*
*Anchin.*

C. 1883 CHARLES FREDERICK WORTH TWO-PIECE EVENING OR
BRIDAL GOWN. Heavy cream satin, tight-boned bodice, tiered back,
bustle skirt with slight train, bodice laces in back, intricately constructed
and boned with 13 stays, skirt with 4 ties which when tied create bustle
silhouette, bodice and skirt lined in silk taffeta, very good condition.
Estimated $4,000
*Courtesy of Sothebys.com*

Wedding Coat. *Courtesy of Mary Troncale, Branford, CT. Photograph by Tom Amico.*

**c. 1915 WEDDING COAT.** Wool, exceptional hand-embroidery, relined, excellent condition. $1,200

*Courtesy of Mary Troncale, Branford, CT.*

Wedding Dress. *Courtesy of Mary Troncale, Branford, CT. Photograph by Tom Amico.*

**1920s WEDDING DRESS.** Ecru, low-waisted, scalloped hem, with needle lace and cutwork, pristine condition. $800
*Courtesy of Mary Troncale, Branford, CT.*

satin stitch in silk floss, edged all around with 23"-wide border of hand-knotted silk fringe, excellent condition. $585
*Courtesy of Linda Ames, Vintage Textile, www.vintagetextile.com*

## *Couture*

c. 1878 ÉMILE PINGAT WEDDING GOWN. Cream silk faille, silk embroidered net lace, Valenciennes lace, pleated silk, muslin, heavy netting, cloth flowers with wax orange blossoms, metal weights, bodice lining with 12 whalebone stays, tan silk twill, silk satin and silk taffeta, silk grosgrain petersham, skirt lining—stiffened cotton, train lining—windowpane buckram, stiffened cotton gauze, cotton cording, a pleated double ruffle of cotton gauze edged with Valenciennes lace, "E. PINGAT, 30 RUE LOUIS LE GRAND 30, PARIS," known provenance, excellent condition. $5,800
*Courtesy of Karen Augusta, Antique Lace & Fashion, www.antique-fashion.com*

## *Menswear*

EARLY TO MID-1800s SILK EMBROIDERED MEN'S WEDDING VEST. Off-white, white-on-white embroidery, excellent detail work, size 36S, excellent condition. $195
*Courtesy of Deborah Burke, Antique & Vintage Dress Gallery, www.antiquedress.com*

# WESTERN STYLES

Western dress styles date back to the American cowboy of the 1890s. The cowboy at this time was already outfitted with a Stetson hat, bandanna, wool or cotton shirt, pocket vest, deerskin gloves or gauntlets, jeans, chaps, and boots. The hat, thought to be the most important item by the cowboy, could be personalized with different bands of trim, by the size of the brim, or height of the crown; even by the way it was creased in the center. Gloves were another way to personalize attire; fringed gauntlets were often beaded in bright colors with tooled work. The shirt was originally plain and tailored with the bib front making an appearance in the 1900s. By the 1930s, film stars glamorized the life of the cowboy and with it came the rodeo fashions associated with Western wear today.

Early movies featuring authentic cowboy garb contributed to the legend of the cowboy in the twentieth century. The movie version of Owen Wister's novel, *The Virginian,* starring Gary Cooper, gave credence to the image of the cowboy as a romantic hero. John Wayne's movies of the thirties added glamour with the western styling of leather vests and buckskin. Two-toned sateen shirts with buttons and flaps were popular in this decade.

Plateau Indian Vest. *Courtesy of Linda Kohn and Joseph Sherwood, High Noon of Los Angeles, www.highnoon.com. Photograph by High Noon.*

**C. 1900s PLATEAU INDIAN VEST.** Finely (small) beaded, multicolored, floral pattern, with original front-ties and fringe around neck and down back, fully lined, fine condition. Estimate $1,500–$2,000
*Courtesy of High Noon of Los Angeles.*

Later, shirts made in gabardine, rayon, cotton, or wool were manufactured. The hatbands were made of silk or were beaded.

In 1938, the Western clothing designer Jack A. Weil added metal snap-buttons to the cowboy shirt, which are still used on the Western shirt today. In 1946 Weil had his own company designing western clothes for men, women, and children under the name Rockmount RanchWear Manufacturing Company. In the forties, cowboy and Western scenes were reproduced on ties, reflecting an interest in the cowboy's life. Photo ties and hand-painted ties were both designed with Western motifs.

There are several well-known designers of the Western shirt. Nathan Turk in Los Angeles made embroidered shirts. Rodeo Ben, a Philadelphia designer of Western wear, produced shirts with mother-of-pearl snaps in the thirties, forties, and fifties. He supplied many of the television cowboys with their clothing, especially Gene Autry. Viola Grae, another designer of Western wear, added jewel and embroidery work to clothing. Nudies brand of Western wear was made in California, primarily for the movies.

With the popularity of television Westerns in the fifties, featuring stars like the singing cowboy Roy Rogers and his wife Dale Evans, Western clothing appeared in clothing stores everywhere. H Bar C and California Ranchwear were popular brands. Children's Western outfits were popular at this time as well. Western fashions also began to encompass Native American wear. Native American clothing included Navajo skirts, authentic pouches, moccasins, beaded shirts and bags. (It is important that these pieces be purchased from a reputable dealer, one who is a member of the Antique Tribal Art Dealers Association.)

Cowboy boots as we know them originated in the 1900s. Tight-fitting high boots were important to the cowboy on the range. This boot style flattered the foot and acted as protection when riding or working on the range. Handles called "mule-ears" were sewn on the tops of the boot to assist in pulling them on. H. J. Justin & Sons featured a square-toed boot with decorative stitching in their 1947 catalog that typified the cowboy boot of the times. Heel and toe shapes changed during the decades but the basic structure of the boot remained the same.

Levi Strauss popularized denim pants during the California Gold Rush of 1849 when he designed a pair of work pants, in a durable indigo-blue cotton called denim. Over time other style elements were added such as orange stitching and copper rivets. After World War II, Levi Strauss & Co. expanded their line of pants, jackets, and jeans. Other companies also made what became known as jeans; Lee in 1927 and Wrangler in 1947.

Western fashions have inspired current fashion designers at different times. In the eighties, Giorgio Armani introduced his version of the cowboy's duster: a long raincoat used by the cowboy for protection on the range. In the seventies, Calvin Klein introduced the designer jeans. Ralph Lauren followed with his popular country Western jeans, jeans skirts, cowboy boots, and prairie skirts all reminiscent of the Old West. Denim jeans, a truly American style of dress, remained a part of American fashion throughout the twentieth century.

## Important Designers and Manufacturers of Western Styles

**CALIFORNIA RANCHWEAR:** In 1936 Seymour Christenfeld of the Christenfeld family started a California branch to the family business of H Bar C. It was called California Ranchwear, the label of which is an indication that the garment was the company's high-end merchandise and manufactured in their Los Angeles facility.

**H BAR C:** In the late 1800s, the Christenfeld family started manufacturing Western pants. They merged with the shirtmaker Halpern, and the company was known as H and C, Halpern and Christenfeld. In 1936 Halpern died and the decision was made to take the corporate name of H Bar C. Margaret and Frank Miele were the designers who originated the styles, patterns, and elaborate embroideries for the H Bar C Company starting in the late forties. H Bar C manufactured the wardrobes for Western television and movie stars in the fifties. The H Bar C Company, although no longer family operated, is in the process of restructuring and will again be producing fine Western wear for upcoming trade shows.

**LEVI STRAUSS & CO.:** This famous company was actually started in the 1860s by Levi Strauss and Jacob Davis. Strauss is credited with bringing indigo blue–dyed denim to the manufacturing of jeans. Copper rivets and orange topstitching were later added to the back pants pockets. In 1886 a leather label was added to the back of the pants and in 1936 a red tab was added to further identify the pants as Levi's. After World War II, Levi Strauss & Co. expanded their designs to include shirts, jackets, and other denim wear.

**NATHAN TURK:** Embroidered Western shirts.

**NUDIE:** Nudie, a Los Angeles designer, provided highly decorative Western wear for film stars in the 1930s and later for country and Western stars.

**ROCKMOUNT RANCHWEAR MANUFACTURING COMPANY:** In 1946, Jack A. Weil opened this manufacturing company specializing in high-quality Western wear. Weil is credited with putting the "Gripper Snap" on Western shirts. In the 1950s he came out with square-dancing costumes for men and women. This family-operated business manufactured children's Western wear as well.

**RODEO BEN:** Rodeo Ben from Philadelphia provided many of the shirts used in television, especially those for Gene Autry. He used mother-of-pearl snaps on his shirts in the thirties, forties, and fifties.

**JOHN B. STETSON COMPANY:** The original maker of what is referred to as the "Stetson" or "John B." hat was created in the 1890s by a hatmaker in Philadelphia, John B. Stetson. He provided many designs for his hats which cowboys often trimmed in their own fashion. His company was bought by Resistol in 1927. Resistol is still producing the Stetson and the Resistol hat; the Stetson for the style-conscious and the Resistol for the working cowboy.

Original Tom Mix–Stetson Hats Advertisement, very good condition. Estimate $200–$300. *Courtesy of Linda Kohn and Joseph Sherwood, High Noon of Los Angeles, www.highnoon.com. Photograph by High Noon.*

**VIOLA GRAE:** Viola Grae was famous for embroidered and jeweled shirts.

**WRANGLER:** A subsidiary of the V.F. Corporation, Wrangler produced their first jeans in 1947. Their goal was to provide proper-fitting jeans for rodeo cowboys, pants that fit over boots, and high pockets that allowed the cowboy to use his pockets while still in the saddle. Wrangler presides as the official sponsor of the Professional Rodeo Cowboys Association.

Barbara Stanwyck's Annie Oakley Dress. *Courtesy of Linda Kohn and Joseph Sherwood, High Noon of Los Angeles, www.highnoon.com. Photograph by High Noon.*

**1935 BARBARA STANWYCK'S ANNIE OAKLEY DRESS.** Barbara Stanwyck's dress from her first film for RKO. Estimate $4,000–$6,000
*Courtesy of Linda Kohn and Joseph Sherwood, High Noon of Los Angeles.*

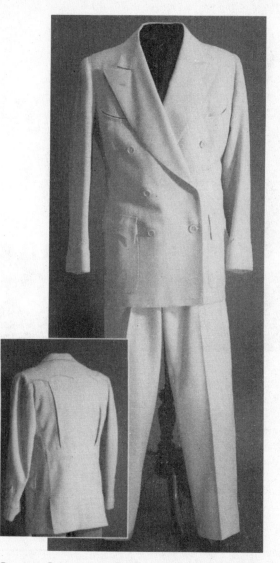

Custom Gene Autry Suit. *Courtesy of Linda Kohn & Joseph Sherwood, High Noon of Los Angeles, www.highnoon.com. Photograph by High Noon.*

**Early 1940s Custom Gene Autry Suit.** Cream colored, tailor-made, marked inside jacket pocket "made expressly for Gene Autry," excellent condition. Estimate $800–$1,200
*Courtesy of Linda Kohn and Joseph Sherwood, High Noon of Los Angeles.*

Ken Maynard's Personal Shirt. *Courtesy of Linda Kohn and Joseph Sherwood, High Noon of Los Angeles, www.highnoon.com. Photograph by High Noon.*

Gene Autry's Nudie Cowboy Shirt. *Courtesy of Linda Kohn and Joseph Sherwood, High Noon of Los Angeles, www.highnoon.com. Photograph by High Noon.*

**KEN MAYNARD'S PERSONAL SHIRT.** By Fay Ward, "The Best 'n Western Garb," red gabardine, green, pink, maroon, and yellow flowers, white trim, used in Ken Maynard Circus, several small holes, runny red color, good condition. Estimate $600–$900
*Courtesy of Linda Kohn and Joseph Sherwood, High Noon of Los Angeles.*

**1962 GENE AUTRY'S NUDIE COWBOY SHIRT.** Gene Autry's personal Nudie cowboy shirt, embroidered thunderbird design, outstanding condition. Estimate $200–$300
*Courtesy of Linda Kohn and Joseph Sherwood, High Noon of Los Angeles.*

Plateau Indian
Gauntlets. *Courtesy of
Linda Kohn and Joseph
Sherwood, High Noon of
Los Angeles,
www.highnoon.com.
Photograph by High Noon.*

Plateau Indian Purse.
*Courtesy of Linda Kohn
and Joseph Sherwood,
High Noon of Los Angeles,
www.highnoon.com.
Photograph by High Noon.*

**1920s PLATEAU INDIAN GAUNTLETS.** Oversized and impressive, finely
(small) floral beading, fringed, contrasting white field, fully lined, outstanding condition. Estimate $1,200–$1,800
*Courtesy of Linda Kohn and Joseph Sherwood, High Noon of Los Angeles.*

**1900s PLATEAU INDIAN PURSE.** Highly visual fine-beaded pictorial
with bow and arrow and buffalo design on front, floral pattern on back,
excellent condition. Estimate $1500–$2,500
*Courtesy of Linda Kohn and Joseph Sherwood, High Noon of Los Angeles.*

BJ's N. Turk Hudson Bay Jacket. *Courtesy of Linda Kohn and Joseph Sherwood, High Noon of Los Angeles, www.highnoon.com. Photograph by High Noon.*

Nudie's Cowboy Boots and Hawk and Butterfly Boots. *Courtesy of Linda Kohn and Joseph Sherwood, High Noon of Los Angeles, www.highnoon.com. Photograph by High Noon.*

Two Wool
Chimayo Coats.
*Courtesy of
Linda Kohn and
Joseph Sherwood,
High Noon
of Los Angeles,
www.highnoon.com.
Photograph by
High Noon.*

**BJ's N. Turk Hudson Bay Jacket.** "BJ's N. Turk Van Nuys, Cal"
marked. Estimate $600–$900
*Courtesy of Linda Kohn and Joseph Sherwood, High Noon of Los Angeles.*

**1930s Two Wool Chimayo Coats.** All-season, bright colors and
bold designs, great condition. Estimate $600–$900 each.
*Courtesy of Linda Kohn and Joseph Sherwood, High Noon of Los Angeles.*

**Nudie's Cowboy Boots.** "Nudie, Rodeo Tailor of North Hollywood,"
custom-made, adorned with inlaid spurs and horses, gold lamé, pink,
blue, turquoise, and rhinestones including pavé heels, 13″ h × 11″ l.
Estimate $1,000–$1,500
*Courtesy of Linda Kohn and Joseph Sherwood, High Noon of Los Angeles.*

**c. 1940s Hawk and Butterfly Boots.** Scalloped tops, bold inlaid
images, minor repair, otherwise fine condition. Estimate $900–$1,300
*Courtesy of Linda Kohn and Joseph Sherwood, High Noon of Los Angeles.*

## MARKET TRENDS FOR WESTERN WEAR

**1940s–1950s GABARDINE COWGIRL COAT.** White leather fringe, iridescent lining, label: "Ranch Maid Western Wear of Denver," excellent condition. $200
*Courtesy of Lynn Pastore, Avenue 13–5 and Dime Vintage, www.510vintage.com*

**1950s COWGIRL SWING SKIRT.** Cotton fabric with great western images, excellent condition. $75
*Courtesy of Lynn Pastore, Avenue 13–5 and Dime Vintage, www.510vintage.com*

**1950s H BAR C COWGIRL WESTERN COAT.** Waist-length jacket, wool with satin lining, old Conmar brass zipper, excellent detail, excellent condition. $75
*Courtesy of Lynn Pastore, Avenue 13–5 and Dime Vintage, www.510vintage.com*

**1950s GABARDINE COWBOY SHIRT.** Black with floral embroidery, pearl snap buttons, famous H Bar C label, excellent condition. $100
*Courtesy of Lynn Pastore, Avenue 13–5 and Dime Vintage, www.510vintage.com*

**1940s—1950s GABARDINE COWBOY JACKET.** Black with diamond-shaped pearl snap buttons, very rockabilly, waist-length, excellent condition. $175
*Courtesy of Lynn Pastore, Avenue 13–5 and Dime vintage, www.510vintage.com*

**1950s GABARDINE WESTERN SHIRT.** Burgundy, pearl snap buttons, Miller Western Wear, excellent condition. $50
*Courtesy of Lynne Pastore, Avenue 13–5 and Dime Vintage, www.510vintage.com*

**1930s HOOT GIBSON CHILD'S OUTFIT.** Rare "Universal Jewel Ranch" faux leopard design complete with hat, vest, and chaps, very good condition. Estimate $400–$600
*Courtesy of Linda Kohn and Joseph Sherwood, High Noon of Los Angeles, www.highnoon.com*

**1900–1910 WILD WEST SHOW VEST.** Northern Plains, Indian-made, front: two butterflies, owl, roses, and vines, back: probably beaded later (1920s), original lining, back fringed and decoratively beaded with cowboy lassoing steer. Estimate $1,500–$2,500
*Courtesy of Linda Kohn and Joseph Sherwood, High Noon of Los Angeles, www.highnoon.com*

**c. 1910 EARLY COWBOY SLICKER.** Corduroy-lined collar, brass buttons, all original, excellent condition. Estimate $1,400–$1,800
*Courtesy of Linda Kohn and Joseph Sherwood, High Noon of Los Angeles, www.highnoon.com*

c. 1890 YAKIMA INDIAN GAUNTLETS. Figural, Elk Dreamer Society, multicolored, beaded and fringed, rich yellow ocher color, pictorial: cowboy wearing hat and boots holding horse with square-skirted, high-back saddle having tapaderos, outstanding condition. Estimate $3,000–$5,000
*Courtesy of Linda Kohn and Joseph Sherwood, High Noon of Los Angeles, www.highnoon.com*

1962 GENE AUTRY'S PERSONAL COWBOY SUIT. Herringbone, marked and dated in pocket by maker—"Tartaglia Bros, Beverly Hills, GENE AUTRY, July 1962," impeccable condition. Estimate $800–$1,200
*Courtesy of Linda Kohn and Joseph Sherwood, High Noon of Los Angeles, www.highnoon.com*

LATE 1940s ARIZONA STATE BOOTS. One of the original 48 "State Boots" to be commissioned by Acme and made by Lucchese. Each pair of boots included a representation of the state's flag, bird, flower, capitol building, and symbols of commerce, industry, and history. Originals were distinguished by holes drilled in the bottoms of the soles that allowed for mounting on a traveling display that toured state fairs, rodeos, and store openings; only 18 of the original 48 pairs are still known to exist. Estimate $4,000–$6,000
*Courtesy of Linda Kohn and Joseph Sherwood, High Noon of Los Angeles, www.highnoon.com*

1960s–1970s WESTERN SHIRT. Blue polyester, "H Bar C," size 15½ × 33, "New Old Stock," excellent condition. $24.
*Courtesy of Art and Janene Fawcett, Vintage Silhouettes, CA, www.vintagesilhouettes.com*

1960s–1970s WESTERN SHIRT. Green floral polyester/cotton blend, "H Bar C," size 15½ × 32, "New Old Stock," excellent condition. $24
*Courtesy of Art and Janene Fawcett, Vintage Silhouettes, CA, www.vintagesilhouettes.com*

1950s WESTERN SHIRT. Gray gabardine, "Miller Western Wear, Denver, CO." $95
*Courtesy of Screaming Mimi's, New York, NY.*

1970s WESTERN SHIRT. Navy permanent press, plaid trim, excellent condition. $45
*Courtesy of Screaming Mimi's, New York, NY.*

# PART THREE

RESOURCES

# *Ways to Buy*

SHOW DEALERS AND STORES THAT SPECIALIZE IN VINTAGE
FASHION AND FABRICS
We recommend calling or checking the websites of the following listings
for their hours. (Dealers are listed with "By appointment only.")

ALASKA
**The Rage Vintage Clothing**
Catherine Shenk
432 G Street
Anchorage, AK 99501
(907) 274-7243
e-mail: no-lemmings01@aol.com
www.no-lemmings.com
*Women's and men's everyday attire as well as formal wear from the teens to the
mid-1970s are all part of The Rage Vintage Clothing's inventory. They also carry
accessories—hats and shoes.*

CALIFORNIA
**High Noon of Los Angeles**
9929 Venice Boulevard
Los Angeles, CA 90034
(310) 202-9010
By appointment only.
e-mail: Highnoon@pacbell.net

FAX: (310) 202-9011

www.highnoon.com

*High Noon's specialty is very fine Western wear. Their inventory includes shirts, jeans, chaps, boots, hats, Indian beadwork, and textiles.*

### Vintage Silhouettes

1301 Pomona Avenue

Crockett, CA 94525

(800) 636-1410

e-mail: stone@ncal.verio.com

www.vintagesilhouettes.com

*Vintage Silhouettes carries men's and women's wearable fashions and accessories from the 1860s through the 1960s, including Edwardian and Victorian fashion and couture. Their online shopping is changed daily.*

### Golyester

136 S. La Brea Avenue

Los Angeles, CA 90046

(323) 931-1339

*Golyester carries women's fashions and accessories from the late 1800s through the 1950s. Among their specialties are women's suits from the 1930s and 1940s, hats from the 1920s to the 1950s, ethnic fashions from the late 1800s, and Spanish and Chinese shawls. They also carry an extensive inventory of textiles, ribbons, buttons, and trims.*

### Madame Butterfly

5474 College Avenue

Oakland, CA 94618

(510) 653-1525

FAX: (510) 594-1684

*With an inventory that covers the Victorian period through the 1970s, Madame Butterfly has women's clothing and accessories (hats, bags, jewelry, and shoes) as well as men's Hawaiian shirts, tuxedos, and bell-bottoms. They also rent costumes.*

### Wear It Again Sam

3922 Park Boulevard

San Diego, CA 92103

(619) 299-0185

e-mail: wearitagainsam@home.com

www.wearitagainsamvintage.com

*Wear It Again Sam carries mint-condition, wearable men's and women's clothing from 1900 to the early 1960s, as well as hats, shoes, and purses. They have Victorian dresses and wedding gowns, and specialize in women's and men's party clothing.*

### Hot Couture
101 Third Street
Santa Rosa, CA 95401
(707) 528-7247
e-mail: hcvintage@sonic.com
*Covering 1900 through 1970, Hot Couture carries men's and women's casual-to-formal wearable fashions and accessories. Please call to ask about their vintage reproductions.*

### Stop the Clock
2110 Addison Street
Berkeley, CA 94704
(510) 841-2142
*Stop the Clock carries both men's and women's clothing and accessories from the 1930s through the 1970s. They also have a special collection of Hawaiian shirts.*

### Paris 1900
2703 Main Street
Santa Monica, CA 90405
(310) 396-0405
*Paris 1900 specializes in women's and children's fashions from the turn of the century through the 1930s. They also carry bridal pieces.*

### Paper Bag Princess
8700 Santa Monica Boulevard
West Hollywood, CA 90069
(310) 358-1985
www.paperbagp.com
*Couture designers such as Yves Saint Laurent, Rudi Gernreich, Gucci, and more are part of this shop's inventory. Paper Bag Princess also specializes in hats of all kinds and accessories.*

### Trappings of Time
470 Hamilton Avenue
Palo Alto, CA 94301
e-mail: info@trappingsoftime.com
www.trappingsoftime.com
*Trappings of Time has an extensive inventory for men and women; among the highlights are "zoot" suits, gangster suits, speakeasy suits, lounge lizard jackets, women's cocktail dresses, and formal wear. Their fashions and accessories are from the 1880s to the 1980s. Their designers, Fortuny, Pucci, Blackwell, and Chanel, can be seen by appointment only. In addition they have authentic costume rentals.*

### Ages Ahead
524 Bryant Street
Palo Alto, CA 94301
(650) 327-4480
e-mail: info@agesahead.com
www.agesahead.com
*Ages Ahead carries wedding dresses and accessories from the late 1880s to the 1960s. They are the sister store to Trappings of Time.*

### The Stage Stop
Janice Stockwell
4330-C Clayton Road
Concord, CA 94521
(925) 685-4440
FAX: (925) 685-4440
e-mail: sakistoc@pacbell.net
*The Stage Stop carries Victorian and turn-of-the-century fashions to the 1960s. They have a fine collection of prom dresses and eveningwear for women and 1930s and 1940s suits. They carry vintage tuxedos for men.*

### Glorious Old Clothes
Gloria Zisch
107 W. Main Street
Grass Valley, CA 95945
(530) 477-9001
e-mail: gzisch@webtv.net
*Quality wearables for men and women from the 1920s to the 1960s; Glorious Old Clothes also carries vintage women's suits and accessories.*

### Departures from the Past
2028 Fillmore Street
San Francisco, CA 94115
(415) 885-3377
*Departures from the Past carries men's and women's vintage fashions. They specialize in formal wear from the 1940s and 1950s. They have a large assortment of lingerie and actual 1960s fashions still in the wrappers. Rental clothing is available.*

### Decades Vintage
8214½ Melrose Avenue
West Hollywood, CA 90046
(323) 655-0223
FAX: (323) 655-0172
www.decadesinc.com
*This upstairs store carries 1960s to 1970s couture fashions for men and women.*

**Resurrection** (sister stores in NYC)
8006 Melrose Avenue
Los Angeles, CA 90046
(323) 651-5516
FAX: (323) 651-2785
e-mail: redsny97@aol.com
*Like its sister stores, Resurrection in L.A. sells mostly designer 1960s and 1970s and accessories.*

## COLORADO

**Avenue 13–5 and Dime Vintage**
606 E. 13th Avenue
Denver, CO 80203
(303) 299-1170
e-mail: Ln51@prodigy.net
*A small shop absolutely overflowing with vintage fashions—Western, Levi's, capri pants, bell-bottoms, designer, platforms, ties, hand-painted swings, etc.*

## CONNECTICUT

**Mary Feq Troncale**
Branford CT
(203) 481-3302
By appointment only.
*Mary Troncale's collection of fine museum-quality pieces includes women's evening-wear, antique gowns, and designer clothing.*

**Lorr Polizzi**
North Branford, CT
(203) 481-3730
FAX: (203) 481-3730
By appointment only.

**Yesterday's Threads**
Branford, CT
(203) 481-6452
FAX: (203) 483-7550
By appointment only.
*Yesterday's Threads carries men's and women's clothing, accessories, and costume jewelry from the 1800s to the 1940s.*

**Retroactive**
58 River Street
Milford, CT 06460

(203) 877-6050
FAX: (203) 877-6050
e-mail: retroactive@att.net
www.designervintage.com
*Retroactive's specialty is European and American designer clothing. They also carry crisp, clean, and wearable fashions from the 1920s to the 1970s.*

### Sophia's
1 Liberty Way
Greenwich, CT 06830
(203) 869-5990
FAX: (203) 869-5990
*Vintage fashions from Victorian to the 1970s—bridal, ball gowns, suits, furs, gloves, and accessories are all part of Sophia's inventory. They also have costume rental.*

## FLORIDA

### Donovan & Gray
3623 South Dixie Highway
West Palm Beach, FL 33405
(561) 838-4442
FAX: (561) 838-9449
e-mail: jafiii@bellsouth.net
*Donovan & Gray has a large inventory of clothing from the 1800s to the 1980s. They carry women's designer labels and all accessories, as well as a selection of vintage lace.*

### Collage Antiques
Carol Canty-Moyse
Graham Moyse
(954) 927-9973
By appointment only.
e-mail: ccmoyse@aol.com
www.antiqnet.com/collage
*Collage Antiques carries suits, dresses, coats, and accessories from the 1900s to the 1960s. They also carry antique jewelry.*

### Orlando Vintage
Lisa Marie Booth
2117 W. Fairbanks Avenue
Winter Park, FL 32789
(407) 599-7225
e-mail: Orlvintage@aol.com
www.fashiondig.com

*Orlando Vintage carries men's and women's vintage clothing from the 1920s to the early 1980s. Their well-stocked inventory includes hats to handbags and everything in between. They also have a rental boutique.*

## ILLINOIS

### Wacky Cats
3109 N. Lincoln Avenue
Chicago, IL 60657
(773) 929-6701
e-mail: wackycats@hotmail.com
*Wacky Cats carries vintage clothing from the 1940s through the 1970s.*

### Carrie's Vintage Clothing
204 North Neil Street
Champagne, IL 61820
(217) 352-3231
e-mail: Carries@advancenet.net
www.advancenets.net/~carries
*You can find men's and women's Victorian as well as 1920s to early 1970s vintage clothing, rockabilly Western wear, furs, gowns, formals, all accessories, and pop culture magazines in this vintage store.*

### Tender Buttons
946 N. Rush Street
Chicago, IL 60611
(312) 337-7033
*An adorable yet spacious shop offering the same unique buttons that are found in its New York store, Tender Buttons specializes in vintage and antique porcelain, glass, Bakelite, wooden, and metal buttons.*

## INDIANA

### Red Rose Vintage Clothing
834 East 64th Street
Indianapolis, IN 46220
(317) 257-5016
www.rrnspace.com
*Red Rose Vintage Clothing has a well-stocked inventory of late 1800s through the 1970s vintage clothing and accessories for men and women. Their website is added to weekly.*

## LOUISIANA

### Trashy Diva
829 Chartres Street
New Orleans, LA 70116

(504) 581-4555
www.trashy-diva.net
*Trashy Diva sells clothing and accessories from the 1900s to the 1960s. Their inventory includes glamour wear, designer fashions, and corsets.*

## MARYLAND

### Antique Textile Resource
Nancy Gewirz
Bethesda, MD
(301) 951-8477
FAX: (301) 951-9095
By appointment only.
*Nancy Gewirz carries antique textiles from 1840 to 1930. She specializes in old Fortuny and antique and vintage clothing for design purposes only. She does deal in sportswear, WW II jeep jackets, and jeans.*

## MASSACHUSETTS

### Cindi St. Clair
Boston, MA
(617) 308-7843
(207) 438-9639 (Maine)
By appointment only.
*An incredible collection of fashions for men, women, and children; Cindi St. Clair shows at the Pier Show in New York City annually.*

### Linda White Antique Clothing
2 Maple Avenue
Post Office Square
Upton, MA 01568
(508) 529-4439
e-mail: info@vintageclothing.com
www.vintageclothing.com
*Impeccable museum-quality pieces are what Linda White is renowned for. Her inventory includes Victorian and Edwardian fashions to 1960s, primarily for women and children. She has elegant eveningwear from the 1920s and 1930s, wedding gowns and accessories, vintage, antique, and estate jewelry.*

### Jean Breen
Massachusetts
(781) 762-4809
e-mail: LVDewy@misn.comp
By appointment only.

*Jean Breen carries Victorian children's wear, 18th century to the 1920s women's clothing, and wedding gowns. She also has accessories, including fans, buttons, and lace.*

### Lynn and Rob Morin
W. Townsend, MA
(978) 597-6935
By appointment only.
e-mail: Ifm@net1plus.com
*The Morins specialize in men's, women's, and children's clothing and accessories from the 18th and 19th centuries. Their collection includes mint and wearable items to pieces of textiles. They also have trade manuscripts of 19th century textiles.*

### Closet Upstairs
223 Newbury Street
Boston, MA 02116
(617) 267-5757
FAX: (617) 267-5757
www.closetupstairs.com
*Closet Upstairs carries men's and women's Victorian to the 1980s—casual, formal, evening, cocktail dresses, prom dresses, tuxedo pants, and accessories.*

### Circa
42 Main Street
Fairhaven, MA 02719
(508) 997-9390
*Circa deals in men's and women's wearable vintage clothing, as well as fabrics and lace. They also have period costumes.*

### The Fainting Couch
250 No. Main Street
Mansfield, MA 02048
(508) 339-7733
e-mail: Faintc@gis.net
www.Faintingcouch.com
*This lovely store specializes in fine, antique apparel and accessories from the 18th century to the 1960s.*

### Northampton Bead Company
2nd Floor, Thorne's Marketplace
at 150 Main
Northampton, MA 01060
(413) 584-5582

*The Northampton Bead Company carries a full selection of antique and vintage buttons. Their inventory includes buttons of Bakelite, jet, metal, and enamel. When available, they also have vintage beads and sequins.*

## MICHIGAN
**Paul Shore**
Lansing, MI 48915
(517) 482-2560
e-mail: rageoftheage@hotmail.com
www.rageoftheage.com
By appointment only.
*Paul Shore's inventory includes 20th century wearable vintage in good condition for men and women. Shore specializes in women's business suits and eveningwear.*

**Everybody's Everything**
1523 Niles Avenue
St. Joseph, MI 49085
(616) 983-3276
e-mail: ee@qtm.net
*Everybody's Everything carries clothing and accessories for men, women, and children from the 1920s to the 1970s. They also rent costumes.*

## MINNESOTA
**Linda and Winona**
**Mid-Town Antique Mall**
301 S. Main Street
Stillwater, MN 55082
(651) 430-0808, (651) 430-1843
You can also call for an appointment.
*Hat lovers take note: Linda and Winona carry hats and bonnets from early Victorian to 1920s cloches. They also have pre-Victorian and Victorian women's and children's clothing and accessories up to the 1920s; post 1920s—high style only. They also specialize in quilts.*

## NEW JERSEY
**Of Times Gone By**
Sharon Schwartz
Cherry Hill, NJ 08003
(856) 795-21445
By appointment only.
*Renowned for her fine handbags and purses, Sharon Schwartz also shows exquisite hats.*

### Time After Time Vintage Clothing
"Clothing from the Past"
81 Main Street
Madison, NJ 07940
(973) 966-6877
*Time After Time carries men's and women's fashions, designer clothes, and accessories from the turn of the century to the 1970s, as well as lace, buttons, trims, and jewelry.*

### Monroes
12 S. Broad Street
Ridgewood, NJ 07450
(201) 251-9400
e-mail: mvintiques@aol.com
*Monroes carries men's and women's vintage fashions and accessories from the 1930s to the 1960s.*

### Rags to Riches
8917 River Road
Edgewater, NJ 07020
(201) 941-3121
e-mail: richesby sheila@aol.com
*Calling their collection funky to elegant, Rags to Riches carries mostly women's clothing from the 1920s to the 1970s.*

### Lisa Victoria
(201) 488-2824
By appointment only.
*Garments from the 1800s to selected 1960s and 1970s, Lisa Victoria offers high-style, glamorous, designer pieces of museum quality.*

## New York
### Eileen Love
Warwick, NY
(845) 988-9609
By appointment only.
e-mail: Love@warwick.net
*Eileen Love has a superb selection of women's dresses and suits from the 1920s to the 1940s, exquisite vintage purses, and other accessories.*

### Lorraine Wohl Collection
860 Lexington Avenue
New York, NY 10021
(212) 472-0191

*The Lorraine Wohl Collection specializes in women's clothing and couture, as well as accessories and jewelry. They also have a special collection of fine, beaded evening pieces.*

## O Mistress Mine

143 Seventh Avenue S.
New York, NY 10014
(212) 691-4327
e-mail: omistres@aol.com
www.omistressmine.com
*In addition to their vintage fashion inventory that covers the turn of the century through the 1960s, O Mistress Mine specializes in fancy Art Deco and thirties gowns, and designer-label pieces.*

## Tender Buttons

143 East 62nd Street
New York, NY 10021
(212) 758-7004
FAX: (212) 319-8474
*A wonderful little store, Tender Buttons has oodles of fascinating unique buttons. They identify themselves as having the largest collection of antique and vintage buttons in America. They now have a sister store in Chicago.*

## Patina

451 Broome Street
New York, NY 10013
(212) 625-3375
FAX: (212) 625-3391
e-mail: patina@banet.net
*Patina has "hand-selected" vintage clothing and accessories from the 1950s to the 1970s—beaded sweaters, French-style jackets, coats, and handbags.*

## Buy-Gone Days

Pine Bush, NY
(845) 744-6422
e-mail: ina@warwick.net
By appointment only.
*Buy-Gone Days carries women's designer clothing and accessories from the 1950s to a select group of designers in the 1980s. Their evening and sport clothing date from the 1920s to the 1950s.*

## Alice's Underground

481 Broadway
New York, NY 10007
(212) 431-9067

*Alice's Underground carries men's and women's fashions and accessories from the 1950s through the 1970s. They also have bins of fabrics and some designer pieces.*

### Cheap Jack's Vintage Clothing
841 Broadway
New York, NY 10003
(212) 777-9564
www.cheapjacks.com
*Carrying "everything from the turn of the century to modern times," Cheap Jack's has men's and women's clothing and accessories.*

### Kathy's Back Room
Elma, NY 14059
(716) 652-3929
By appointment only.
*Specializing in 1950s, this dealer carries men's, women's, and children's vintage fashions. Kathy's Back Room can also be found at Antique World, 10995 Main Street, Clarence, NY 14031. (716) 759-8483.*

### Quincy Kirsch
30 West 26th Street (LL)
New York, NY 10010
(917) 553-3614
*This shop carries men's, women's, and children's clothing from the 1800s to the 1960s. They also carry accessories and costume jewelry.*

### Sara Daha
(917) 501-7343
By appointment only.
*Fashions include men's and women's from the 1940s to the 1970s.*

### From Around the World Vintage
209 West 38th Street, Suite 1207
New York, NY 10018
(212) 354-6536
FAX: (212) 354-6541
By appointment only.
e-mail: Fatwvintag@aol.com
*Quality clothing from the 1930s to the 1980s for both men and women, From Around the World Vintage is for the hip, fashionable shopper. They carry athletic wear, casual wear, eveningwear, and tropical. They also serve as a resource for fashion designers.*

### Collage Antiques
Carol Canty-Moyse
Graham Moyse

(631) 907-0743
By appointment only.
e-mail: ccmoyse@aol.com
www.antiqnet.com/collage
*Collage Antiques carries suits, dresses, coats, and accessories from the 1900s to the 1960s. They also carry antique jewelry.*

### Right to the Moon, Alice
Ron and Alice Lindholm
Cooks Falls, NY
(607) 498-5750
By appointment only.
e-mail: rightothemoonalice@yahoo.com
eBay user name <ragman55>
*Men's, women's, and children's clothing are all included in this vintage clothing company's inventory. Their specialty is providing costumes for films and theaters.*

### Pepper
(718) 972-3225
FAX: (718) 972-3225
By appointment only.
e-mail: vintagecouture1@aol.com
*With an inventory of over 6,000 pieces, Pepper carries mint-condition turn-of-the-century to the 1990s high-quality clothing, textiles, and accessories.*

### Foley & Corinna
108 Stanton
New York, NY 10002
(212) 529-2338
*Anna Corinna carries women's designer vintage clothing and accessories from the 1960s through the 1990s.*

### Marie A. Bradley
Bronx, NY
(718) 798-2680
By appointment only.
*Men's, women's, and children's collectible fashions and accessories from the Victorian days to the 1950s are included in Marie Bradley's vintage collection.*

### Vintage by Stacey Lee
White Plains, NY
(914) 328-0788
FAX: (914) 741-2461

e-mail: vintagesl.aol.com
By appointment only.
*A pristine collection of designer vintage from 1900 to 1970, Vintage by Stacey Lee also has clothing fashions for movies and design. She also has an amazing collection of handbags and gloves.*

## Muriel Fleming
New York, NY
(212) 689-3676
By appointment only.
*Muriel Fleming specializes in Victorian and 1920s to 1930s women's eveningwear.*

## M. Catalina Vintage Loft
New York, NY
(212) 352-0275
By appointment only.
e-mail: marybcatalina@hotmail.com
*Men's, women's, and children's twentieth century fashions as well as document and beading swatches are included in Vintage Loft's inventory.*

## Cherry
Radford Brown and Cesar Padilla
185 Orchard Street
New York, NY 10002
(212) 358-7131
www.eros.com/hotcherry/
*Cherry carries fine designer vintage from the 1960s to the 1970s for both men and women. They carry designer labels, handbags, all accessories, and specialize in shoes—Joseph La Rose shoes, still in the original boxes.*

## What Comes Around Goes Around
351 West Broadway
New York, NY 10013
(212) 343-9303
FAX: (212) 966-7130
e-mail: Vdl@earthlink.net
www.nyvintage.com
*An eclectic store in SoHo, What Comes Around Goes Around carries men's and women's fashions and accessories from the 20th century. Their inventory includes everything from high-end Victorian to 1960s Sears polyester. Their wholesale and rental vintage clothing showroom is called Vintage Design and is located at:*
*13–17 Laight Street 5th Fl.*
*New York, NY 10013*
*(212) 274-8340*

## Jean Hoffman Antiques

207 East 66th Street
New York, NY 10021
(215) 535-6930
e-mail: markanet@nac.net
www.jeanhoffmanantiques.com
*Jean Hoffman Antiques has a special collection of beautiful vintage wedding gowns, in addition to their inventory of decorative fabrics and laces, parasols, walking sticks, shawls, vintage handbags, and couture garments.*

## Screaming Mimi's

382 Lafayette Street
New York, NY 10003
(212) 677-6464
www.screamingmimisnyc.com
*Screaming Mimi's carries both men's and women's clothing and accessories from the 1950s through the 1970s.*

## Star Struck

47 Greenwich Avenue
New York, NY 10014
(212) 691-5357
*With specialties in Hawaiian shirts, gabardine suits and jackets, Western wear, and vintage blue jeans, Star Struck's inventory includes men's and women's clothing from the 1930s to the 1970s.*

## Fashion Dig Studio

561 Broadway 6th Floor
New York, NY 10012
(212) 334-0346
FAX: (212) 274-1624
e-mail: janet@fashiondig.com
www.fashiondig.com
*Fashion Dig is a vintage shopping mall representing vintage clothing from a variety of dealers. Their website has an advice column and an online newsletter.*

## Resurrection (two locations in Manhattan)

217 Mott Street
New York, NY 10012
(212) 625-1374
FAX: (212) 625-1376
e-mail: resny97@aol.com

123 East 7th Street
New York, NY 10009
(212) 343-1658
*Both stores specialize in 1960s, 1970s, and some 1980s couture pieces.*

**Atomic Passion**
430 East Ninth Street
New York, NY 10009
(212) 533-0718
email: atomicpas@aol.com
*Atomic Passion carries a wide assortment of shoes and a kicky collection of vin-tage clothing from the 1940s to the 1980s.*

OHIO
**Suite Lorain**
**The Vintage Department Store**
7105 Lorain Avenue
Cleveland, OH 44102
(216) 281-1959
*Suite Lorain carries men's, women's, and children's vintage fashions and acces-sories from the 1930s to the 1970s.*

**Talk of the Town**
9111 Reading Road
Reading, OH 45215
(513) 563-8844
*A spacious store, Talk of the Town carries both men's and women's elegant and fun-loving fashion and accessories from the 1850s to the 1970s. Period costume reproductions are available for rent.*

OREGON
**Lady Luck Vintage**
1 Southeast 28th Street
Portland, OR 97214
(503) 233-4041
*This roomy vintage shop showcases a soft-pink glamour room and an "oriental-inspired" room. Lady Luck Vintage carries men's and women's casual-to-dressy fashions from the 1920s to the 1980s as well as lingerie, handbags, and shoes.*

**Hattie's Vintage**
2721 SE 26th Street
Portland, OR 97202
(503) 235-5305
e-mail: Hattie@teleport.com

*Hattie's Vintage carries men's and women's fashions from the 1940s to the 1970s. Their specialty is fashions from the 1960s.*

### Keep 'Em Flying
510 NW 21st Avenue
Portland, OR 97209
(503) 221-0601
*Men's and women's Victorian fashions throughout the 1980s is found in this shop. Specialties of theirs are hats and jewelry.*

### Puttin on the Ritz
350 East 11th Avenue
Eugene, OR 97401
(541) 686-9240
*Puttin on the Ritz carries men's, women's, and children's fashions from the turn of the century to the mid-1960s. They also carry accessories and vintage fabric and notions.*

### Reflections in Time
1114 NW 21st Avenue
Portland, OR 97209
(503) 223-7880
e-mail: reflectionintime@hotmail
*In business for fifteen years, Reflections in Time's specialty is 1960s and 1970s vintage. Their inventory includes all accessories as well as 1940s and 1950s vintage.*

## PENNSYLVANIA
### Ballyhoo Vintage
213 New Street
Philadelphia, PA 19106
e-mail: gwest@sprynet.com
www.ballyhoovintage.com
*Ballyhoo Vintage carries men's and women's wearables from the 1930s to the 1970s. They have a large selection of men's shirts and jackets, women's wear including lingerie, halter tops, and swimsuits.*

### Decades
1511 South Street
Philadelphia, PA 19146
(215) 545-6867
e-mail: decadesv@hotmail.com
*Decades's inventory includes dressmaking fabrics, textiles, high-quality 1960s and 1970s vintage clothing as well as designer "modern" vintage for men and women. Their specialties are accessories—shoes, bags, belts, and costume jewelry.*

**Katy Kane**
New Hope, PA 18938
(215) 862-5873
FAX: (215) 862-9093
www.katykane.com
By appointment only.
*Katy Kane carries women's twentieth-century formal wear, couture, and daywear. She also has Adrian suits, accessories, and luggage. Please call for her show schedule.*

**Timeless Textiles**
343 Lincolnway West
New Oxford, PA 17305
(717) 624-1560
e-mail: ttextiles@aol.com
www.timelesstextiles.com
*Specializing in historic fabrics both retail and wholesale, Timeless Textiles has a research library on the premises and does consulting work. Classes on clothing and fabric are available on the weekends.*

**Zap & Co.**
315 North Queen Street
Lancaster, PA 17603
(717) 397-7405
FAX: (717) 393-9132
e-mail: zapandco@aol.com
www.zapandco.com
*With an inventory of over 10,000 pieces, Zap & Co. has clothing and accessories from Victorian to the 1960s, designer labels, gloves, jewelry, and a special collection of handbags.*

**The Cat's Pajamas**
335 Maynard Street
Williamsport, PA 17701
(570) 322-5580
e-mail: catspjs@suscom.net
www.catspajamas.com
*The Cat's Pajamas features men's, women's, and children's wearable fashions from the 19th century through the 1970s.*

TEXAS
**Blast from the Past**
1801 Fort Avenue
Waco, TX 78704
(254) 714-1183

*Blast from the Past carries men's, women's, and children's vintage from the 1940s through the 1990s.*

## WASHINGTON

### Isadora's Antique Clothing
1915 First Avenue
Seattle, WA 98101
(206) 441-7711
e-mail: isadoras@earthlink.com
www.isadoras.com
*Isadora's carries high-end pristine fashions for men and women from the turn of the century to the late 1960s. They also have an inventory of bridal, accessories, furs, and designer clothing. One of several specialties is their selection of gabardine suits.*

### Madame & Co.
Seattle, WA
(206) 281-7908
By appointment only.
*With a wide selection of items, Madame & Co. carries ladies' fashions from many eras. Among their tempting offerings are lingerie, white petticoats, pantaloons, and wedding dresses—Edwardian, Victorian, and Art Deco—as well as other Art Deco garments. They also carry antique laces, buttons, and trims.*

### Fritzi Ritz
3425 Freemont Place N.
Seattle, WA 98103
(206) 633-0929
*With a specialty in fashions and accessories that date to the 1970s, Fritzi Ritz has items for both men and women. Included in their inventory are vintage fabrics sold by the piece.*

### Rudy's Vintage Clothing and Watches
1424 First Avenue
Seattle, WA 98101
(206) 682-6586
e-mail: rudysvin@uswest.net
www.rudysvintage.com
*With the largest selection of vintage wristwatches in the Northwest, Rudy's is a tough one to beat. In addition to timepieces, they carry men's and women's vintage fashions, as well as vintage fabrics.*

## Internet Shopping

Please check the store and show dealer listings for additional websites.

### Antique Lace & Fashion

Karen Augusta

(802) 468-4958

www.antique-fashion.com

*This site is a catalog of the exquisite and the unusual in antique clothing, lace, and textiles from the 18th century to the mid-20th century. Couture pieces, museum-quality descriptions, detail photos, measurements, and fashion links to educational sites are included.*

### Vintage Textile

Linda Ames

(603) 352-6338

www.vintagetextile.com

*Vintage Textile specializes in antique costume, decorative textiles, antique jewelry, and fine vintage apparel for the discriminating collector. Victorian, Edwardian, 1920s, 1930s, and 1940s clothing as well as designer clothing that includes 1980s. Excellent detailed descriptions and detail photos, measurements, and sizing are also included with every item.*

### Isadora's Antique Clothing

(206) 441-7711

www.isadoras.com

*Isadora's showcases high-style pristine fashions from the 1900s through the 1960s, including designer. Their inventory includes hand-selected dresses, suits, gowns, cocktail dresses, furs, bridal, and accessories. Their beautiful photographs and detail photos are accompanied with descriptions and sizing.*

### Antique & Vintage Dress Gallery

Deborah Burke

(617) 630-0299

www.antiquedress.com

*Antique Dress sells Victorian, Edwardian, vintage designers including the 1990s, wedding attire and accessories, museum pieces, celebrity pieces, prom dresses, hats, and jewelry. Deborah gives very spirited and informative descriptions that include measurements and condition of the vintage pieces as well as detail photos.*

### Vintage Silhouettes

(800) 636-1410

www.vintagesilhouettes.com

*Vintage Silhouettes has a large inventory that includes fabulous men's fashions, ladies' wearables, couture, and accessories. They work with movie, theater, and television. Measurements and detail photos are included with their descriptions.*

### Enokiworld
Vintage Clothing for Modern Women
(314) 725-0735
www.enokiworld.com
*Enokiworld sells 1950s to 1980s vintage designer clothing and accessories. Their extensive inventory features dresses, suits, separates, outerwear, eyewear, handbags, swimsuits, and lingerie. A very contemporary site with lively, yet exacting descriptions that include designer information, style suggestions, and measurements for every item. The photographs include detail photos of fabrics. A nice shopping feature is the way in which items you are considering stay lit while you continue browsing.*

### Kitty Girl Vintage
Find What You're Looking For
(415) 386-6774
www.kittygirlvintage.com
*Specializing in women's rayon day dresses, dinner dresses, and party dresses, Kitty Girl Vintage sells women's fashions from the 1920s to the 1960s. The site is updated weekly. Lovely photographs with detail photos accompany the description, measurements are included for every item.*

### Cookie's Closet
Fabulous Vintage–Modern Appeal
(415) 970-5030
www.cookiescloset.com
*Cookie's Closet sells high-end designer vintage (Schiaparelli, Gucci, Pucci, Courrèges, Dior, Blass, to name a few), accessories, and lingerie. Women's styles date from Victorian to the 1970s. Men's fashions include cashmere and resort wear. Be sure to check out the style guide. Detailed descriptions, detail photos, and sizes are included.*

### Vintage Textiles
www.vintagetextiles.com
*Vintage Textiles specializes in museum-quality antique and vintage fabrics from around the world.*

### 5 and Dime Vintage
(303) 299-1170
www.510vintage.com
*A large inventory of vintage fashions for men and women—sweaters, bathing suits, lingerie, skirts, couture, sportswear (Adidas, Puma, Nike, etc.), denim, Western, accessories, and an extensive inventory of Levi's are sold on this website. Have fun with the easy-to-follow charts that include descriptions, measurements, and realistic detail shots. Buy or sell on this site.*

### Fashion Dig Studio
www.fashiondig.com
*Fashion Dig's site is devoted to "the fashion and style enthusiast." There is an advice column and an online newsletter. They describe themselves as a vintage shopping mall, offering many different shopping opportunities.*

### Cat's Pajamas
(570) 322-5580
www.catspajamas.com
*Cat's Pajamas features wearables—men's, women's, and children's fashions from the 19th century through the 1970s. Descriptions, sizes, and detail photos are included for each item.*

### The Fainting Couch
(508) 339-7733
www.faintingcouch.com
*The Fainting Couch specializes in fine, antique apparel and accessories from the 18th century to 1960s.*

### Reminiscing Vintage Fashions
www.reminiscing.com
*This Internet shop carries wearable fashions and sizes for women that include Edwardian to 1940s vintage fashion, wedding attire, and a "Forgotten Woman Boutique." They have a clearance room of bargain items. Detailed descriptions, measurements, and close-up photos.*

### Davenport and Company Online
www.davenportandco.com
*There are many shopping opportunities at this site for men and women—fashions from the 1840s to 1980s including Victorian, wedding gowns, evening and formal wear, 1970s polyester, hats, and other vintage accessories, sewing items, lingerie, and magazines. The site has descriptions, sizes, and close-up photos.*

### Patterns from the Past
www.oldpatterns.com
*Patterns from the Past sells original vintage sewing patterns and older knitting, crochet, and tatting patterns.*

### Just Say When
www.justsaywhen.com
*Just Say When sells vintage fashions for women from the 1900s to the 1980s. Their inventory includes: Pucci, designer suits and accessories, lingerie, swimwear, coats, fashion links, and a flea market.*

### Ballyhoo Vintage
(215) 627-1700

www.ballyhoovintage.com

*An extensive inventory of men's shirts and jackets and women's vintage, couture pieces, accessories, swimsuits, halter tops, and lingerie from the 1930s to the 1970s are sold at this site. They have descriptions and close-up photos.*

### Bittersweet Boutique
www.bittersweetboutique.com

*Bittersweet Boutique's website sells men's, women's, and children's clothing from the 1800s to the 1970s including lingerie, accessories, and furs with detail photos and descriptions.*

### Red Rose Vintage Clothing
www.rrnspace.com

*A well-stocked inventory of late 1800s through the 1990s—women's couture, coats, lingerie, accessories, and men's fashions. They have descriptions, sizing, and detail photos. Their website is added to weekly. eBay connection.*

### The Paper Bag Princess
www.paperbagp.com

*The Paper Bag Princess sells couture designer clothing like Gucci and Rudi Gernreich. In addition, they are also known for their hats. Also find on their site— celebrity clothing, valuable vintage, fashion news, and the vintage calendar of events.*

### What Comes Around Goes Around
www.nyvintage.com

*The inventory of What Comes Around Goes Around includes vintage denim, women's couture, and designer vintage from the 1920s to 1970s, as well as military and leather.*

### Decades
www.decadesinc.com

*A great site for couture vintage fashion, Decades specializes in the 1960s and the 1970s. They do not, however, sell online. They take requests for certain designer items.*

## EBAY
www.ebay.com

*There is a tremendous amount of merchandise for sale every day on eBay. You will want to familiarize yourself with vintage fashion before going online so you know what you are looking at. You will also want to get to know the sellers or dealers you will be buying from. You can and should check the previous sales the seller has made to read customers comments. If you have questions regarding the merchandise don't hesitate to e-mail the seller for further information.*

*To leave a bid on an item you must first register with eBay online. You will need to give a name and an e-mail address to register.*

*eBay is the ultimate shopping experience for the nonstop shopper. Remember there are good things and not good things for sale. The drawback with buying clothing this way is that you can't try it on or see the condition for yourself. Check the conservation guidelines we have given you. Look up designers' names. Know the clothing and accessory styles in the decade you want to buy from.*

## RESALE AND CONSIGNMENT SHOPS

Now that vintage fashion is thought by many to include fashions from the entire 20th century, you may want to check out resale and consignment shops for the most recent styles. Look in the yellow pages in your local telephone directory to find listings in your area.

### Michael's Resale
1041 Madison Avenue
New York, NY 10021
(212) 737-7273
FAX: (212) 737-7211
www.michaelsconsignment.com
*Michael's sells only designer fashions less than two years old, with the exception of Chanel.*

### Bis
1134 Madison Avenue
New York, NY 10028
(212) 396-2760
www.bisbiz.com
*Bis carries current high-end designer resale, some vintage.*

### Encore
1132 Madison Avenue, 2nd Floor
New York, NY 10028
(212) 879-2850
FAX: (212) 879-2374
www.encoreresale.com
*Encore is the oldest designer and consignment business in the U.S.; founded in 1954. Jackie Kennedy brought her clothing to Encore. Encore's clothing is all designer labels only, international as well as American and are never more than 1½ years old.*

## SHOWS

Show dates and times can be found on the websites or by calling.

### ARIZONA

**High Noon**
9929 Venice Boulevard
Los Angeles, CA 90034
(310) 202-9010
FAX: (310) 202-9011
www.highnoon.com

*Wild West Collectors Show and Auction*
Centennial Hall
Mesa, AZ
January Show

### CALIFORNIA

**Vintage Expositions**
(707) 793-0773
www.vintagefashionexpo.com

*Vintage Fashion Expo*
Civic Auditorium
1855 Main at Pico
Santa Monica, CA
October, February, and May Shows

*Vintage Fashion Expo*
The Concourse
8th and Brannan
San Francisco, CA
March and September

### CONNECTICUT

**The Maven Company, Inc.**
(914) 248-4646
www.mavencompany.com

*Semi-annual Show and Sale*
*of Vintage Clothing, Jewelry, and Textiles*
The Westchester County Center
White Plains, NY
January and March

*Semi-annual Show and Sale*
*of Vintage Clothing Jewelry and Textiles*
National Guard Armory
Armory Road and Route 180
Stratford, CT
September and February

**Barrows Show Promotional, Ltd.**
Box 141
Portland, CT 06480
(860) 342-2540

*Greater Hartford Vintage Clothing and Jewelry Show and Sale*
Emanuel Synagogue
Mohegan Drive
West Hartford, CT
November, January, April, July, August

ILLINOIS
**Cat's Pajamas Productions**
P.O. Box 392
Dundee, IL 60118
(847) 428-8368
e-mail: catspjs@mailcity.com
www.catspajamasproductions.com

*Vintage Clothing and Jewelry Show and Sale*
Hemmens Cultural Center
Grove Avenue at the Fox River
Elgin, IL
February

**Dolphin Promotions**
P.O. 7320
Ft. Lauderdale, FL 33338
(954) 563-6747 or (708) 366-2710
e-mail: dolphinpromotionn@worldnet.att.net
www.dolphinfairs.com or www.antiquenet.com

*Vintage Clothing and Antique Textile Show*
Rosemont Convention Center
Chicago, IL
August

**MASSACHUSETTS**
**Linda Zukas**
**Show Associates**
P.O. Box 729
Cape Neddick, ME 03902-0729
(207) 439-2334
www.vintagefashionandtextileshow.com

*Sturbridge Antique Textile and Vintage Clothing Extravaganza*
Host Hotel—Sturbridge
Route 20, Sturbridge, Mass. (junction Mass Pike 90 and I-84)
May, July, and September

**NEW JERSEY**
**Brimfield Associates**
P.O. Box 1800
Ocean City, NJ 08226
(609) 926-1800
e-mail: atlantiquecity@aol.com
www.atlantiquecity.com

*Atlantique City Show*
New Atlantic City Convention Hall
1 Ocean Avenue
Atlantic City, NJ
March and October

**NEW YORK**
**Stella Show Management Co.**
147 West 24th Street
New York, NY 10011
(212) 255-0020
FAX: (212) 255-0002
e-mail: stellashows@aol.com
www.stellashows.com

*Manhattan Triple Pier Expo*
Terminals 88, 90, and 92
New York, NY
March and November

**Metropolitan Arts and Antiques Pavilion**
125 West 18th Street
New York, NY 10011
(212) 463-0200 ext. 222
www.metropolitanevents.com

*Vintage Fashion and Antique Textile Show and Sale*
Metropolitan Pavilion
125 West 18th Street
New York, NY
January, April, and September

## OREGON
### JR Promotions
Portland, OR
(360) 574-3984
e-mail: vintage@xpert.net

*Best of the Past Vintage Clothing and Textile Sale*
Portland, OR
March

### Right Foot, Left Foot Productions
Portland, OR
(888) 343-0383
www.neens.com/NWExpo

*NW Vintage Expo*
Memorial Coliseum
Portland, OR
August

## AUCTION HOUSES
### Sotheby's
1334 York Avenue
New York, NY 10021
(212) 606-7000
www.sothebys.com

### William Doyle Galleries
175 East 87th Street
New York, NY 10128
(212) 427-2730
www.williamdoyle.com

### Christie's
20 Rockefeller Plaza
New York, NY 10020
(212) 636-2000
www.christies.com

# Resource Guide

**MUSEUMS**

The museums listed below house nationally known collections. Individuals with research interests may make an appointment to see the holdings. Many of the museums have rotating exhibits.

ARIZONA

**The Phoenix Art Museum**
Arizona Costume Institute
(a predominantly Western collection)
1625 North Central Avenue
Phoenix, AZ 85004
(602) 257-1222
www.phxart.org/

CALIFORNIA

**Los Angeles County Museum**
Costume and Textile Department
5905 Wilshire Boulevard
Los Angeles, CA 90036
(213) 937-4250
www.lacma.org

**M. H. de Young Memorial Museum**
Golden Gate Park
75 Tea Garden Drive
San Francisco, CA 94118-4501
(415) 750-3614

**The Oakland Museum**
1000 Oak Street
Oakland, CA 94607
(510) 238-3842
www.museumca.org/

CONNECTICUT
**Wadsworth Atheneum**
600 Main Street
Hartford, CT 06103
(203) 278-2670
www.wadsworthatheneum.org

ILLINOIS
**The Art Institute of Chicago**
Michigan Avenue and Adams Street
Chicago, IL 60603
(312) 443-3600
www.artic.edu

**Chicago Historical Society**
Clark Street at North Avenue
Chicago, IL 60614
(312) 642-4600
www.chicagohs.org/chshome.html

MASSACHUSETTS
**The Boston Museum of Fine Arts**
465 Huntington Avenue
Boston, MA 02115
(617) 267-9300
www.mfa.org

NEW YORK
**Brooklyn Museum of Art**
Eastern Parkway
Brooklyn, NY 11238
www.brooklynmuseum.org

**Cooper-Hewitt Museum**
Smithsonian Museum of Design
2 East 91st Street
New York, NY 10128
(212) 860-6868
www.si.edu/ndm

**The Fashion Institute of Technology**
The Edward C. Blum Design Laboratory
227 West 27th Street
New York, NY 10001
(212) 760-7708
www.fitnyc.suny.edu/

**Metropolitan Museum of Art**
Costume Institute
Fifth Avenue at 82nd Street
New York, NY 10001
www.metmuseum.org/

**Museum of the City of New York**
Fifth Avenue at 103rd Street
New York, NY 10029
(212) 534-1672
www.mcny.org

OHIO
**Cincinnati Art Museum**
Eden Park
Cincinnati, OH 45202-1596
www.cincinnatiartmuseum.com

**Kent State University Museum**
Rockwell Hall
East Main and South Lincoln Streets
Kent, OH 44240
(330) 672-3450
www.kent.edu/museum

**Western Reserve Historical Society**
**The Chisholm Halle Costume Wing**
10825 East Boulevard
Cleveland, OH 44106
(216) 721-5722
www.wrhs.org

PENNSYLVANIA
**Philadelphia Museum of Art**
Benjamin Franklin Parkway, Box 7646
Philadelphia, PA 19101
(215) 763-8100
www.philamuseum.org

TEXAS

**The Texas Fashion Collection**
North Texas State University
Denton, TX 76203
(817) 565-2732

WASHINGTON

**University of Washington**
**Historical Costume and Textile Collection**
Seattle, WA 98195
(206) 357-3185 (Costume Division)

WASHINGTON, D.C.

**The National Museum of American History**
Smithsonian Institution
Constitution Avenue, between 12th and 14th Streets
Washington, D.C. 20560
(202) 357-3185 (Costume Division)
www.americanhistory.si.edu/

**The Textile Museum**
2320 S Street NW
Washington, D.C. 20008-4088
(202) 667-0441
www.textilemuseum.org

## MUSEUMS OF SPECIAL INTEREST

**Maidenform Museum**
200 Madison Avenue
New York, NY 10016
(212) 856-8900

**The Glove Museum at Lacrasia**
6 East 32nd Street, 6th Floor
New York, NY 10016
(212) 532-1956

**Hoguet Fan Museum and Atelier**
2, Franie boulevard Strasbourg
75010 Paris, France
33-1-42-08-19-89

## WESTERN MUSEUMS

### Gene Autry Western Heritage Museum
47 Western Heritage Way
Los Angeles, CA 90027
(323) 667-2000

### Pro Rodeo Hall of Champions and Museum of the American Cowboy
101 Pro Rodeo Drive
Colorado Springs, CO 80919
(719) 528-4761

### National Cowboy Hall of Fame and Western Heritage Center
1700 NE 63rd Street
Oklahoma City, OK 73111
(405) 478-2250

### National Cowgirl Hall of Fame and Western Heritage Center
111 West 4th Street, Suite 300
Fort Worth, TX 76102
(817) 336-4475

### Roy Rogers and Dale Evans Museum
15650 Seneca Road
Victorville, CA 92392
(760) 243-4547

## SOCIETIES AND ORGANIZATIONS

The following societies and organizations offer memberships:

### ENGLAND

**The Fan Circle**
24, Asmuns Hill
London, NW1 16ET, England, UK

### INDIANA

**International Old Lacers, Inc.**
2409 South Ninth Street
Lafayette, IN 47905

MARYLAND
## The Costume Society of America
55 Edgewater Drive, P.O. Box 73
Earleville, MD 21919
(800) CSA-9447
FAX: (410) 275-8936
e-mail: national.office@costumesocietyamerica.com
www.costumesocietyamerica.com

## NEWSLETTERS
Listed below are newsletters from societies around the nation that deal solely with issues of vintage clothing and textiles. To receive any of these publications, write to the address or search the website and request information.

### Vintage!
Federation of Vintage Fashion
3684 Wetseka #101
Los Angeles, CA 90034
(707) 793-0773

### The Vintage Gazette
Molly's Vintage Promotions
194 Amity Street
Amherst, MA 01002
(413) 549-6446

## MAGAZINES
The following magazines include vintage clothing and/or fabrics in their publications. They may be found in bookstores or by subscription.

### Ornament
P.O. Box 2349
San Marcos, CA 92079
(800) 888-8950

### Piecework
Interweave Press, Inc.
201 East Fourth Street
Loveland, CO 80537
(970) 669-7672

### Victoria
P.O. Box 7150
Red Oak, IA 51597
(800) 876-8696

**Surface**
P.O. Box 360
Sebastopol, CA 95473-0360
(707) 829-3110

## CONSERVATORS, CONSERVATION STUDIOS, AND CONSERVATION SUPPLIERS

It is important to keep in mind that there are professionals who are trained in conservation to restore antique and vintage pieces.

**A. Newbold Richardson**
Appraisals and Conservation of Historic Textiles
602 South View Terrace
Alexandria, VA 22314
(703) 684-0863
e-mail: pastcrafts@yahoo.com
By appointment only.

**Bryce Reveley**
Gentle Arts
4500 Dryades Street, Studio B
New Orleans, LA 70115
(504) 895-5628
FAX: (504) 895-6047
By appointment only.

**Judith Eisenberg**
Textile Conservator
New York, NY
(212) 691-2638
By appointment only.

*If you need to find a conservator in your area, a referral service is offered by the American Institute for the Conservation of Historic and Artistic Works. When contacting them please be specific as to what your needs are and the exact piece you want to have restored, so that they can give you a conservator who specializes in your area of concern.*

**American Institute for the Conservation of Historic and Artistic Works**
1717 K Street NW, Suite 200
Washington, D.C. 20006
(202) 452-9545
FAX: (202) 452-9328

e-mail: info@aic-saic.org
http://aic.stanford.edu

## CONSERVATION STUDIOS
**Textile Conservation Laboratory**
Cathedral of St. John the Divine
1047 Amsterdam Avenue
New York, NY 10025
(212) 316-7400

## CONSERVATION SUPPLIES
Acid-free tissue and boxes can be ordered directly from suppliers.

**Light Impressions**
Rochester, NY
(800) 828-9859

**University Products**
P.O. Box 101
Holyoke, MA 01041
(800) 628-1912

**Talas**
568 Broadway
Suite 107
New York, NY 10012
(212) 219-0770

## CLEANING AND RESTORATIONS
**J. Scheer & Co.**
561 Broadway, New York, NY 10012
23 Market Street
Rhinebeck, NY 12572
(800) 448-7291
www.jscheer.com
*Specialists in the cleaning and preservation of museum textile collections, wedding gowns, and 20th-century couture.*

# Glossary

**A-LINE:** skirt or dress shaped like a capital A.

**AIGRETTE:** a stiff tuft of egret or osprey tail feathers used as an ornament usually on a hat.

**ANILINE DYES:** synthetic dyes which yield bright colors; produced in England in 1856 by William Perkin.

**APPLIQUÉ:** pieces of fabric sewn on to a garment for decoration.

**APRON:** a small piece of fabric worn over the front of clothing that ties in the back with fabric self-ties.

**ART DECO:** a bold, geometric style of decoration popular from 1925 to 1940.

**ART NOUVEAU:** a decorative style popular in the late nineteenth century and early twentieth century which is distinguished by the use of flowing lines and flowers.

**ARTIFICIAL SILK:** a term given to rayon from 1890 to 1920.

**BAKELITE:** trade name for material made from heating phenol with formaldehyde; a popular pressed plastic for jewelry, buckles, and buttons in the thirties.

**BALL GOWN:** a full-skirted, ankle-length gown with décolleté neckline, usually made in rich fabrics.

**BALLET-LENGTH:** mid-calf length.

**BALLETS RUSSES:** a series of ballets in Russia in the early twentieth century. Inspired by the Orient, the costumes with their rich fabrics and bright colors greatly influenced fashion.

**BANDANNA:** a large colored handkerchief, often figured.

**BASQUE:** also known as a peplum; a short skirt gathered or pleated onto the bodice of a dress or jacket.

**BATTLE JACKETS:** (Eisenhower, bomber jacket) waist-length jacket, generously cut over shoulders with long sleeves and pockets, buttons or zips up the front.

**BATWING SLEEVE:** a dolman sleeve which is cut as an extension of the bodice, making a sleeve that extends from the waist to the wrist.

**BERET:** a knitted or woven circular hat without a brim.

**BERMUDA SHORTS:** shorts ending just above the knee.

**BERTHA:** a wide, deep lace collar, falling from an oval neckline and covering the shoulders of a dress.

**BETTINA BLOUSE:** designed by Givenchy and named for his top Parisian model, Bettina Graziani. The blouse was made of shirting and had ruffled broderie anglaise sleeves and an open neck.

**BIAS CUT:** material cut diagonally across the grain allowing it to fall into a vertical drape that could be sculpted to the body; popular in films of the thirties; originally designed by Madeleine Vionnet.

**BIKINI:** a very brief two-piece bathing suit.

**BISHOP SLEEVE:** popular style from the mid-nineteenth century to the 1970s; a long dress sleeve that is full below the elbow and gathered at the wrist.

**BLOOMERS:** full, loose trouser garments gathered at the ankle or knee.

**BLOUSON TOP:** a dress top that is pulled together at the waist causing it to puff out over the skirt.

**BOATER:** popular hat for men in the late nineteenth century to 1940s and for women in the 1920s; a hard, circular hat made of straw with a flat crown and ribbon band.

**BOBBIN LACE:** a handmade lace made with bobbins of thread; the pattern is outlined on the cushion with pins and the bobbin threads are drawn and twisted around the pins.

**BOBBY SOCKS:** short, white socks popular with teenagers in the fifties.

**BODICE:** the upper part of a dress; in the nineteenth century, the bodice was boned and fitted; in the twentieth century, bodice is used as a dressmaker's term for the top, front, and back sections of a garment.

**BODYSTOCKING:** a leotard-shaped, fine knitted, pull-on garment worn under semi-transparent clothing; introduced in the sixties.

**BOLERO:** a short Spanish-style sleeveless bodice, worn open.

**BONING:** stays sewn into garment for stiffening and to provide shape.

**BONNET:** a hat that covers the whole head and ties under the chin; popular in many styles in the nineteenth century.

**BOUCLÉ:** Fr. (to curl): a fabric that is knitted or woven from looped yarn, giving a nap to the fabric.

**BOUFFANT STYLE:** full or puffed-out style.

**BOWLER:** a derby; a hard, round hat with crown and rolled brim; worn by men in the late nineteenth century up to WWII.

**BROCADE:** a rich, jacquard fabric with raised design, usually of figures or flowers in silk, gold, or silver threads.

**BRODERIE ANGLAISE:** also known as Swiss or Madeira embroidery; a white on white embroidery often used as trim.

**BUBBLE SKIRT:** Pierre Cardin designed stiffened short-skirted bubble-shaped dresses in 1957.

**BURNOUS:** a full cloak with a hood that is embellished with embroidery and tassels, originally of North African origin.

**BUSK:** a knife-shaped piece of whalebone which was inserted in the front of a corset held in place by the lacing.

**BUSTLE:** a pad of stuffing worn under the skirt at or just below the waist to expand fullness to the back.

**CAFTAN:** an ankle-length, silk or cotton garment with long, wide sleeves and sash waist; used in various fashion designs.

**CALICO:** a sturdy, durable fabric of coarse cotton; usually dyed having figured patterns.

**CAPE:** a sleeveless outer garment fastened at the neck and worn like a cloak.

**CAPRI PANTS:** popular women's pant style in the fifties; pants tapered to mid-calf.

**CARDIGAN:** long-sleeved knitted sweater without a collar; made popular for women in the twenties by Gabrielle "Coco" Chanel.

**CARTWHEEL HAT:** a hat with a shallow crown and exaggerated, straight brim, usually in straw.

**CASHMERE:** a natural fiber of soft wool combed from the cashmere goat which is raised in Kashmir, India, Pakistan, Tibet, Mongolia, China, Iran, and Iraq. Cashmere is often blended with other fibers like wool for increased durability and to lower the expense of the garment.

**CATSUIT:** a zippered or buttoned front garment that is all in one piece.

**CELANESE RAYON:** Celanese is the trademark name for the manufacture of rayon.

**CHAMBRAY:** a class of plain-weave, yarn-dyed fabrics having a colored warp and white cotton or manufactured fiber filling; chambray comes in solid colors or in figured, checked, and striped patterns.

**CHANTILLY LACE:** a bobbin lace often in black with a floral and dot motif on a fine background; design outlined by a heavier thread (cordonnet).

**CHAPS:** leg coverings, usually of leather, worn by cowboys for protection.

**CHARMEUSE:** the trade name for a lightweight, lustrous cotton, rayon, or silk fabric.

**CHATELAINE:** popular in the nineteenth century to carry practical items by the woman of the household; made of steel and hung down from the waistband.

**CHEMISE:** a shirt-like garment worn as an undergarment by women.

**CHEMISE DRESS:** a no-waisted straight-lined dress with a belt that tied under the bust, around the waist, or at the hip. Made popular in the twenties by Gabrielle "Coco" Chanel.

**CHENILLE:** Fr. (caterpillar): the chenille yarn has a pile protruding on all sides; it is produced by weaving a tightly twisted fabric with a strong warp and cotton, silk, rayon, or wool.

**CHESTERFIELD COAT:** (after WWI) a long black velvet-collared coat worn by young women. In the nineteenth century, a man's gray wool overcoat with a fitted waist and velvet collar.

**CHEVIOT:** woolen fabric used for coats and suits.

**CHIFFON:** a light, gauzy fabric made from finely twisted threads of silk, wool, or synthetics; popular for scarves or eveningwear.

**CHINA SILK:** a lustrous fabric that is a soft lightweight silk, made in China and Japan.

**CHINOISERIE:** an ornamentation style originating in the eighteenth century in Europe; it is characterized by intricate patterns with Chinese motifs.

**CINCH BELT:** a wide elastic belt worn with skirts, popular in the fifties.

**CIRCLE SKIRT:** a round skirt cut from one or two pieces of fabric; popular in the fifties.

**CLOAK:** a full-cut outer garment that covers the body.

**CLOCHE:** Fr. (bell): a tight-fitting hat covering the head, with or without a brim and worn low over the brow, popular from 1915 to 1935.

**CLOISONNÉ:** enameling done with thin metal bands dividing the colors.

**CLOQUE:** a fabric that is embossed or quilted or has a quilted effect.

**CLUTCH PURSE:** a handbag without straps; popular in a variety of shapes and sizes.

**CONFECTIONS:** nineteenth-century women's outer garments such as cloaks, mantles, and capes.

**COOLIE HAT:** a cone-shaped, one-piece hat often made of straw.

**CORDUROY:** a durable cut-pile cotton or rayon with vertical ribbing of wide or narrow cords.

**CORSET:** a garment worn under a dress in the nineteenth century to achieve a smaller waist; made of stays inserted into the fabric and then laced tightly.

**COSSACK-STYLED:** fashions influenced by Russian dress; characterized by full, flowing skirts, tied with sashes, full pants tucked in boots, and tall fur hats.

**COTTON:** a fabric produced from the fibers of the cotton plant, used especially for summer garments and underwear.

**COUTURE:** an abbreviation for haute couture, a term used for custom-made or high-fashion clothing as opposed to clothes that are mass-produced.

**COWL:** a drape attached to the neck of a garment that can be used as a hood or neckline drape.

**CRAVAT:** man's necktie.

**CREPE:** a general classification of fabrics that can be made from natural and synthetic materials; a soft fabric with a crinkled texture or grained surface.

**CRÊPE DE CHINE:** Fr. (crêpe of China): a fine silk woven in a plain weave used for dresses.

**CREPE GEORGETTE:** a sheer silk or manufactured fiber that is woven into a plain-weave fabric; used for blouses, dresses, skirts, gowns, and millinery.

**CRINOLINE CAGE:** made popular by Empress Eugénie in the 1850s, it allowed skirts to stay very full and round.

**CROCHET:** needlework made by looping yarn or thread with a hooked needle.

**CUBAN HEELS:** short, chunky, straight heels.

**CUBISM:** an abstract art movement developed in Paris in the early twentieth century that influenced textile designers to use bold, flat, geometric shapes and patterns.

**CUIRASS:** a jacket bodice that is fitted to the hipline.

**CULOTTE:** a skirt divided into two legs but giving the effect of a full skirt.

**CUMMERBUND:** a wide waistband worn by both men and women in the twentieth century; a substitute for the man's previously worn waistcoat.

**CUT-AWAY:** a man's formal coat with tails, where the front of the coat is cut away from the waist to the back.

**DACRON:** the trade name of DuPont manufacturing for a polyester fabric from the early fifties.

**DAMASK:** a luxurious decorative woven silk fabric with the pattern as part of the weave; self-colored. In the nineteenth century, it was used for women's clothing. In the twentieth century, damask is usually used in home furnishings.

**DART:** a pointed tuck sewn inside a garment to shape the garment to the body.

**DÉCOLLETAGE:** décolleté neckline, low-cut neckline of a blouse or dress, exposing the neck and back or shoulders.

**DENIM:** a sturdy cotton twill fabric woven from white and blue threads.

**DEPARTMENT STORES:** in the mid-nineteenth century department stores developed; these stores played an important role in the promotion of fashion during the twentieth century.

**DÉSHABILLÉS:** very fancy tea gowns popular in the late nineteenth and early twentieth centuries.

**DIRNDL:** a skirt that is full and loosely pleated at the waist.

**DJELLABAH:** a long, hooded cloak of Moroccan origin having full wide sleeves, worn with an open neck; popular style in the sixties and seventies.

**DOLMAN SLEEVE:** a sleeve that is not set into the armhole but is an extension of the bodice; a full wide sleeve that is narrow at the wrist; popular in the thirties.

**DOUBLE-BREASTED:** a jacket with two rows of buttons for front closure.

**DRAWERS:** knickers made of cotton or linen and worn as underwear.

**EDWARDIAN:** an elaborate style of dress associated with clothing styles during the reign of King Edward VII of England (1901–1910).

**EISENHOWER JACKET:** a jacket introduced in WWII and made popular by General Eisenhower. Also called the battle or bomber jacket.

**ELIZABETHAN COLLAR:** a decorative, high-necked collar.

**EMBROIDERY:** decorative needlework done on fabric by hand or machine.

**EMPIRE WAIST:** a low-cut dress gathered under the bustline.

**EMPRESS EUGÉNIE HAT:** a small hat designed by Adrian and worn tilted forward to one side; named for the Empress Eugenie of France.

**ENSEMBLE:** a coordinated outfit.

**ENVELOPE BAG:** a rectangular purse without a strap and with an envelope-style closure.

**EPAULETTE:** an ornamental strap sewn onto the shoulder of a coat or jacket for decoration.

**ETON SUIT:** originally a suit worn by boys at Eton College in England in the late nineteenth century and early twentieth century; the popular style was characterized by a short, square jacket.

**EYELET:** a lightweight fabric with small threadbound holes making up the design.

**FAILLE:** a soft, medium-weight, slightly ribbed fabric with a slight luster; woven in silk, cotton or rayon.

**FAIR ISLE SWEATER:** a sweater with a knitted band across the neck, shoulders, and chest in a multicolored geometric pattern.

**FAUVISM:** an art movement of the early 1900s that influenced fashion and fabric design with the use of flat, two-dimensional shapes in bright colors.

**FEDORA:** a soft felt hat with brim and tapered crown with a center crease; a popular men's style at the end of the nineteenth century until the 1950s.

**FELT:** a fabric made by bonding fibers of cotton, fur, or wool; used primarily in making hats.

**FEZ:** a cylinder-shaped hat with tassel on top.

**FILET LACE:** a hand- or machine-made lace characterized by patterns of animals, trees, and leaves.

**FISHNET:** large open-weave knitted net stockings.

**FISHTAIL TRAIN:** a train shaped like the tail of a fish.

**FLANNEL:** a household term for woolen fabrics; a light to medium weight of plain or twill weave with a slightly nappy surface.

**FOULARD:** a printed design on soft-finished silk; used to make neckties and scarves.

**FRENCH SEAM:** a seam where the raw edges are totally covered by sewing them together on both the right and the wrong sides.

**FROCK COAT:** nineteenth century formal men's attire: knee-length coat with tails, collar, and back vents; an inspiration for the design of women's coats in the twentieth century.

**GABARDINE:** a strong tightly woven fabric having a fine-ribbed effect; made of cotton, wool, or rayon twill.

**GEORGETTE:** a lightweight and sheer fabric in plain-weave silk or in a manufactured fiber with a crepe face.

**GIGOT:** leg-of-mutton sleeve.

**GIMP:** a flat cord of silk or wool used in the decoration of clothing.

**GINGHAM:** a medium-weight cotton/linen fabric woven into checks with pre-dyed yarns.

**GODET:** fabric cut in a triangular shape that is inserted into a garment to give it fullness.

**GORED SKIRTS:** skirts made from tapered strips of fabric that widen toward the hemline, popular in the nineteenth and early twentieth century.

**GRANNY GOWN:** an old-fashioned clothing style with long, full skirts; popular in the late sixties and early seventies.

**GROMMET:** metal-made eyelet in a garment.

**GROSGRAIN:** heavily ribbed, closely woven silk fabric used in millinery.

**HACKING JACKET:** a fitted, single-breasted jacket that flares from the waist with a single back vent; originally worn as a riding jacket.

**HALO HAT:** a hat worn at the back of the head with the brim acting as a frame for the face.

**HALTER:** a neckline style that is high in front, ties at the back of the neck and reveals the back and shoulders.

**HAREM PANTS:** a full, ankle-length divided skirt or pants based on Turkish women's trousers.

**HARRIS TWEED:** originally refers to a handwoven woolen fabric from the Outer Hebrides Islands off the northern coast of Scotland.

**HAUTE COUTURE:** French for high-quality fashion design and craftsmanship that is highly labor intensive and expensive. In the late twentieth century some couturiers licensed manufacturers to use their names on general fashion items, jewelry, cosmetics, and the like.

**HAWAIIAN SHIRT:** colorful shirts depicting fruit, flowers, and island themes.

**HELMET:** a hat that covers and fits close to the head.

**HOBBLE SKIRT:** a skirt style introduced by Paul Poiret that was narrow and tight-fitting from the knee to the ankle, making walking difficult; popular between 1910 and 1914.

**HOMBURG:** a man's stiff felt hat with a thin rolled brim and a center crease crown; popularized by Edward VII, Prince of Wales, after visiting Homburg, Germany.

**HORSESHOE COLLAR:** a collar with a deep U shape.

**HOT PANTS:** short pants worn in the 1970s.

**IKAT:** a resist type of fabric decoration.

**IVY LEAGUE:** an American dress style worn by college students on the East Coast; characterized for men by gray flannel suits and button-down shirts with narrow striped ties; for women by the kilt, blazer, sweater, and string of pearls.

**JACQUARD:** a decorative weave created on a jacquard loom, especially for brocades and damasks which have woven-in patterns.

**JAMS:** men's brightly colored bathing suits styled as shorts with drawstring waists; popular in the sixties.

**JERSEY:** a soft, stretchy, plain knitted fabric popularized in the twenties by Gabrielle "Coco" Chanel. Jersey originally was made from wool and manufactured on the Isle of Jersey in the Channel Islands off the English coast and used for the clothing of fishermen.

**JUMPER:** a sleeveless dress with a round or square neckline worn over a blouse.

**JUMPSUIT:** all-in-one-piece suit with long sleeves and legs and a zippered front.

**KATE GREENAWAY:** (1846–1903) an English book illustrator who influenced children's dress styles in the nineteenth century with Empire-line dresses, bonnets, smocks, and ruffles.

**KILT:** a tartan cloth skirt which is pleated and made to overlap in the front where it is secured by buckles and a large pin.

**KIMONO:** (Japanese) a loose-fitting robe with wide sleeves worn with a wide waist sash.

**KNICKERBOCKERS:** knickers.

**KNICKERS:** full-cut pants gathered at the knees.

**LAMÉ:** usually a gold or silver fabric woven with metallic threads; popular in the thirties for eveningwear.

**LAPEL:** a part of a jacket neckline that can turn back or fold over.

**LASTEX:** U.S. Rubber Co. trade name for elastic yarn fabrics.

**LAWN:** a fine, plain-woven, sheer cotton or linen fabric with a crisp finish.

**LEG-OF-MUTTON SLEEVE:** a sleeve that is tight-fitting from the wrist to the elbow and very full from elbow to shoulder where it is gathered to fit into the armhole; used in late nineteenth century on blouse or bodice.

**LEOTARD:** a one-piece, long- or short-sleeved Spandex suit, fitted between the legs.

**LINEN:** a strong natural fabric woven from fibers of the flax plant that can be made in fine or coarse textures.

**LOUIS HEEL:** a woman's medium-height French heel, widened at the base, named for Louis XV.

**LUCITE:** transparent plastic.

**LUREX:** Registered trade name of Rockwood Industries for its metallic fiber and yarn.

**MADRAS PLAID:** Indian cotton plaid.

**MAILLOT:** a one-piece bathing suit that is tight-fitting.

**MALACCA:** a type of palm used to make canes and parasol handles in the nineteenth century.

**MANDARIN JACKET:** a Chinese-styled jacket, with small stand-up collar fastened in front or on the shoulder.

**MANTLE:** a woman's outer garment of the late nineteenth century in the form of a waist- or hip-length cloak with hood.

**MAXI:** an ankle- or floor-length skirt, popular in the late sixties.

**MICRO:** a very short skirt, popular in the sixties.

**MIDI:** a mid-calf-length skirt, popular in the late sixties.

**MINI:** an above-the-knee-length skirt, popular from 1962 to 1970.

**MOHAIR:** a loosely woven fabric made from angora wool.

**MOIRÉ:** Fr. (watered): a finishing process that produces a wavy pattern; usually applied to ribbed fabrics of cotton, acetate, rayon, silk, and some manufactured fabrics; it is permanent only if heat or chemically set.

**MONASTIC DRESS:** Claire McCardell design of 1938; the style is very full and flared from the shoulders, optional belt.

**MONDRIAN, PIET:** (1872–1944) an artist who painted in grid-like divisions of flat color which influenced fashion designer Yves Saint Laurent in the sixties.

**MOTIF:** a recurring figure in the pattern of a design.

**MOUSSELINE:** a fine plain-woven fabric in cotton, silk, or wool which has a stiff finish; popular in the nineteenth century.

**MUFF:** a popular accessory in the nineteenth century used to keep the hands warm and made in a variety of pillow-like shapes.

**MUSLIN:** a plain-woven cotton material made in a variety of weights.

**NEHRU SUIT:** a suit with a jacket having a stand-up collar and button front that was popular in white in the sixties.

**NORFOLK JACKET:** a wool tweed, hip-length jacket with large patch pockets, front and back box pleats, and self-material belt. It was worn by men in the nineteenth century and worn by women for sporting events in 1890.

**NYLON:** household term for fabric made from synthetics; used in hosiery and apparel. Nylon was developed by W. H. Carothers for the DuPont Co., marketed in 1938, it was the first of the fully synthetic fibers.

**OP ART:** an art style of the sixties that influenced fashion and fabrics with optical circles, squares, and spirals.

**ORGANDY:** a sheer, light cotton fabric made of fine count that is stiffened by chemicals; similar fabrics are made of rayon, silk, or other fibers.

**OTTOMAN:** used in coats, suits, evening wraps, and dresses; a firm and lustrous fabric with horizontal cords.

**PAGODA SLEEVE:** a three-quarter-length sleeve, wider at the elbow and often with tiers of flounces and lace undersleeve.

**PANNIERS:** the framework used to expand the upper sides of a skirt.

**PAREO:** brightly covered wrapped skirts.

**PARURE JEWELRY:** a set of jewels that match and are worn together; in the nineteenth century it consisted of necklace, earrings, bracelet, brooch, rings, and head ornament.

**PASSEMENTERIE:** decorative trim for an article of clothing such as braiding, beads, gimp, cording in various combinations.

**PATENT LEATHER:** high-gloss material used for shoes and purses since the twenties.

**PAVÉ:** in jewelry—setting stones very close together.

**PEA COAT:** a heavy, double-breasted, hip-length jacket originally worn by sailors.

**PETERSHAM:** a thin belting in the tops of skirts.

**PENCIL SKIRT:** a slim skirt cut in one line from hips to hem.

**PEPLUM:** a short skirt attached to the bodice or jacket that flares out over the hip.

**PETER PAN COLLAR:** a flat collar, about two or three inches deep, with rounded edge.

**PETTICOAT:** a nineteenth century woman's underskirt made from fine fabrics.

**PICTURE HAT:** a wide-brimmed hat with high crown and usually decorated with ribbons and flowers.

**PILLBOX HAT:** a small, brimless hat with straight sides and a flat top.

**PIPING:** a thin tube-like strip of fabric cut on the bias and used as an edging on a garment.

**PIQUÉ:** woven cotton, silk, or spun rayon with lengthwise cording.

**PLATFORM SOLE:** a thick sole on a shoe; popular in the forties and the seventies.

PLIQUE-À-JOUR: enameling that looks like stained glass.

POINT DE GAZE: needlepoint lace with a floral motif; worked on a net ground.

POKE BONNET: a bonnet with a projecting brim, tying under the chin.

PONCHO: a square fabric with a center opening for the head.

PONGEE: a plain-woven ecru-colored fabric with irregular crosswise ribbing, originally made from silk but popular in twentieth century cotton blends.

POPLIN: a sturdy, ribbed plain-woven fabric made from combinations of silk, rayon, wool, or cotton.

POPOVER DRESS: Claire McCardell dress design of 1942; wraparound front and large pockets designed to be worn in the home.

PORKPIE: a hat usually made from felt which is characterized by a snap-brim and a round, flat crown.

POUF: a style popularized by Christian Lacroix: a short full skirt, sometimes tucked up at the back.

PRAIRIE LOOK: Ralph Lauren design of the seventies; white petticoat under denim skirt.

PRINCESS LINE: a slim-fitting dress line made without a waist seam; the waist was created by vertical panels of fabric.

PROVENANCE: the source or location of origin can include the names of the designer, maker, and owner.

PSYCHEDELIC: popular sign of the sixties, irregular shapes and bright colors.

PUNK: a dress style that began in the mid-seventies in London, England, with teenagers, the unemployed, and students. It is characterized by unisex hairstyles dyed in bright colors, backcombed, or cropped; the clothing styles were meant to frighten, hence black studded leather and torn trousers. Refined styles were seen in the fashion designs of the 1980s.

QUIANA: a wrinkle-free nylon introduced by DuPont in the 1960s.

RAYON: a synthetic fabric made by cellulose solution; often referred to as artificial silk.

RAYON CREPE: rayon with a crinkled surface.

READY-MADES: a term used in the nineteenth century for partly made clothing that could be bought at a department store and then completed to one's own specifications. Mourning clothes were the first ready-mades.

**READY-TO-WEAR:** a term used to describe pre-made clothing that can be bought and worn "off the rack." Also used to describe the ready-to-wear industry. The French term for ready-to-wear is prêt-à-porter.

**RETICULE:** nineteenth century small purse made of soft fabrics with cord ties and worn held from the wrist.

**RETRO:** a word used to describe fashions from a previous era.

**RHINESTONE:** glass or imitation stone used for decoration.

**ROBE DE STYLE:** a full-skirted, calf-length dress with a close fitting bodice and natural or low waistline.

**SACK DRESS:** a loosely shaped dress which tapers at the knees.

**SAILOR SUIT:** children's dress style at the turn of the century based on the navy uniform.

**SARI:** an Indian woman's outer garment made from one length of fabric of colored silk or cotton that is wrapped at the waist to make the skirt, with the remaining part worn over the shoulder.

**SARONG:** a length of fabric wrapped around the body and tied at the waist.

**SASSOON, VIDAL:** an English hairstylist popular in the sixties and seventies for his layered and sculptured cuts that were compatible with the fashions.

**SATEEN:** usually a cotton weave made with satin that is strong and glossy.

**SATIN:** a smooth, lustrous fabric made from finely woven silk or rayon threads; the underside is dull.

**SEERSUCKER:** a cotton fabric with permanent woven stripes that are crinkled.

**SEQUIN:** a small disc of shiny metal or plastic that is used for trim.

**SERGE:** a worsted fabric of twill weave originally made in silk or wool; the term is used especially for a clear-finished worsted suiting fabric made in a variety of qualities. It can be constructed from wool, cotton, rayon, silk, and manufactured fibers.

**SHAWL:** a square or rectangular piece of fabric worn wrapped around the shoulders.

**SHEATH:** a straight, figure-fitting dress.

**SHEPHERDESS STYLE:** a high-waisted dress with a bell-shaped skirt.

**SHIFT:** a simple unconstructed dress in twentieth century fashion.

**SHIRRING:** two or more rows of gathering used as decoration on a garment.

**SHIRTWAISTS:** women's blouses in the late nineteenth century and early twentieth century.

**SHIRTWAIST DRESS:** a tailored, knee-length dress with long sleeves, a collar, and usually a belt; first popular in the forties.

**SHRUG JACKET:** abbreviated jacket.

**SILK:** a fine fabric having a sheen and made of natural fibers produced by silkworms.

**SINGLE-BREASTED:** a row of single buttons for closure on a jacket.

**SLASH POCKETS:** side pockets.

**SMOCKING:** a panel of fabric gathered by embroidery stitching.

**SNOOD:** a knotted or woven net used to cover and encase hair at the back of the head; sometimes attached to hats.

**SOUTACHE:** a trimming made from a narrow rounded braid.

**SPAGHETTI TIES:** thin fabric strings that tie on the shoulders.

**SPANDEX:** introduced in 1958 by DuPont: a manufactured fiber that is strong and light in weight; used in swimwear, lingerie and hosiery.

**SPENCER JACKET:** a nineteenth century woman's short, waist-length jacket worn as an outer garment or indoors over an evening dress.

**SPORTSWEAR:** American term for everyday or casual wear.

**STETSON:** American manufacturer's trade name; a brand of felt hat that has a broad brim and high crown; cowboy hat.

**STILETTO HEEL:** a shoe with a high narrow heel; originated in Italy.

**STOLE:** a long, rectangular wrap worn around the shoulders.

**STREET STYLE:** an important influence on clothing in the late twentieth century. Streetwear was the clothing worn by teens that was inexpensive yet gave them individual styles representative of their group or cult. Street style was incorporated into the designs of couture and ready to wear.

**SURPLICE:** a fashion style where the two halves of the front of the garment cross diagonally.

**SURREALISM:** a twentieth century art and literature movement characterized by fantasy or dream-like qualities. Elsa Schiaperelli's fashions often had surrealistic themes.

**SWEATER SET:** matching pullover and cardigan sweaters, worn together.

**SWEETHEART NECKLINE:** heart-shaped neckline, first popular in the forties.

**TABLE-TOP NECKLINE:** a sculptured neckline.

**TAFETTA:** a finely woven silk or faux silk fabric that is stiff and glossy.

**TAMBOUR EMBROIDERY:** embroidery made of linked chain stitches.

**TATTING:** handmade knotted lace made with cotton or linen thread.

**TEA GOWNS:** mid-nineteenth century at-home gowns designed to be worn with a loosened corset; by the 1870s gowns became very elaborate with fancy fabrics, lace, and ruffles.

**TENCEL:** a trademark of Courtauld's; Tencel is a cellulosic fiber, solvent-spun, known for its high performance; used for high-end apparel.

**TACTEL:** trademark of the DuPont company; a filament nylon fiber.

**TIARAS:** small crowns.

**TOOLED WORK:** designs carved into leather.

**TOPPER:** a full, hip-length coat with shawl collar and turned-up cuffs; popular in the forties and fifties.

**TOPSTITCHING:** decorative row of hand- or machine-made stitching.

**TOQUE:** head-hugging hat without a brim.

**TOREADOR PANTS:** tight pants laced at the knee.

**TOURNURE:** Fr. (bustle): term popular in the late nineteenth century.

**TRAIN:** a long rectangular piece of fabric attached to the back of a dress at the waist or shoulders.

**TRAPEZE DRESS:** Yves Saint Laurent designed this dress in 1958: a tent-shaped dress that was cut wide and full, knee-length, and fell free from the shoulders in the back.

**TRENCHCOAT:** a military style of raincoat of lightweight wool or cotton blend.

**TROMPE L'OEIL:** an optical illusion created by knitting a design into a garment.

**TUCKS:** a series of folds sewn and pressed down on fabric; used as a decoration on a dress.

**TULLE:** a fine machine-made net fabric of silk, gauze, or nylon.

TUNIC: a straight, sleeveless, loose-fitting garment with many fashion manifestations.

TURBAN: originally a long scarf wrapped around the head; used by milliners to construct a hat style, especially popular in the thirties and forties.

TWEED: a textured fabric woven of different-colored wools.

TWILL: a durable weave used often for cottons and wools; a twill pattern is usually recognizable by its diagonal wales.

TWINSET: matching sweater and cardigan.

TYVEK: the registered trademark of the DuPont Company for "spun-bonded olefin" fabric.

VALENCIENNES LACE: a light bobbin lace worked in one piece, named for a lace-making town on the French and Belgium border. The ground of fine mesh is usually square- or diamond-shaped. The lace is characterized by small holes surrounding the toiles (design), no cordonnet (raised outlining thread), and is usually made in a floral motif.

VAREUSE DRESS: a Dior design in the fifties based on the French fisherman smock; a loose hip-length garment with a stand-away collar.

VEIL: a thin piece of fabric that covers the face; made in a variety of fabrics and lengths.

VELOUR: a velvet-like fabric made from natural or synthetic fibers.

VELVET: a soft fabric made from a warp pile weave; the warp forms a smooth, dense pile of loops which may be pressed one way (panne) or stand erect; made from silk, cotton, or synthetics; the underside is plain.

VINYL: plastic.

WAIST: a blouse.

WAISTCOAT: a man's sleeveless garment that is worn under a jacket and over a shirt; often embroidered and made of silk.

WARP PRINTS: a patterning method whereby dyes are printed on a warp before weaving into cloth; the warp threads shift in the process and produce a somewhat blurred pattern.

WASP WAIST: tiny waist.

WATTEAU: a dress style named for the dresses in the eighteenth century paintings of Jean-Antoine Watteau having a sacque back (deeply pleated back) and a tight-fitted bodice.

**WET-LOOK:** ciré Fr. (waxed): fabrics made by the combination of wax, heat, and pressure on the fabric to produce a wet-like effect.

**WOOL:** strong fibers obtained from sheep.

**WORSTED WOOL:** a woolen fabric made from smooth yarn that is particularly durable.

**WRAPAROUND DRESS:** twentieth century dress style that overlaps at the waist.

**YOKE:** the upper part of a piece of clothing that fits across the bust, across the back behind the shoulders and holds up the rest of the garment.

# Bibliography

Armstrong, Nancy. *The Book of Fans*. New York: Mayflower Books, 1978.

Baudot, Chanel. *Chanel*. New York: Universe Publishing, 1996.

Beard, Tyler. *100 Years of Western Wear*. Salt Lake City: Gibbs-Smith Publishers, 1993.

Beckerman, Ilene. *Love, Loss and What I Wore*. Chapel Hill, N.C.: Algonquin Books of Chapel Hill, 1995.

Bendure, Zelma and Gladys Pfeiffer. *America's Fabrics: Origin and History, Manufacture, Character and Uses*. New York: The Macmillan Company, 1947.

Blum, Dilys and H. Kristina Haugland. *Best Dressed*. Philadelphia: Philadelphia Museum of Art, 1997.

Blum, Stella. *Everyday Fashions of the Twenties*. New York: Dover Publications, Inc., 1981.

Boucher, François. *20,000 Years of Fashion: The History of Costume and Personal Adornment*. New York: Harry N. Abrams, Inc., 1987.

Boston, Lloyd. *Men of Color: Fashion, History, Fundamentals*. New York: Artisan, 1998.

"Bridal Sweet: John F. Kennedy, Jr., realizing that no man is an island, sneaks off to one in Georgia to wed longtime love Carolyn Bessette," *People* (7 October 1996, v46, n15): 46–56.

Buxbaum, Gerta, Editor. *Icons of Fashion: The 20th Century*. New York: Prestel, 2000.

Callan, Georgina O'Hara. *The Thames and Hudson Dictionary of Fashion and Fashion Designers*. New York: Thames and Hudson, 1998.

Clancy, Deirdre. *Costume Since 1945: Couture, Street Style, and Anti-Fashion*. New York: Drama Publishers, 1996.

Clark, Fiona. *Hats.* London: Batsford, 1982.

Coleman, Elizabeth. *The Opulent Era: Fashions of Worth, Doucet and Pingat.* New York: Thames and Hudson, 1990.

Constantino, Maria. *Fashions of a Decade: The 30s.* New York: Facts on File, 1992.

Craughwell-Varda, Kathleen. *Looking for Jackie.* New York: Hearst Books, 1999.

De La Haye, Amy and Cathie Dingwall. *Surfers, Soulies, Skinheads & Skaters.* New York: The Overlook Press, 1996.

Dorner, Jane. *Fashion: The Changing Shape of Fashion Through the Years.* London: Octopus Books, Ltd., 1974.

Earnshaw, Pat. *The Identification of Lace.* Buckinghamshire, UK: Shire Publications, Ltd., 1994.

Eisman, Lawrence. Of Milwaukee, Wisconsin, telephone interview with author, October 3, 2000.

Engelmeier, Regine and Peter W., Editors. *Fashion in Film.* New York: Prestel, 1990.

Epstein, Diana and Millicent Safro. *Buttons.* New York: Harry N. Abrams, Inc., 1991.

Ettinger, Roseann. *Handbags.* West Chester, Pa.: Schiffer Publishing Ltd., 1991.

Ewing, Elizabeth. *History of Children's Costume.* New York: Charles Scribner and Sons, 1977.

_____. *History of 20th Century Fashion.* London: Batsford, Ltd., 1974. (reprinted 1992)

Fontanel, Béatrice. *Support and Seduction: A History of Corsets and Bras.* New York: Harry N. Abrams, Inc., 1997.

Fox, Patty. *Star Style at the Academy Awards.* Santa Monica: Angel City Press, Inc., 2000.

Gibbings, Sarah. *The Tie: Trends and Traditions.* New York: Barron's, 1990.

Gioello, Debbie Ann. *Understanding Fabrics: From Fiber to Finished Cloth.* New York: Fairchild Publications, 1982. (reprinted 1996)

Greenlaw, M. Jean. *Ranch Dressing: The Story of Western Wear.* New York: Lodestar Books, 1993.

Grimble, Frances. "Collecting Victorian Men's Wear," *The Antique Trader Weekly* (13 January 1993): 62–64.

Handley, Susannah. *Nylon: The Story of a Fashion Revolution.* Baltimore, Maryland: The Johns Hopkins University Press, 1999.

"How Fashion Broke Free: A Special Report on a Half-Century of Fashions of the Times," *New York Times Magazine* (24 October 1993): 113–195.

Hochswender, Woody and Kim Johnson Gross. *Men in Style.* New York: Rizzoli, 1993.

Holborn, Mark. *Issey Miyake.* Köln: Taschen, 1995.

Howell, Georgina. *In Vogue: 75 Years of Style*. London: Condé Nast Books, 1991.

_____. *Diana: Her Life in Fashion*. New York: Rizzoli, 1998.

Hunt, Marsha. *The Way We Wore: Styles of the 1930s and '40s*. Fallbrook, Ca.: Fallbrook Publishing, Ltd., 1993.

Kennett, Frances. *The Collector's Book of Fashion*. New York: Crown Publishers, Inc., 1983.

Ketchum, William C. Jr. *Western Memorabilia: Collectibles of the Old West*. Maplewood, N.J.: Hammond, 1980.

Klaiman, Marianna. Of New York, N.Y., telephone interview with author, October 3, 2000.

Lee, Sarah Tomerlin. *American Fashion: The Life and Times of Adrian, Mainbocher, McCardell, Norell, and Trigère*. New York: The Fashion Institute of Technology, 1975.

Leneck, Lena and Gideon Bosker. *Making Waves*. San Francisco: Chronicle Books, 1989.

Martin, Richard. *The St. James Fashion Encyclopedia: A Survey of Style from 1945 to the Present*. Detroit: Visible Ink Press, 1997.

Martin, Richard and Harold Koda. *Jocks and Nerds: Men's Style in the Twentieth Century*. New York: Rizzoli, 1989.

_____. "Waist Not: The Migration of the Waist 1800–1960." New York: The Metropolitan Museum of Art, 1994.

Mayor, Susan. *A Collector's Guide to Fans*. Secaucus, N.J.: Wellfleet Books, 1990.

McBride-Mellinger, Maria. *The Wedding Dress*. New York: Random House, 1993.

Meller, Susan and Joost Elffers. *Textile Designs*. New York: Harry N. Abrams, Inc., 1991.

Mendes, Valerie. *Dressed in Black*. New York: Harry N. Abrams, Inc., 1999.

Mendes, Valerie and Amy De La Haye. *20th Century Fashion*. London; New York: Thames and Hudson, 1999.

"Men's Fashions: Hollywood." Cable Channel, American Movie Classics, (AMC) television (23 July '00) 12:30 a.m.

Milbank, Caroline Rennolds. *New York Fashion: The Evolution of American Style*. New York: Harry N. Abrams, Inc., 1989.

_____. *Couture: The Great Designers*. New York: Stewart, Tabori and Chang, Inc., 1985.

Mohrt, Françoise. *The Givenchy Style*. New York: The Vendome Press, 1998.

Mulvagh, Jane. *Vogue: History of Twentieth Century Fashion*. New York: Viking, 1988.

Nunn, Joan. *Fashion in Costume 1200–2000*. Chicago: New Amsterdam Books, 2000.

O'Hara, Georgina. *The Encyclopedia of Fashion*. New York: Harry N. Abrams, Inc., 1986.

O'Keeffe. *Shoes.* New York: Workman Publishing, 1996.

Morris, Bernadine. *Valentino.* New York: Universe Publishing, 1996.

Mulvagh, Jane. *Vogue: History of Twentieth Century Fashion.* New York: Viking, 1988.

Peacock, John. *Men's Fashion: The Complete Sourcebook.* London: Thames and Hudson, Ltd., 1996.

_____. *The 1980s.* New York: Thames and Hudson, 1998.

Pochna, Marie-France. *Christian Dior: The Man Who Made the World New.* New York: Arcade Publishing, 1996.

Reedstrom, Ernest Lisle. *Historic Dress of the Old West.* New York: Blandford Press, 1986.

Richardson, A. Newbold. Of Alexandria, Virginia, telephone inteview with author, December 7, 2000.

Schaut, Jim and Nancy. *Collecting the Old West.* Iola, Wi.: Krause Publications, 1999.

Schields, Jody. *Hats.* New York: Clarkson Potter, 1991.

Shaeffer, Claire B. *Couture Sewing Techniques.* Newton, Ct.: Taunton Press, 2001.

Shapiro, Dan. Of Santa Monica, California, telephone interview with author, July 18, 2001.

Sichel, Marion. *History of Children's Costume.* London: Batsford Academic and Educational, Ltd., 1983.

Sotheby's. "Nothing to Wear" Auction catalog, April 8, 1998. New York.

Steele, Valerie. *Fifty Years of Fashion: New Look to Now.* New Haven: Yale University Press, 1997.

_____. *Women of Fashion: Twentieth Century Designers.* New York: Rizzoli, 1991.

Taylor, Lou. *Mourning Dress: A Costume and Social History.* London; Boston: G. Allen and Unwin, 1983.

Thieme, Otto Charles, Elizabeth Ann Coleman, Michelle Oberly, Patricia Cunningham. *With Grace & Favour.* Cincinnati: Cincinnati Art Museum, 1993.

Tober, Barbara. *The Bride: A Celebration.* New York: Harry N. Abrams, Inc., 1984.

Tortora, Phyllis G. and Robert S. Merkel. *Fairchild's Dictionary of Textiles,* 7th Edition. New York: Fairchild Publications, 1995.

Vermorel, Fred. *Vivienne Westwood: Fashion, Perversity and the Sixties Laid Bare.* New York: The Overlook Press, 1996.

Versace, Gianni. *Designs.* New York: Abbeville Press, 1994.

Villa, Nora. *Bambini Vestiti a Festa* (Children in Their Party Dress). Modena, Italy: Zanfi, 1989.

Yohannan, Kohle and Nancy Nolf. *Claire McCardell: Redefining Modernism.* New York: Harry N. Abrams, Inc., 1998.

# Index

0-609-80772-2

# FIND THOSE HIDDEN TREASURES!

*The Official® Guide to Flea Market Prices* is the essential resource for bargain hunters *and* seasoned dealers! Expert Harry L. Rinker shows us how to shop *and* have fun.

- Up-to-date values for more than 500 categories
- How to find and evaluate flea markets
- Hundreds of photographs
- A complete flea marketeer's reference library
- A special report on Internet flea markets

**Buy It • Use It • Become an Expert™**

**HOUSE OF COLLECTIBLES**

**Available at bookstores everywhere!**